EXAM CRAM™ 2

PMP

Michael Solomon

que®

CERTIFICATION

PMP Exam Cram 2

Trademarks

Warning and Disclaimer

Bulk Sales

Que Certification offers excellent discounts on this book when ordered in quantity for bulk purchases or special sales. For more information, please contact

U.S. Corporate and Government Sales
1-800-382-3419
corpsales@pearsontechgroup.com

For sales outside the United States, please contact

International Sales
international@pearsoned.com

Publisher
Paul Boger

Executive Editor
Jeff Riley

Acquisitions Editor
Steve Rowe

Development Editor
Steve Rowe

Managing Editor
Charlotte Clapp

Project Editor
Dan Knott

Production Editor
Megan Wade

Indexer
Erika Millen

Proofreader
Brad Engels

Technical Editor
Steve Maloney

Publishing Coordinator
Cindy Teeters

Multimedia Developer
Dan Scherf

Interior Designer
Gary Adair

Cover Designer
Anne Jones

Page Layout
Kelly Maish

About the Authors

Michael Solomon, CISSP, PMP, CISM, TICSA, is a full-time security and project management speaker, consultant, and trainer with more than 17 years of industry experience. He holds an MS in mathematics and computer science from Emory University (1998) and a BS in computer science from Kennesaw State University (1987). Michael has written several IT and project management books, including *Information Security Illuminated* (Jones & Bartlett, 2005), *Security+ Lab Guide* (Sybex, 2005), *Computer Forensics JumpStart* (Sybex, 2005).

Kelvin J. Arcelay is a founder and managing partner at CITASGroup LLC, specializing in audit, compliance, interim CIO, and project management services. He has more than 21 years of business technology implementation experience and has worked with well-known companies such as Global Payments, Cumulus Media, Siemens, TYCO, Fruit of the Loom, and Bristol-Myers Squibb. In addition, he holds active certifications in project management (PMP), Information Security (CISM, CISSP), and Six Sigma Green Belt.

Tina Dacus has worked for 10 years in information technology, specializing in project management, quality assurance, and process improvement. She has training in and experience using the Capability Maturity Model Integrated (CMMI) and the Project Management Body of Knowledge (PMBOK). She is a member of the Project Management Institute (PMI).

Bob Tarne, PMP, is a senior consultant with Project Management Solutions, where he oversees implementation of project management initiatives with clients to help optimize their business performance. He is also the chair of PMI's Information Technology and Telecommunications Specific Interest Group and a graduate of PMI's Leadership Institute. Bob has also worked in project management roles at Sprint and Owens-Illinois. Bob's career began as an officer in the U.S. Navy, where he served for seven years as a cryptologist. He holds an MS in business from Johns Hopkins University and a BS in electrical engineering from the University of Illinois. Bob earned his PMP in 2001.

Acknowledgments

We would all like to acknowledge our families for their unyielding love and support while writing this book. We couldn't do it without you.

We Want to Hear from You!

As the reader of this book, *you* are our most important critic and commentator. We value your opinion and want to know what we're doing right, what we could do better, what areas you'd like to see us publish in, and any other words of wisdom you're willing to pass our way.

As an executive editor for Que Publishing, I welcome your comments. You can email or write me directly to let me know what you did or didn't like about this book—as well as what we can do to make our books better.

Please note that I cannot help you with technical problems related to the topic of this book. We do have a User Services group, however, where I will forward specific technical questions related to the book.

When you write, please be sure to include this book's title and author as well as your name, email address, and phone number. I will carefully review your comments and share them with the authors and editors who worked on the book.

Email: feedback@quepublishing.com

Mail: Jeff Riley
         Executive Editor
         Que Publishing
         800 East 96th Street
         Indianapolis, IN 46240 USA

For more information about this book or another Que Certification title, visit our website at www.examcram2.com. Type the ISBN (excluding hyphens) or the title of a book in the Search field to find the page you're looking for.

Contents at a Glance

Table of Contents

Introduction

The Project Management Professional (PMP) certification is a valued asset in the ever-evolving professional project management field. PMP certification in the professional arena ensures employers are hiring a project manager with thorough, tested knowledge in project management principles; years of hands-on, specific experience performing project management tasks; and a commitment to continuing education in the field of project management. Among fellow PMP-certified practitioners, PMP certification allows colleagues a commonality of experience and opportunities for networking. PMPs share the same frame of reference in project management, regardless of the field of endeavor.

PMP-certified individuals work in a wide array of industries, from aerospace to telecommunications. Many hiring supervisors specify PMP certification as a preferred skill set when soliciting project managers.

Both private and public sector employers recognize the value a PMP-certified employee brings to a project. Corporations embrace the consistent application of project management methodologies for initiating, planning, executing, controlling, and closing projects. The Project Management Institute (PMI) project framework is highly praised by companies and government entities whether they are engaged in large-scale development projects or simply undertaking small, reengineering initiatives. In both scenarios, the PMI approach offers a consistent project management methodology that can be tailored to the size and complexity of the project. This framework, coupled with the PMP certification program, ensures that PMP-certified practitioners are in high demand in the workforce.

PMI has brought the art and science of project management full circle through its PMP certification program and methodology, the Project Management Body of Knowledge (PMBOK). PMI seeks to evaluate project management professionals through the application and certification process to ensure a dependable workforce with solid credentials. The PMP

Certification Examination tests for comprehensive project management knowledge as well as a thorough understanding of the PMBOK. This approach ensures that PMP-certified practitioners have comparable qualifications and strategic competencies in all aspects of project management. PMI advocates the practice of project management as a discipline, not unlike engineering or any other precise, science-based course of study. As such, PMI developed the PMBOK as an all-encompassing standard for the practice of project management regardless of the specific industry.

The Project Management Institute

PMI is the premier project management organization in the world. It is a nonprofit, educational group intent on advancing the practice of project management through the promotion and promulgation of widely accepted standards. It has more than 150,000 members in over 150 countries with 247 charter-based local chapters. This is quite a feat for an organization that started in 1969 with five volunteers!

PMI establishes professional standards, provides continuing education opportunities for members, engages industry-specific research, and offers certifications aimed at unifying and strengthening the discipline of project management.

If you consider yourself a project management professional and want to earn your PMP, consider joining PMI. You will receive a reduced rate when sitting for your PMP examination as well as all the other benefits of PMI membership. These benefits include a community of peers offering valuable information exchange about industry trends and access to the latest knowledge through a monthly magazine and quarterly research journals.

Depending on your location, PMI offers seminars, workshops, and other continuing education opportunities as well as networking through local chapter and specific interest group involvement.

Your local chapter might also offer tutorials and other study courses in preparation for taking your PMP Certification Examination. Study groups and examination assistance through local chapters can augment the information you are learning in this book by offering opportunities to apply your newly acquired knowledge. To learn more about PMI and membership, visit PMI's website at http://www.pmi.org.

What's New in the PMBOK, Third Edition

PMI, as a member-driven organization, is continually evolving to meet the needs of its membership and the project management profession. To this end, the PMBOK has been revised to incorporate feedback from members and reflect current industry practice and developments since the last edition. For those readers familiar with the last edition—the PMBOK, 2000 Edition, in effect the second edition of the PMBOK—you will want to acquaint yourself with the changes in the third edition. This is particularly important if an earlier edition of the PMBOK was used in preparation for the PMP certification examination.

According to PMI, the new edition reflects the evolution from "generally accepted on most projects, most of the time" to "generally recognized as good practice on most projects" as the criteria for inclusion of information within the PMBOK. The use of the terminology "generally recognized" over "generally accepted" implies a higher degree of acceptance and recognition for the value and applicability of the knowledge and practices contained within this updated PMBOK.

New material has been added to reflect changes, adaptations, and additions to tools and techniques used in the current practice of project management. The number of processes increased from 39 to 44. Thirteen processes were renamed, two processes were deleted, and seven processes were added. The added processes are

➤ Develop Project Charter—Section 4.1

➤ Develop Preliminary Project Scope Statement—Section 4.2

➤ Monitor and Control Project Work—Section 4.5

➤ Close Project—Section 4.7

➤ Create Work Breakdown Structure—Section 5.3

➤ Activity Resource Estimating—Section 6.3

➤ Manage Project Team—Section 9.4

PMI avoided changing all the process names in favor of incremental change to minimize confusion. A clarification was provided between project management process groups and the knowledge areas placing greater distinction on process groups. The process designations—"facilitating processes" and "core processes"—have been discontinued. All project management process groups have the same level of importance.

All the process inputs, tools, techniques, and outputs were revised and updated to support improved integration and process mapping. In addition, project management processes were mapped to show process integration. Also, process flow diagrams have been added to Chapters 4–12 of the PMBOK.

All these changes are the result of input from PMPs that was used to streamline and clarify the PMBOK. A complete listing of all changes to the PMBOK, Third Edition is available in Appendix A of the PMBOK, and we will also discuss these changes in more detail in Chapter 1 of this book. Each change is identified in its respective chapter in the PMBOK.

The new PMP Certification Examination goes into effect on September 30, 2005 based on the PMBOK, Third Edition.

The PMP Certification Process

PMP certification entails a number of steps, beginning with an application to PMI detailing a prospective PMP candidate's qualifications, experience, and training. Once approved by PMI to sit for the examination, a candidate registers for the exam and must comply with various procedures set forth for the actual test. The PMP certification process concludes with the passage of the examination and issuance of PMP credentials by the PMI.

Registering for the PMP Certification Exam

Prior to actually taking a PMP Certification Examination, you must submit an application to PMI for approval. Your application to the PMI for PMP certification is not a mere formality; you are asked to provide detailed documentation supporting your professional project management experience and training in specific areas of expertise.

Application Submittal

An application is included in the *PMP Handbook*, available on the PMI website. This handbook provides detailed information on every step of the application process. Your application will document your qualifications based on your education, work experience, and training. The *PMP Handbook* states the policies and procedures that must be adhered to by all applicants for PMP certification. If you believe you meet the requirements necessary for PMP candidates, you are ready to apply to the PMI.

Read the *PMP Handbook* prior to applying for PMP certification to ensure that you have a full understanding of the procedures necessary for exam signup.

The application can be submitted online through the PMI website or in hard-copy format through postal mail. The PMI processes PMP certification applications within 10–14 business days of receipt for individuals and within 20 days for applications received from corporations. PMP applicants requesting a scheduled paper-pencil examination are processed within 30 calendar days of receipt.

Apply online through the PMI website at www.pmi.org to save time.

Your PMP certification application is necessary to ensure you meet specific educational requirements and minimum experience criteria. PMI sets forth minimum standards for applicants to ensure all PMP-certified practitioners are experienced in the field of project management.

Candidates for PMP certification must meet both the educational and experience requirements for one of two categories. Verification forms showing compliance with these criteria must be submitted with your application for either category. Both categories are detailed in Tables I.1 and I.2.

Category One, shown in Table I.1, is for applicants possessing a bachelor's degree or equivalent. In this category, less personal project management experience is necessary, although you must possess a minimum of 4,500 hours of hands-on project management activity. Category Two, shown in Table I.2, is ideal for candidates with longer work histories but not in possession of a university degree. In this category, you can use 7,500 hours of project management performance to substitute for a college degree.

Table I.1 Category One Applicants		
Criteria	**Minimum**	**Explanation**
Bachelor's degree		Or equivalent from a university.
Personal project management experience within five process groups	4,500 hours	Within the last 6 years from the date of application.

(continued)

Table I.1 Category One Applicants *(continued)*

Criteria	Minimum	Explanation
Nonoverlapping months of personal project management experience	36 months	Individual months count toward the 36 months requirement once, even if you worked on multiple projects during the same month.
Specific instruction that addresses learning objectives in project management	35 contact hours	Must include instruction on project quality, scope, time, cost, human resources, communications, risk, procurement, and integration management.

Table I.2 Category Two Applicants

Criteria	Minimum	Explanation
Personal project management experience within five process groups	7,500 hours	Within the last 8 years from the date of application.
Nonoverlapping months of personal project management experience	60 months	Individual months count toward the 36 months requirement once, even if you worked on multiple projects during the same month.
Specific instruction that addresses learning objectives in project management	35 contact hours	Must include instruction on project quality, scope, time, cost, human resources, communications, risk, procurement, and integration management.

In the next section of this book, the PMP Exam Self-Assessment will assist you in evaluating your ability to meet these qualifications. Additional information related to the educational and experience mandates for PMP certification eligibility are provided in the *PMP Handbook.*

Application Fee and PMI Membership

The application also requires a fee tiered for PMI members and non-PMI members, with the latter paying a higher rate. As of this writing, PMI members pay $405 for the examination while nonmembers pay $555.

As part of the application process, you will be asked whether you are a PMI member and, if not, given the opportunity to join. There are many benefits to PMI membership, including a discounted rate when applying for PMP certification. If you are pursing your PMP certification, you already believe there is benefit to the PMI and should consider joining. Furthermore, the annual cost for PMI membership is $119, which is actually cheaper than the difference between the examination cost for a nonmember. The total cost for joining PMI and sitting for PMI examination is $524. (This does not include chapter, special interest groups, and college membership that require additional fees.)

Audit

A random sample of applicants is chosen for audit prior to issuing eligibility letters. If you are selected for an audit you will be asked to provide additional information about your work experience, including supporting documentation from your supervisors detailing your work on specific projects.

Examination Administration

The PMP Certification Examination is offered globally. Computer-based administration is available within North America and other countries. PMI offers the PMP Certification Examination through computer-based administration at Prometric (formerly Sylvan Technology). In addition, a paper-pencil examination is offered at specific locations. A complete list of testing sites and vendors is available on the PMI website. More information regarding paper-pencil testing is also available in the *PMP Handbook*.

You must apply for certification through PMI prior to scheduling a PMP certification examination at Prometric. Prometric requires a PMI identification code to register; it is provided to PMP candidates by PMI when approval is granted to sit for an exam. PMP candidates can then register online or using Prometric's interactive voice-response telephone registration system.

Registration with Prometric is straightforward. Your approval letter from PMI to sit for the PMP certification exam includes an active link to Prometric's website as well as a toll-free telephone number for its interactive voice-response system. Specific instructions for registering are also included in your approval letter from PMI.

Prometric's website and telephone registration system provide the same instructions guiding you through the process of registration. It is important to register after you become approved to do so because testing locations, dates, and times are offered on a first-come, first-served basis at Prometric. The sooner you register, the more likely you will obtain your preferred testing location, testing date, and time.

To learn more about Prometric and its administration of the PMP certification examination, visit Prometric's website at www.prometric.com.

The *PMP Handbook* also includes information on registering for the PMP certification examination with Prometric.

After your application has been approved by PMI as eligible for certification, passage of the actual PM Certification Examination constitutes the final step in becoming a PMP.

Reexamination

Candidates who do not pass the PMP certification exam can apply to the PMI for reexamination using a form on its website. This form must be submitted within 1 year of the original examination date.

Cancellation

Candidates within North America can cancel and reschedule an exam 2 business days prior to the scheduled testing. Candidates outside North America must do so 7 calendar days in advance.

Candidates unable to appear for a scheduled examination due to a medical emergency must submit written notification to the PMI Certification Program Department within 72 hours of the scheduled exam. A rescheduling fee will be charged, and all circumstances are reviewed on a case-by-case basis.

Refund

A refund can be obtained by written request to the PMI 1 month before your exam eligibility expires. (You have 1 year from the date of your eligibility letter in which to take the PMP certification exam.) A $200 processing fee will be retained from your original application fee.

Arriving at the Exam Site

Prior to departing for the exam site, be sure you have a form of identification with a picture and a signature (preferably your state driver's license) to show the testing center administrator. If you do not have proper identification, you will not be allowed to take the exam. Your approval letter from PMI and your registration confirmation from Prometric detail which forms of identification are acceptable.

In addition to your identification, bring a simple calculator, a watch, and pencils. Programmable calculators are not allowed. You might not have cause to use a calculator, but it is always best to be prepared. You will not want to perform even simple calculations on paper for fear of making a nervous error. Take a watch to time yourself during the examination. Some testing centers have clocks in the room, but it is best to have your own watch to ensure accuracy. A stopwatch or timer feature might also be beneficial if you fear you cannot manually keep up with elapsed time. Take a couple of sharpened pencils to take notes.

Wear comfortable clothing and layer your clothing. You should be able to add a sweater or long-sleeve shirt or conversely remove a layer of clothing to adjust to the climate in the room. You will be spending up to 4 hours in the examination room, and your ability to concentrate and focus on the task at hand can be dramatically impacted by the room temperature and your sense of comfort.

Get to your exam site early so you can review the PMP Cram Sheet provided in this book and any additional notes you might create to quickly focus your mind on specific topics prior to the test. An early arrival will ensure you have ample time to relax and mentally prepare for the examination.

Your approval letter from PMI and your registration confirmation from Prometric instruct you to arrive at least 30 minutes prior to your exam time for check-in. You will be asked to present your identification information, your PMI identification code provided in your approval letter from PMI, and possibly your Prometric registration confirmation number.

In the Exam Room

Do not start the examination immediately. Sit down at your computer terminal and acclimate to the examination room and your immediate environment. Organize your peripherals for your comfort. Are the mouse and keyboard set correctly? Does your chair need adjusting? Is the monitor at the correct eye level for you? A few minor corrections can make all the difference over the next few hours.

Prior to the start of the examination, the test administrator will review any specific instructions and inform you what is and is not allowed during the examination period. You will be allowed to take breaks and use the restrooms as necessary.

Pretest Tutorial

Prior to beginning the examination you will be provided with a briefing and 15-minute online tutorial designed to familiarize you with the computer and operational procedures for the test. If you have taken a computer-based test previously or participated in computer-based training, you should feel comfortable in this environment. The pretest tutorial shows you how to navigate through the test using your computer mouse. You are shown how to select an answer to a question, move forward to a new question, return to a previous question, and similar functions. The clock begins after completion of the tutorial, so if you feel comfortable with the information presented, move forward to the actual examination.

Time Allotted for the Test

You will have up to 4 hours to complete the examination. Pace yourself. There are 200 multiple-choice questions, which breaks down to 50 questions per hour and a little over a minute per question. Not all questions will require equal time. Don't agonize over every question; read the question and each possible answer in its entirety prior to selecting an answer.

Answer the PMI Way

More than one answer can seem plausible and correct. You are not asked to select the correct answer but rather the *best* answer from those provided. Attempt to rule out any obviously wrong choices immediately to narrow your field of best answers. You should strive to select the best answer based on how you believe PMI and the PMBOK would respond given the question and not necessarily from your own project management experience.

It cannot be emphasized enough that the PMI answer is the correct answer. You might do some task a certain way in real practice, and that method might even be one of the answer choices. But for purposes of the PMP Certification Examination, the PMBOK answer is the only correct answer. Don't get caught off guard here!

The best answer as determined by PMI is provided as one of the four possible responses. Be suspicious of answers offering definitive responses like *"never"* and *"always."* Some answers might tout non-PMI methods and reflect common project management misconceptions. Some answers might offer correct information, but the information is not pertinent to the question at hand. Similarly, some questions might contain factually correct information that has no bearing on the possible answers.

Pace Yourself During the Exam

After the first hour you will be able to determine your speed and make adjustments as necessary. It is important to be aware of your time so you won't have to rush at the end to complete the examination. You should leave adequate time to review any responses you were unsure of and to return to unanswered questions. If you are spending more than 1 minute on a question, it is better to skip over the question and mark it for review later than to agonize over the question and lose the opportunity to answer other questions you know the answers to.

The examination allows you to mark questions for later review and make multiple passes through the exam. Mark every question you are unsure of even if you have selected an answer. This approach will save you time when you review your responses because you will not need to review any unmarked questions. If, on a second review, you determine an answer, unmark the question. Continue this process of going through all the marked questions until you have answered all the questions or are nearing the end of the allotted time period.

Save the last 20 minutes or so of the test to finalize any unmarked answers and ensure you have provided an answer to each question. Try to make a best guess by ruling out definitely wrong answers, as discussed earlier, but do not give up. Select an answer for each question—even if you have to guess. There is no penalty for guessing.

 Remember, there is no penalty for guessing. So, be sure all questions have been answered—even if you have to guess. You at least give yourself an opportunity to get it right if you have an answer marked!

Throughout the testing period keep an eye on the clock or use your watch timer to remind you at discreet intervals to take a break. It is amazing what simply standing up and stretching for a few minutes can do for your concentration.

At the conclusion of the test, candidates can opt to complete a satisfaction survey.

Exam Room Surveillance

You will probably be under surveillance during the examination. Some testing centers use both videotape and human monitors to ensure the validity of the test. After you get underway with your examination and start to concentrate on the task at hand, you will be unaware of any other activity. Any monitoring by the testing center will be unobtrusive.

Grading Your Exam

At the end of the examination period, the administrator will immediately score your exam and provide you with a printed copy of your results indicating pass or fail status. The scores will be submitted to PMI by the end of the business day. If you have passed the exam, a PMP credential packet is mailed to you in 6–8 weeks by PMI.

If you are taking a paper-pencil examination, answer sheets are scored when they are returned to the test administrator. You can request that your exam be hand-scored for an additional $45 fee.

Any questions regarding your score using either computer-based testing or paper-pencil examination should be addressed to PMI's exam supervisor.

Study and Exam Preparation

The PMP certification examination consists of 200 four-option, multiple-choice questions developed by PMPs. Examinees must score 81.7% to pass the test, which requires answering 164 questions correctly.

There are no prescribed guidelines for a course of study because the examination is objective in scope and intended to test your knowledge of the project management field; however, emphasis is strongly placed on the PMBOK.

Do note that in March 2002, the PMP Certification Examination changed to include an additional performance requirement specific to professional responsibility in the practice of project management. The PMI PMP Code of Professional Conduct is not a component of the PMBOK; rather it is a one-page standalone document available on the PMI website which you will be tested on as part of the examination.

The PMP Certification Examination tests for professional responsibility and five process groups:

➤ Project initiation ➤ Project control

➤ Project planning ➤ Project closing

➤ Project execution

The most significant knowledge areas are project planning, project execution, and project control:

➤ **Project planning and project execution**—Each of these sections accounts for 23.5% of the test material. These two areas comprise 94 exam questions collectively.

➤ **Project control**—This section follows closely with 46 questions, totaling 23% of the test questions.

Overall, 70% of the examination deals exclusively with planning, executing, and controlling projects.

Of the six test areas, professional responsibility accounts for 14.5% of the PMP Certification Examination. This equates to 29 of the 200 multiple-choice questions.

Project initiation and project closing represent the smallest percentage of test questions at 8.5% and 7%, respectively. Approximately 17 questions will address project initiation activities, while 14 questions will focus on completing a project.

A new PMP Certification Examination goes into effect on September 30, 2005, based on the PMBOK, Third Edition. A blackout period will commence on September 25, 2005, during which the PMP Certification Examination will not be offered. All applications submitted after August 29, 2005 will be required to take the new PMP Certification Examination.

About the Book

This book offers you tools, techniques, tips, and other information to assist you in passing the PMP Certification Examination and becoming PMP certified. The emphasis is on reconciling your approach to the exam with PMI's viewpoint and perspective on the examination. This book is not a guide to general project management but rather a specific study tool aimed at distilling PMI's approach to project management as set forth in the PMBOK, Third Edition. Project initiation, planning, execution, control, and closing are the core topics in this book offered in parallel to those same key areas in the PMBOK.

Using This Book

This book prepares you to pass the PMP certification exam by highlighting important project management principles, providing insight into proven test-taking strategies, and emphasizing key information you can expect to see on the test. You will get guidance and clarification on PMBOK concepts and learn their relationships to other project management methodologies. Additional resources are cited for you in each chapter, and you will get many opportunities to apply your knowledge through practice exams and test questions.

Two practice exams are offered in this book, as well as practice questions at the end of each chapter. After you complete a chapter, take the practice questions to determine how well you comprehended the information in the chapter. If you missed more than one or two questions, work your way through the chapter again focusing on the concepts you missed.

Similarly, you can test your knowledge and evaluate your level of preparation for the PMP certification exam by taking the practice exams under real conditions. After you've worked your way through this book once, take one practice exam. Evaluate your results. Then, based on your strengths and weaknesses, reread the chapters of this book related to those areas of the practice examination where you were less certain or did not select the correct answer. Then take the second practice exam to see whether your understanding of the material improved.

In each chapter of this book, there is a "Need to Know More?" section identifying additional resources. The books, websites, and other reference materials cited in the "Need to Know More?" section within each chapter are also collected comprehensively in Appendix B, "Additional Resources." If you feel you need more information related to any project management topic, these are the materials to consult. Some sources are cited in multiple chapters because they are seminal works in the field of project management. These resources, used in conjunction with the PMBOK, provide well-rounded preparation for any test material.

Finally, the Cram Sheet condenses the concepts, knowledge areas, process groups, terminology, and formulas presented throughout this book down to a tear-out sheet you can take with you to the exam site for quick review prior to entering the testing facility. The Cram Sheet is also a valuable tool for use in quick daily reviews after you have completed this book. Review the Cram Sheet every day; if there are any terms that seem vague, go to that particular topic in the book for a refresher course.

Chapter Formats

Each *Exam Cram 2* chapter follows a regular structure, along with graphical cues about especially important or useful material. The structure of a typical chapter is as follows:

➤ **Hotlists**—Each chapter begins with lists of the terms you'll need to understand and the techniques and concepts you'll need to master before you can be fully conversant with the chapter's subject matter. We follow these "hotlists" with a few introductory paragraphs, setting the stage for the rest of the chapter.

➤ **Topical coverage**—After the opening hotlists, each chapter covers the topics related to its subject.

➤ **Exam alerts**—Throughout the topical coverage section, we highlight the material most likely to appear on the exam by using a special exam alert layout that looks like this:

This is what an exam alert looks like. An exam alert stresses concepts, terms, or activities that will most likely appear in one or more exam questions. For that reason, we think any information offset in exam alert format is worthy of extra attentiveness on your part.

Even if material isn't flagged as an exam alert, all the content in this book is associated in some way with test-related material. What appears in the chapter content is critical knowledge.

➤ **Notes**—This book is an overall examination of the topics covered on the PMP. Where a body of knowledge is deeper than the scope of the book, we use notes to indicate areas of concern or specialty training. The following is an example of a note:

This is an example of a note.

➤ **Tips**—We provide tips that will help you build a better foundation of knowledge or focus your attention on an important concept that will reappear later in the book. Tips provide a helpful way to remind you of the context surrounding a particular area of a topic under discussion. The following shows you what a tip looks like:

This is what tips look like. The intent of tip elements is to provide you with alternative ways to approach project management duties. These can be quicker ways of doing tasks or new methods that are not as well known. These elements bring real-world PM content into the boundaries of an exam prep book, too!

➤ **Exam Prep Questions**—This section presents a short list of test questions related to the specific chapter topic. Each question has a following explanation of both correct and incorrect answers. The practice questions highlight the areas we found to be most important on the exam.

The bulk of the book follows this chapter structure, but there are a few other elements we would like to point out:

➤ **Practice exams**—There are two full practice tests found at the end of this book. The questions are designed to challenge your knowledge and readiness for the PMP exam.

➤ **Answer keys**—These provide the answers to the practice exams, complete with explanations of both the correct responses and the incorrect ones.

➤ **Glossary**—This is an extensive glossary of important terms used in this book.

➤ **The Cram Sheet**—This appears as a tear-away sheet, inside the front cover of this *Exam Cram 2* book. It is a valuable tool that represents a collection of the most critical items we think you should memorize before taking the test. Remember, you can dump this information out of your head onto the margins of your test booklet or scratch paper as soon as you enter the testing room.

You might want to look at the Cram Sheet in your car or in the lobby of the testing center just before you walk into the testing center. The Cram Sheet is divided under headings, so you can review the appropriate parts just before each test.

Self-Assessment

Are you qualified to take the PMP Certification Examination? As noted in the Introduction, candidates for certification must meet specific qualifications regarding education, project management experience, and training to sit for PMP certification. An application must be submitted to PMI for approval detailing your qualifications prior to taking the PMP Certification Examination. The PMP Exam Self-Assessment will assist you in evaluating your ability to meet these qualifications.

PMP in the Real World

The PMP certification and PMI membership are for project management professionals of all disciplines. Whether your professional experience is in information technology or construction, you are eligible for PMP certification; however, you must prepare for the examination. It is easy to believe that your experience performing project management in any industry will be a sufficient knowledge base for taking and passing the PMP Certification Examination.

This is not always the case, though. The PMP Certification Examination is very structured to the PMBOK and project management processes and concepts as advocated by PMI. PMI specifies an all-encompassing role for project management professions including extensive planning (project initiation) activities and project closing processes. Procurement, quality control, and risk management are also emphasized.

Depending on the size of your organization and your role on a project team, you might not have hands-on experience with all the processes deemed essential by PMI. You might not engage in, nor have experience with, implementing the complete life cycle of a project as outlined by the PMBOK. Comparably, your corporation might use a PMI-modified methodology for project management based on industry experience or even combine PMI tools with other management techniques, resulting in a hybrid model. These approaches can result in successful project implementation in your company, but they will not be effective in achieving your PMP certification. It is imperative that you understand all the PMBOK procedures and the manner in which PMI believes these processes should be practiced to pass the PMP Certification Examination.

Throughout this book, you will be asked to learn and apply PMI's vision for project management. The PMI answer is the only correct response on exam day. Your experience and qualifications might result in you tailoring the PMBOK and other project management concepts to meet your organization's needs. You might have valid hands-on job experience to support your preference, but in terms of preparing for the PMP Certification Examination, you need to reorient your thinking in terms of the PMBOK and PMI. The correct answer is the PMI answer. After you successfully achieve your PMP certification, you can resume your tailoring or modifying of the PMBOK and PMI's framework to meet the needs and goals of your organization and your practice of project management.

The Ideal PMP Candidate

There is no "ideal" PMP candidate. The requirements for the PMP certification allow for a broad range of applicants with a mix of qualifications; however, minimal levels for experience, education, and training must be met. You can apply to PMI based on your hands-on experience in the field of project management or use your educational background to offset less experience in your discipline.

Education and Project Management Experience

Candidates for PMP certification must meet both educational and experience requirements. Candidates possessing a university degree apply under Category One and have a lower threshold for work experience. Candidates without a university degree are deemed Category Two and can substitute years of work experience for the degree requirement. Verification forms showing compliance with these criteria must be submitted with your PMI application for either category.

Applications with a University Degree

Category One is for applicants possessing a bachelor's degree or equivalent. In this category, fewer personal project management experience hours are necessary, although you must possess a minimum of 4,500 hours of hands-on project management activity within each of the five PMI process groups (initiating, planning, executing, monitoring/controlling, and closing). You must have led and directed specific tasks within all five process groups. This must occur within a minimum of 36 nonoverlapping (unique) months within the last 6 years.

Table 1 Category One		
Criteria	**Minimum**	**Explanation**
Bachelor's degree		Or equivalent from a university.
Personal project management experience within five process groups	4,500 hours	Within the last 6 years from the date of application.
Nonoverlapping months of personal project management experience	36 months	Individual months count toward the 36 months requirement once, even if you worked on multiple projects during the same month.
Specific instruction that addresses learning objectives in project management	35 contact hours	Must include instruction on project quality, scope, time, cost, human resources, communications, risk, procurement, and integration management.

Applications Without a University Degree

Category Two allows applicants with significant work experience to submit additional work history in lieu of a university degree. In essence, your extended period of job experience serves as your educational requirement.

In this category, you can use 7,500 hours of project management performance to substitute for holding a college degree. You must validate that this work occurred within the last 8 years, of which 60 months must support nonoverlapping periods of personal project management experience. Your work experience must cover all five process groups as noted in category one. A high school diploma or equivalent and/or an associate's degree or equivalent are a requirement of this category.

Table 2   Category Two

Criteria	Minimum	Explanation
Personal project management experience within five process groups	7,500 hours	Within the last 8 years from the date of application.
Nonoverlapping months of personal project management experience	60 months	Individual months count toward the 60 months requirement once, even if you worked on multiple projects during the same month.
Specific instruction that addresses learning objectives in project management	35 contact hours	Must include instruction on project quality, scope, time, cost, human resources, communications, risk, procurement, and integration management.

Regardless of whether you opt for category one or two, you must complete 35 contact hours of project management education. This training must provide specific instruction addressing project quality management, scope management, time management, cost management, human resources management, communications management, risk management, procurement management, and integration management within the learning objectives.

Courses, workshops, and training sessions in one or more of the following categories satisfy the education requirement:

➤ University/college academic and continuing education program

➤ Courses or programs offered by training companies or consultants

➤ Courses or programs offered by PMI Component organizations (not including chapter meetings)

➤ Courses or programs offered by PMI Registered Education Providers

➤ Courses or programs offered by employer/company-sponsored program

➤ Courses or programs offered by distance-learning companies

Experience Verification

To document your qualifications, you will be asked to complete an experience verification form as part of your PMI application. For the training component, you will document your training by providing the institution name, the name of the course attended, the dates of attendance, and the contact hours earned. You should save any document related to the course, such as a completion certificate in the event that you are randomly selected for an audit by PMI.

For your work experience, the experience verification form will ask you to note the project title, your role on the project, the approximate number of hours spent working in each of the five process areas, the project start date, the project end date, and contact information for the company where the work was performed. You will also be asked to summarize the deliverables you managed on the project and provide contact information for each project.

Prior to starting your experience verification form, compile all relevant information. Your résumé, work records, time-management tools, and related documentation will be essential to detailing your professional experience. Any work breakdown structures and resource allocation spreadsheets detailing the time you spent on each process area can be particularly helpful. Be thorough in your explanations of your work experience. This will be beneficial if you are selected for an audit.

Review each of the process groups in the PMBOK to ensure you are correctly documenting your work experience. The PMI might differentiate between process groups in a manner contrasting with your past work experience, so it is imperative that your work experience aligns with the correct PMI process groups.

For your education component, you are simply asked to name the institution from which you graduated, your field of study, and your date of graduation. A photocopy of your diploma or transcript should suffice if you are asked to verify your degree as part of a PMI audit.

Testing Your Exam Readiness

The more experience you have responding to PMBOK-type questions, the greater your likelihood of passing your PMP Certification Examination. You should take one of the practice examinations in this book prior to beginning a course of study to gauge your strengths and weaknesses. This will enable you to develop a study plan in conjunction with this book to target your vulnerable knowledge areas.

After you have completed your initial study plan and read this book in its entirety, take the second practice exam. Evaluate your results. Did you do better than the initial test? Have your strengths and weaknesses improved?

Have your strengths and weakness changed? Study your responses to the questions that were incorrect. Are there any patterns evident in the questions you missed? Did you debate between two answers, ultimately opting for the wrong answer? Did you pick answers that appear correct but are simply not the best answer by the standards of the PMBOK and the PMI? Based on this analysis, go back and revise your study plan, concentrating on those areas where you need more knowledge and improvement.

Take your practice examinations under testing conditions. This is a key factor for success during your PMP Certification Examination. When you take a practice test, do so in a quiet area at your desk or dining room table free of distractions. You do not want to be interrupted by the doorbell, phones, email, or your dog during this time.

Set a timer on your watch to ensure you are complying with the time requirement. Based on your time trials, you can train yourself to take more time with each question, or less as the case might be. You can make sure you are saving ample time to review your answers. Most importantly, you will be able to alleviate some of the nervousness and pressure you will feel on exam day by orienting yourself to the conditions under which you will be taking the examination. You will also have more confidence that you are monitoring your time and moving through the exam at a proper rate of speed.

With each practice exam you will see improvement. However, be careful when taking the same practice exam more than once so that your improvement is not based simply on memorizing the answer for that specific exam. Two practice exams are offered in this book, and you can purchase additional practice examinations through the PMI bookstore on the PMI website.

Pretest

To end the Self Assessment section, we recommend that you answer the following questions. These questions are intended to help you measure your knowledge of fundamental project management concepts and techniques. If you don't score well on these questions, we recommend reading some books on fundamental project management or spending some more time on the job to gain the fundamental knowledge you need to begin your pursuit of the PMP exam. Some fundamental project management books are cited throughout this book in the "Need to Know More?" sections of each chapter as well as in Appendix B, "Additional Resources." Answer these questions:

➤ Do you know the difference between a project charter and a project plan?

➤ Do you know the difference between initiating and planning a project?

➤ Do you know the difference between backward pass and forward pass to find the critical path in your project?

➤ Do you know when scope verification is performed?

➤ Do you know how to develop and utilize a WBS?

➤ Do you know when to apply a change control system?

➤ Do you know how to use schedule network analysis?

➤ Do you know the difference between earned value and planned value?

➤ Do you know what a Gantt chart is?

➤ Do you know when to fast track a schedule or when crashing would be the better option?

Project Management Framework Fundamentals

Terms you'll need to understand:

✓ Functional organization

✓ Matrix organization

✓ Portfolio

✓ Program

✓ Project

✓ Project knowledge area

✓ Project life cycle

✓ Project management

✓ Project management office (PMO)

✓ Project manager

✓ Project process groups

✓ Project risk

✓ Projectized organization

✓ Stakeholder

✓ Triple constraint

Techniques and concepts you'll need to master:

✓ Project management framework

✓ Differences between projects and operational activities

✓ Project management interaction with general management

✓ Project characteristics throughout the life cycle

✓ Stakeholder responsibilities

✓ Triple constraint interactions and dependencies

This chapter introduces the basic terminology and topics the PMBOK covers and provides a general outline for the PMP exam material. The topics in this chapter correspond to the first three chapters of the PMBOK, including project introduction, project life cycle, and project processes.

Understanding the Project Management Framework

The Project Management framework is the first section of the PMBOK and serves as the foundation for the document. Briefly stated, it presents the structure used to discuss and organize projects. The PMBOK uses this structure to document all facets of a project on which consensus has been reached among a broadly diverse group of project managers. The PMBOK is not only the document that defines the methods to manage projects, but is also the most widely accepted project management foundation. This document provides a frame of reference for managing projects and teaching the fundamental concepts of project management. Note that the PMBOK does not address every area of project management in all industries. It does, however, address the recognized best practices for the management of a single project. Most organizations have developed their own practices that are specific to their organization.

It is important that you read the PMBOK. Although many good references and test preparation sources can help prepare for the PMP exam, they are not substitutes for the PMBOK itself.

The PMP exam tests your knowledge of project management in the context of the PMBOK and PMI philosophy. Regardless of the experience you might have in project management, your answers will only be correct if they concur with PMI philosophy. If the PMBOK presents a method that differs from your experience, go with the PMBOK's approach. That being said, the PMP exam will also contain questions that are not specifically addressed in the PMBOK. It is important that you coordinate your understanding of project management with that of PMI. This book will help you do just that.

What a Project Is and What It Is Not

The starting point in discussing how projects should be properly managed is to first understand what a project is (and what it is not). According to the PMBOK, a *project* has two main characteristics that differentiate it from regular, day-to-day operation. Know these two characteristics of projects.

A Project Is Temporary

Unlike day-to-day operation, a project has specific starting and ending dates. Of the two dates, the ending date is the more important. A project ends either when its objectives have been met or when the project is terminated due to its objectives not being met. If you can't tell when an endeavor starts or ends, it's not a project. This characteristic is important because projects are, by definition, constrained by a schedule.

A Project Is an Endeavor Undertaken to Produce a Unique Product or Service

In addition to having a discrete timeframe, a project must also have one or more specific products or services it produces. A project must "do" something. A project that terminates on schedule might still not be successful—it must also produce something unique.

The PMP exam will contain a few questions on the definition of a project. Simply put, if an endeavor fails to meet both of the project criteria, it is an operational activity. Remember this: Projects exist to achieve a goal. When the goal is met, the project is complete. Operations conduct activities that sustain processes, often indefinitely.

Programs, Portfolios, and the PMO

It is common practice for an organization to have more than one project active at a time. In fact, several projects that share common characteristics or are related in some way are often grouped together to make management or the project more efficient. A group of related projects is called a *program*. If there are multiple projects and programs in an organization, they can further be grouped together into one or more portfolios. A *portfolio* is a collection of projects and programs that satisfy the strategic needs of an organization.

The PMP exam and the PMBOK only cover techniques to manage single projects. You need to know what programs and portfolios are, but you will only address single project management topics in regards to the exam.

Many organizations are finding that project management is so effective that they maintain an organization unit with the primary responsibility of managing projects and programs. The unit is commonly called the *project management office (PMO)*. The PMO is responsible for coordinating projects and, in some cases, providing resources for managing projects. A PMO can make the project manager's job easier by maintaining project management standards and implementing policies and procedures that are common within the organization.

What Project Management Is

According to the PMBOK, "Project management is the application of knowledge, skills, tools, and techniques to project activities to meet project requirements." In other words, project management is taking what you know and proactively applying that knowledge to effectively guide your project through its life cycle.

The purpose of applying this knowledge is to help the project meet its objectives. Sounds pretty straightforward, doesn't it? The PMP exam will test your project management knowledge. But it's more than just a test of your knowledge. It is a test that evaluates your ability to *apply* your knowledge through the use of skills, tools, and techniques. The application of project management knowledge is what makes the exam challenging.

Understanding project management is more than just memorization. You do have to memorize some things (and we'll let you know what those are). But it's more important to know how to apply what you know. Some of the hardest questions on the exam look like they have two, or even three, right answers. You really have to understand the PMBOK to choose the most correct answer.

Did you notice I said the *most correct answer*? The PMP exam will throw several questions at you that seem to have more than one correct answer. In fact, many questions on the exam do have multiple answers that can be considered correct. But you will need to be able to choose the one that best satisfies the question as asked. Read each question carefully. And always remember that the PMBOK rules.

Project Management Knowledge Areas

The PMBOK organizes all the activities that define a project's life cycle into 44 processes. These processes represent content from 9 knowledge areas. It is important to have a good understanding of each of the project processes and how they relate to one another. We'll go into more details of each process in a later section. For now, understand the 9 knowledge areas and what purposes they serve for the project.

The PMBOK itself is organized by knowledge areas. There is a separate chapter for each knowledge area. Table 1.1 shows the 9 knowledge areas and gives a brief description of each.

Table 1.1 Project Knowledge Areas	
Knowledge Area	**Description**
Project Integration Management	Processes and activities that pull the various elements of project management together, including developing plans, managing project execution, monitoring work and changes, and closing the project.
Project Scope Management	Processes that ensure the project includes the work required to successfully complete the project, and no more. This includes scope planning, definition, verification, and control. This area also includes the work breakdown structure creation.
Project Time Management	Processes that ensure the project completes in a timely manner. Activity sequencing and scheduling activities occur in this area.
Project Cost Management	Processes that ensure the project completes within the approved budget. Basically, any cost management activity goes here.
Project Quality Management	Processes that ensure the project will meet its objectives. This area includes quality planning, assurance, and control.
Project Human Resource Management	Processes that organize and manage the project team.
Project Communications Management	Processes that specify how and when team members communicate and share information with one another and others not on the team.
Project Risk Management	Processes that conduct risk management activities for the project. These activities include risk analysis, response planning, monitoring, and control.
Project Procurement Management	Processes that manage the acquisition of products and services for the project, along with seller and contract management.

Figure 1.1 shows each of the project management knowledge areas and the specific processes associated with it.

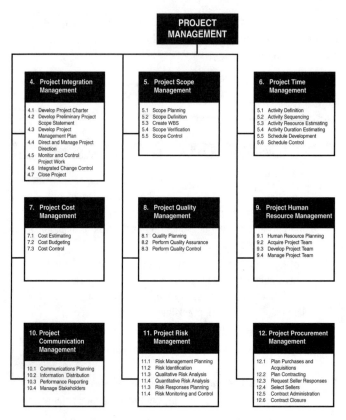

Figure 1.1 Project management knowledge areas and processes.

Knowledge Area Changes in the PMBOK Guide, Third Edition

PMI is constantly reviewing its documents and exams for currency and applicability to today's project management practices. The PMBOK Guide, Third Edition was released in 2005 as an update to the previous edition, the PMBOK 2000. There are several changes in the new edition. None of the changes are major, although the PMBOK has been slightly reorganized to better reflect current project management practices. The changes from the PMBOK 2000 focus on newly added processes and process alignment changes. Here is a summary of the knowledge area changes that are included in the PMBOK Guide, Third Edition:

➤ Has expanded focus on process groups.

➤ Has expanded coverage of integration and initiation processes.

➤ Has added 7 new processes and deleted 2. The PMBOK Guide, Third Edition defines a total of 44 processes (up from 39 defined in the PMBOK 2000).

➤ Has renamed 13 processes to enhance clarity.

➤ Has added process flow diagrams.

➤ Has increased consistency in the placement of inputs, tools and techniques, and outputs.

 As of this writing, PMI will transition to the new exam on September 30, 2005. All PMP exams after the transition date will be based on the PMBOK Guide, Third Edition. If you have been studying another reference that is based on the PMBOK 2000 Edition, make sure you review the newer PMBOK before taking the exam. (Of course, this reference does cover the new PMBOK material.)

To summarize the process additions, deletions, and name changes, Table 1.2 lists the processes that have changed in the PMBOK Guide, Third Edition. (Some processes only change the section number where they appear in the document. We'll only highlight name changes here.)

Table 1.2 Changes in the PMBOK Guide, Third Edition	
2000 Edition Process Name	**Third Edition Process Name**
(none)	4.1 Develop Project Charter
(none)	4.2 Develop Preliminary Project Scope Statement
4.1 Project Plan Development	4.3 Develop Project Management Plan
4.2 Project Plan Execution	4.4 Direct and Manage Project Execution
(none)	4.5 Monitor and Control Project Work
(none)	4.7 Close Project
5.1 Initiation	(Moved to PMBOK Chapter 4)
(none)	5.3 Create WBS
5.5 Scope Change Control	5.5 Scope Control
(none)	6.3 Activity Resource Estimating
7.1 Resource Planning	(Moved to Project Time Management in PMBOK Chapter 6)
8.2 Quality Assurance	8.2 Perform Quality Assurance
8.3 Quality Control	8.3 Perform Quality Control
9.1 Organizational Planning	9.1 Human Resource Planning
9.2 Staff Acquisition	9.2 Acquire Project Team

(continued)

Table 1.2 Changes in the PMBOK Guide, Third Edition *(continued)*

2000 Edition Process Name	Third Edition Process Name
9.3 Team Development	9.3 Develop Project Team
(none)	9.4 Manage Project Team
10.4 Administrative Closure	10.4 Manage Stakeholders
12.1 Procurement Planning	12.1 Plan Purchases and Acquisitions
12.2 Solicitation Planning	12.2 Plan Contracting
12.3 Solicitation	12.3 Request Seller Response
12.4 Source Selection	12.4 Select Sellers
12.6 Contract Closeout	12.6 Contract Closure

In addition to the process name changes, each knowledge area incorporates changes from the PMBOK 2000 Edition that help to clarify the document and make the various sections more cohesive. Of all the knowledge areas, Project Integration Management and Project Risk Management probably underwent the most changes. Be sure you focus on the newer material, especially in these two knowledge areas, as you study for the exam.

How Project Management Affects Other Areas of Management

The PMBOK only represents a part of the expertise required to manage projects effectively. Other areas of expertise are necessary to allow a management team to apply the knowledge in the PMBOK and manage one or more projects. The PMBOK specifically focuses on managing single projects. Because most organizations need to manage multiple simultaneous projects, the need exists for management expertise beyond what the PMBOK addresses. Although other areas of knowledge and expertise are beyond the scope of the PMP exam, you will likely be asked a few questions that test your general awareness of other management requirements.

In addition to the PMBOK and an understanding of the project environment, there are at least three additional areas of expertise necessary to manage a project well. They include

➤ Application area knowledge and standards

➤ General management knowledge and skills

➤ Interpersonal skills

Each of these additional areas of expertise is important to effectively managing projects. This is true even though they are not directly related to the processes and activities most closely related to project management. For example, it is extremely difficult to manage a project without an understanding of general management principles. Likewise, poor interpersonal skills will likely result in project team issues and have an overall negative effect on the project.

For the purpose of the PMP exam, know the areas of expertise required for effective project management.

Understanding Application Area Knowledge and Standards

Each project has characteristics that make it unique and distinct from other projects. Although projects in general share many common needs, each project's objectives can require specific expertise to reach a successful conclusion. Projects often need knowledge of areas that are specific to the product produced—knowledge that would not be needed in other projects. The application area of expertise covers any knowledge, standards, or regulations that are specific in nature and apply to a project but are not general enough to all projects to be considered core product management knowledge.

Some examples of application knowledge and standards are

➤ Specific departments and the services or support they provide. Examples of application area functional departments are legal, manufacturing, marketing, and security. These departments contribute to some, but not all, projects.

➤ Technical elements, including software development and engineering services.

➤ Specific types of management services for specialized areas of production or manufacturing.

➤ Standards and regulations that apply to any work performed in a project.

This topic is often a part of an exam question, as opposed to the main focus of a question. When building your project team, you often need to recruit members based on their application knowledge and experience. The value any team member brings to the project is generally evaluated in terms of one or more areas of expertise.

Understanding General Management Skills

The ability to manage a project effectively is contingent on the performing organization's ability to manage general processes.

Without an understanding of general management topics, specific study of the processes of project management will not be very successful. The discipline of project management builds on the principles of general management and relies on the understanding of basic management. For the exam, be aware that successful project management depends on some disciplines that are outside the standard project management processes and activities.

General management knowledge and skills include the management of any ongoing activities that support the project as it moves through its life cycle. The environment in which projects operate can be different among organizations. Regardless of the specific type of environment, organizations should provide several common products and services that support project activities. Activities in the general management area of expertise include

➤ Accounting

➤ Health, safety, and regulatory compliance practices

➤ Human resources services

➤ Information technology services and support

➤ Legal issues

➤ Logistics

➤ Manufacturing and distribution

➤ Purchasing and procurement

Many general management activities support each project. While not technically part of project management, the general management processes and activities are crucial as a foundation for projects to exist.

Understanding Interpersonal Skills

Another important area of expertise is that of interpersonal skills. As we discuss the various processes of project management, it should become clear that in all cases project team members contribute to the project's success. Likewise, project team members can reduce a project's effectiveness through poor team interaction. It is necessary to posses or develop methods of managing the relationships among project team members.

Although the PMP exam doesn't specifically test knowledge of general interpersonal skills, you are expected to understand the need for good leadership skills and a sound understanding of proper communication techniques. These skills are key to interaction among team members. You'll also need to put these skills into practice when working with stakeholders. One of the most important responsibilities of the project manager is to meet the needs of both the stakeholders and project team—at least in the perspective of keeping both groups productive with respect to the project. These two groups can sometimes be difficult to motivate and bring together. That is why strong leadership and communication skills are important to the interpersonal relationships you will encounter.

The interpersonal skills area includes all areas of interaction between people. Managing interpersonal skills includes

➤ Fostering effective communication

➤ Influencing decisions

➤ Developing and providing leadership

➤ Providing individual and team motivation

➤ Managing conflict

➤ Solving problems

The success of a project can be dramatically influenced by the effectiveness of the team. Positive team dynamics are built on proper development and management of interpersonal skills. Although this area of expertise is not a core project management concern, it can have a material impact on a project. Make sure you understand its importance to the project's overall effectiveness.

Understanding Project Life Cycles

The project manager and project team have one shared goal: to carry out the work of the project for the purpose of meeting the project's objectives. Every project has an inception, a period during which activities move the project toward completion, and a termination (either successful or unsuccessful). Taken together, these phases represent the path a project takes from the beginning to its end and are generally referred to as the project *life cycle*.

The project life cycle is often formally divided into phases that describe common activities as the project matures. The activities near the beginning of a project look different from activities closer to the end of the project. Most projects share activity characteristics as the project moves through its life cycle. You might see several questions on the exam that ask you to compare different phases in a project's life cycle. In general, here are the common comparisons of early and late project life cycle activities:

➤ **The least is known about the project near its beginning**—As the project matures, more is learned about the project and the product it produces. This process is called *progressive elaboration*. As you learn more about the project, all plans and projections become more accurate.

➤ **The level of uncertainty and risk is the highest at the beginning of a project**—As more is learned about the project and more of the project's work is completed, uncertainty and risk decrease.

➤ **Stakeholders assert the greatest influence on the outcome of a project at the beginning**—After the project starts, the stakeholder influence continually declines. Their influence to affect the project's outcome is at its lowest point at the end of the project.

➤ **Costs and personnel activity are both low at the beginning of a project, are high near the middle of the project, and tend to taper off to a low level as the project nears completion.**

➤ **The cost associated with project changes is at its lowest point at the project's beginning**—No work has been done, so changing is easy. As more and more work is completed, the cost of any changes rises.

One of the more important relationships to understand throughout the project life cycle is the relationship between project knowledge and risk. As stated earlier, knowledge of a project increases as more work is done due to progressive elaboration, and risk decreases as the project moves toward completion. Figure 1.2 depicts the relationship between knowledge and risk:

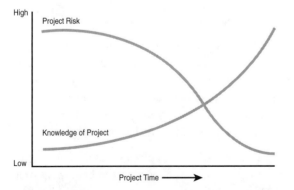

Figure 1.2 Project risk versus knowledge of project.

Another important relationship present in a project's life cycle is the relationship between the declining influence of stakeholders on the outcome of a project and the cost of changes and error corrections. Because little or no work has been accomplished near the beginning of a project, changes require few adjustments and are generally low in cost. At the same time, stakeholders can assert their authority and make changes to the project's direction. As more work is accomplished, the impact and cost of changes increase and leave stakeholders with fewer and fewer options to affect the project's product. Figure 1.3 shows how the influences of stakeholders and cost of changes are related to the project life cycle:

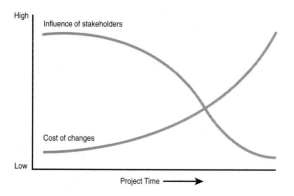

Figure 1.3 Stakeholder influence and cost change impact through the life of a project.

Although all projects are unique, they do share common components or processes that are normally grouped together. Here are the generally accepted process groups defined by PMI (we'll cover each of these process groups in the coming chapters):

➤ Initiation

➤ Planning

➤ Executing

➤ Controlling

➤ Closing

Moving from one phase in the life cycle to another is generally accompanied by a transfer of technical material or control from one group to another. Most phases officially end when the work from one phase is accepted as sufficient to meet that phase's objectives and is passed onto the next phase. The work from one phase could be documentation, plans, components necessary for a subsequent phase, or any work product that contributes to the project's objectives.

Who Are the Stakeholders?

A project exists to satisfy a need (remember that a project produces a unique produce or service). Without a need of some sort, there is no need for a project. Such needs originate with one or more people; someone has to state a need. As a result, a project will fill the need and likely affect some people or organizations. All people and organizations that have an interest in the project or its outcome are called project *stakeholders*. The stakeholders provide input to the requirements of the project and the direction the project should take throughout its life cycle.

The list of stakeholders can be large and can change as the project matures. One of the first requirements to properly manage a project is the creation of a key stakeholder list. Be very careful to include all key stakeholders. Many projects have been derailed due to the political fallout of excluding a key stakeholder. Every potential stakeholder cannot be included in all aspects of a project, so it is important to identify the stakeholders who represent all stakeholders.

Although it sounds easy to create a list of stakeholders, they are not always easy to identify in reality. You will often need to ask many questions of many people to ensure you create a complete stakeholder list. Because stakeholders provide input for the project requirements and mold the image of the project and its expectations, it is vitally important that you be as persistent as necessary to identify all potential stakeholders. Key stakeholders can include

➤ **Project manager**—The person responsible for managing the project.

➤ **Customer or user**—The person or organization that will receive and use the project's product or service.

➤ **Performing organization**—The organization that performs the work of the project.

➤ **Project team members**—The members of the team who are directly involved in performing the work of the project.

➤ **Project management team**—Project team members who are directly involved in managing the project.

➤ **Sponsor**—The person or organization that provides the authority and financial resources for the project.

➤ **Influencers**—People or groups not directly related to the project's product but with the ability to affect the project in a positive or negative way.

➤ **Project management office (PMO)**—If the PMO exists, it can be a stakeholder if it has responsibility for the project's outcome.

The Project Manager

One of the most visible stakeholders is the project manager. The *project manager* is the person responsible for managing the project and is a key stakeholder. Although the project manager is the most visible stakeholder, he does not have the ultimate authority or responsibility for any project. Senior management has the ultimate authority for the project. Senior management issues the project charter (we'll discuss that in the next chapter) and is responsible for the project itself. The project manager is granted the authority by senior management to get the job done and to resolve many issues. The project manager is also in charge of the project but often does not control the resources.

Look at these chapters in the PMBOK for more detailed information on the project manager's roles and responsibilities:

➤ The Project Management Framework Introduction, Chapter 1

➤ Project Life Cycle and Organization, Chapter 2

➤ Project Human Resources Management, Chapter 9

You must have a clear understanding of the project manager's roles and responsibilities for this exam. Go through the PMBOK, search for "Project Manager," and look at all the responsibilities defined. Know what a project manager must do, should do, and should not do.

The PDF version of the PMBOK allows you to easily search for terms. Use it to search for any terms you are unsure of.

Working with Organizational Politics and Influences

In nearly all cases, the project exists within a larger organization. Some group or organization creates each project, and the project team must operate within the larger organization's environment. Several factors impact the extent to which the project is affected.

First, the extent to which the initiating organization derives revenue from projects affects how projects are regarded. In an organization where the primary stream of revenue comes from various projects, the project manager generally enjoys more authority and access to resources. On the other hand, organizations that create projects only due to outside demands will likely make it more difficult for the project manager to acquire resources. If a particular resource is needed to perform both operational and project work, many functional managers will resist requests to assign that resource to a project.

Another factor that influences how projects operate with respect to sponsoring organizations is the level of sponsorship from the project's origin. A project that has a sponsor who is at the director level will typically enjoy far less resistance than one with a sponsor who is a functional manager. The reason for this is simple: Many managers tend to protect their own resources and are not willing to share them without sufficient motivation. The more authority a project sponsor possesses, the easier time the project manager will have when requesting resources from various sources.

In addition to the previous issues, the sponsoring organization's maturity and project orientation can have a substantial effect on each project. More mature organizations tend to have more general management practices in place and allow projects to operate in a stable environment. Projects in less mature organizations might find that they must compete for resources and management attention due to fewer established policies. There can also be many issues related to the culture of an organization, such as values, beliefs, and expectations that can affect projects.

The last major factor that has a material impact on how projects exist within the larger organization is the management style of the organization itself. The next section introduces the main types of project management organizations and their relative strengths and weaknesses.

Differentiating Functional, Matrix, and Projectized Organizational Structures

Each organization approaches the relationship between operations and projects differently. The PMBOK defines three main organizational structures that affect many aspects of a project, including

➤ The project manager's authority

➤ Resource availability

➤ Control of the project budget

➤ The project manager and administrative staff roles

Functional Organizational Structure

A *functional* organization structure is a classical hierarchy in which each employee has a single superior. Employees are then organized by specialty and work accomplished is generally specific to that specialty. Communication with other groups generally occurs by passing information requests up the hierarchy and over to the desired group or manager. Of all the organizational structures, this one tends to be the most difficult for the project manager. The project manager lacks the authority to assign resources and must acquire people and other resources from multiple functional managers. In many cases, the project's priority is viewed lower than operations by the functional manager. In these organizations, it is more common for the project manager to appeal to the senior management to resolve resource issues.

Matrix Organizational Structure

A *matrix* organization is a blended organizational structure. Although a functional hierarchy is still in place, the project manager is recognized as a valuable position and is given more authority to manage the project and assign resources. Matrix organizations can be further divided into weak, balanced, and strong matrix organizations. The difference between the three is the level of authority given to the project manager (PM). A *weak* matrix gives more authority to the functional manager (FM), whereas the *strong* matrix gives more power to the PM. As the name suggests, the *balanced* matrix balances power between the FM and the PM.

Projectized Organizational Structure

In a *projectized* organization, there is no defined hierarchy. Resources are brought together specifically for the purpose of a project. The necessary resources are acquired for the project, and the people assigned to the project work only for the PM for the duration of the project. At the end of each project, resources are either reassigned to another project or returned to a resource pool.

There are many subtle differences between each type of structure. Table 1.3 compares the various organizational structures.

Table 1.3 Organizational Structures

	Functional	Weak Matrix	Balanced Matrix	Strong Matrix	Projectized
Description	Traditional organization with a direct supervisor.	The PM and FM share responsibility, with the FM having more authority.	The PM and FM share responsibility, with each having equal authority.	The PM and FM share responsibility, with the PM having more authority.	Projects do not exist under functional departments. The PM has sole management authority.
Authority of project manager	Very low.	Low.	Low to medium.	Medium to high.	High.
Resource availability	Very low.	Low.	Low to medium.	Medium to high.	High.
Project manager involvement	Part-time.	Part-time.	Full-time.	Full-time.	Full-time.
Staff involvement	Part-time.	Part-time.	Part-time.	Full-time.	Full-time.
Advantages	The FM holds accountability for the project.	The PM gets some authority to manage the project.	The PM and FM share the responsibility of the project.	The PM gets more authority to assign resources and manage the project.	The PM has full authority to staff and manage the project.
Disadvantages	The PM holds little or no authority.	The FM can see the PM as a threat and cause conflict.	The PM and FM can be confused about who manages what.	The FM may feel out of the loop.	The PM holds accountability for the project.

Understanding the Project Environment

It is the responsibility of the project manager to understand the project environment. All projects operate within a specific environment, or blend of environments. In addition to understanding the organizational structure, a project manager needs to understand the effects other outside forces play in managing projects. The most obvious external factors for projects are

➤ **Cultural and social environment**—The team needs to understand differences among team members such as language and customs. Any characteristics that set team members apart are potential areas for conflict.

➤ **International and political environment**—Team members might be from different countries or political systems. As with cultural differences, such differences among team members can cause conflict. These differences can also result in regulatory confusion due to different legal systems in place.

➤ **Physical environment**—Team members might not be physically located in the same place. Physical separation requires modified strategies for communication. Time zones and communication media support can be issues when communicating with separate team members.

Managing the Triple Constraint

The PMBOK mentions the three main variables of a project several times. Each of these variables is related to the other two and directly affects the quality of the project. The three variables are called the *triple constraints* and must all be managed to successfully complete a project. Each of these three variables tends to compete with one the others. Too much attention on one generally means one or both of the others suffer. A major concern of the project manager is to ensure each of these variables is balanced with the other two at all times. The three variables of the triple constraint are

➤ **Project scope**—How much work is to be done? Increasing the scope causes more work to be done, and vice versa.

➤ **Time**—The schedule of the project. Modifying the schedule alters the start and end dates for tasks in the project and can alter the project's overall end date.

➤ **Cost**—The cost required to accomplish the project's objectives. Modifying the cost of the project generally has an impact on the scope, time, or quality of the project.

Any change to one of the variables will have some effect on one, or both, of the remaining variables. Likewise, a change to any of the three variables has an impact on the overall quality of the project. The key to understanding the triple constraints is that they are all interrelated. For example, if you decrease the cost of your project, you will likely decrease the quality and perhaps even decrease the scope. With less money, less work gets done. Or, you might find that it takes more time to produce the same result with less money. Either way, a change to cost affects other variables.

Even though this concept is fairly straightforward, a project manager must stay on top of each one to ensure they are balanced. In addition to managing the triple constraints, the project manager is also responsible for explaining the need for balance to the stakeholders. All too often, stakeholders favor one constraint over another. You'll have to ensure that the stakeholders understand the need for balancing all three.

Figure 1.4 shows how the triple constraints are often depicted as a triangle, with quality in the center.

Figure 1.4   The triple constraints.

Understand how the triple constraints require balance to ensure a change does not negatively impact another variable.

Project Management Process Groups

As we discussed earlier in this chapter, work executed during the project can be expressed in specific groups of processes. Each project moves through each of the groups of processes, some more than once. These common collections of processes that the PMBOK defines are called *process groups*. Process groups serve to group together processes in a project that represent related tasks and mark a project's migration toward completion.

The five process groups defined by the PMBOK are

➤ **Initiating**—Defines the project objectives and grants authority to the project manager

➤ **Planning**—Refines the project objectives and scope and plans the steps necessary to meet the project's objectives

➤ **Executing**—Puts the project plan into motion and performs the work of the project

➤ **Monitoring and controlling**—Measures the performance of the executing activities and compares the results with the project plan

➤ **Closing**—Documents the formal acceptance of the project's product and brings all aspects of the project to a close

Figure 1.5 depicts how the five process groups provide a framework for the project.

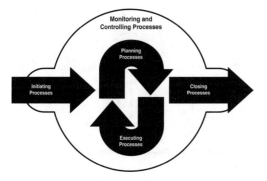

Figure 1.5   Process groups flow.

Each process group will be discussed in detail throughout the rest of this book. Be sure you are comfortable with how a project flows from inception through each of the process groups. The PMBOK, Third Edition has added new figures that depict process flows, inputs and outputs, and interaction between process groups. Look at the PMBOK, Third Edition Chapter 3 for these figures. Use them—they will help you remember how the processes flow throughout the project.

Understanding Project Life Cycle and Project Management Processes Relationships

The PMBOK defines 44 project processes, grouped into five process groups. These processes define the path a project takes through its life cycle. The processes are not linear; some overlap others. In fact, some processes are iterative and are executed multiple times in a single project. It is important to become comfortable with the process flow and how it defines the project life cycle.

Throughout the life of a project, different processes are needed at different times. A project starts with little activity. As the project comes to life, more tasks are executed and more processes are active at the same time. This high level of activity increases until nearing the completion of the project (or project phase). As the end nears, activity starts to diminish until the termination point is reached.

Figure 1.6 shows how the process groups interact in a project.

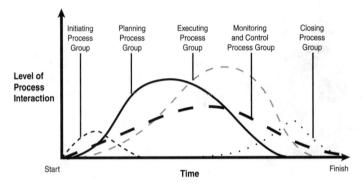

Figure 1.6 Process group interactions.

Processes, Process Groups, and Knowledge Areas

The best way to prepare for questions that test your knowledge of the project management processes is to know and understand each of the processes, along with its process group and knowledge area assignment.

Table 1.4 shows how all 44 processes are grouped by process group and related to the knowledge areas.

Table 1.4   Grouping Processes by Group and Related to Knowledge Areas

Knowledge Area	Initiating Process Group	Planning Process Group	Executing Process Group	Monitoring and Controlling Process Group	Closing Process Group
Project Management Integration	Develop Project Charter (4.1) Develop Preliminary Project Scope Statement (4.2)	Develop Project Management Plan (4.3)	Direct and Manage Project Execution (4.4)	Monitor and Control Project Work (4.5) Integrated Change Control (4.6)	Close Project (4.7)
Project Scope Management		Scope Planning (5.1) Scope Definition (5.2) Create WBS (5.3)		Scope Verification (5.4) Scope Control (5.5)	
Project Time Management		Activity Definition (6.1) Activity Sequencing (6.2) Activity Resource Estimating (6.3) Activity Duration Estimating (6.4) Schedule Development (6.5)		Schedule Control (6.6)	
Project Cost Management		Cost Estimating (7.1) Cost Budgeting (7.2)		Cost Control (7.3)	
Project Quality Management		Quality Planning (8.1)	Perform Quality Assurance (8.2)	Perform Quality Control (8.3)	
Project Human Resources Management		Human Resource Planning (9.1)	Acquire Project Team (9.2) Develop Project Team (9.3)	Manage Project Team (9.4)	

(continued)

Table 1.4   Grouping Processes by Group and Related to Knowledge Areas *(continued)*

Knowledge Area	Initiating Process Group	Planning Process Group	Executing Process Group	Monitoring and Controlling Process Group	Closing Process Group
Project Communications Management		Communications Planning (10.1)	Information Distribution (10.2)	Performance Reporting (10.3) Manage Stakeholders (10.4)	
Project Risk Management		Risk Management Planning (11.1) Risk Identification (11.2) Qualitative Risk Analysis (11.3) Quantitative Risk Analysis (11.4) Risk Response Planning (11.5)		Risk Monitoring and Control (11.6)	
Project Procurement Management		Plan Purchases and Acquisitions (12.1) Plan Contracting (12.2)	Request Seller Responses (12.3) Select Sellers (12.4)	Contract Administration (12.5)	Contract Closure (12.6)

Understanding Process Interaction Customization

The five process groups defined in the PMBOK are general in nature and common to projects. However, all projects are unique and some do not require all 44 individual project processes. The processes defined in the PMBOK are there for use when needed. You should need the majority of the processes to properly manage a project, but in some cases you will not require every process.

Because projects differ from one another, a specific process can differ dramatically between projects. For example, the process of developing a communication plan will be simple and straightforward for a small project with local team members. However, the process will be much more involved and complicated if the team is large and located in several countries.

Understand the five process groups and 44 processes as defined in the PMBOK. But, more importantly, understand when and how to use each process. The exam will focus more on process implementation than process memorization. Be prepared to really think about which processes you will need for a particular project.

Exam Prep Questions

1. You are a project manager working for a large utility company. You have been assigned the responsibility to manage a project that performs monthly security vulnerability assessments and addresses any identified vulnerabilities. You question the assignment because:

   ❏ A. Security vulnerability assessments do not materially contribute to your organization's products and should not be considered important enough to be classified as a project.

   ❏ B. This endeavor cannot be considered a project because no start date is specified.

   ❏ C. The recurring nature of the assessment with no ending date means this endeavor is not a project at all.

   ❏ D. Because a security vulnerability assessment produces no specific product, it is not a project.

2. You are managing a project that will implement a new accounting software package. You have assigned the resources, both personnel and equipment, and want to keep the IT manager in the loop by informing her of your decisions. Which type of organizational structure are you working in?

   ❏ A. Projectized

   ❏ B. Strong matrix

   ❏ C. Weak matrix

   ❏ D. Functional

3. Which process group contains the processes that ensure the project includes the work required to successfully complete the project, and no more?

   ❏ A. Project scope management

   ❏ B. Project quality management

   ❏ C. Project integration management

   ❏ D. Project risk management

4. While building your project team, you decide to include a business analyst with extensive experience implementing, using, and managing tasks with the new chosen accounting software. This individual has managed and participated in other projects that are similar and knows how to work well with users, technical personnel, and management to get the software up and running. Your choice to include him is due to the fact that he possesses expertise in which PMI knowledge area?

   ❏ A. General management knowledge and skills

   ❏ B. Interpersonal skills

   ❏ C. Application knowledge and standards

   ❏ D. Software implementation

5. At what point in a project do you have the highest probability that it will fail?

- ❏ A. The beginning of the project
- ❏ B. After the initial project plan is published but before work actually begins
- ❏ C. After the halfway point of the project is reached
- ❏ D. Just before the end of the project

6. Which of the following statements best describes the influence of stakeholders over the life of a project?

- ❏ A. Stakeholders ultimately direct all project activities.
- ❏ B. Stakeholder influence is low at the beginning and tends to grow throughout the project.
- ❏ C. Stakeholder influence is the highest at the beginning and tends to decrease throughout the project.
- ❏ D. Stakeholders do not directly influence the project's outcome; they only provide authority and resources.

7. During your accounting software implementation project, you find that training is not progressing as quickly as the schedule requires and the users not well trained after the sessions are over. After investigating the cause, you find that the trainers you have retained do not have the proper experience and knowledge to effectively train your users. Which statement best describes the effect on the project and the effect of the action required to fix the problem?

- ❏ A. The schedule is suffering. To fix the situation, you will have to hire more experienced trainers and schedule extra training sessions. Your schedule will return to planned values while cost will increase.
- ❏ B. The quality and schedule are being negatively impacted. To fix the situation, you will likely have to hire more experienced trainers at a higher rate and schedule extra training sessions. Quality and schedule will return to planned values while cost will increase.
- ❏ C. This problem is the responsibility of the organization that provided the trainers. They will provide replacement trainers who are qualified at the same price to continue the training required.
- ❏ D. Although your training looks like it is behind schedule, you wisely built in enough slack time to cover such a problem. You simply find replacement trainers and continue the training.

8. During your accounting software implementation project, two project team members have difficulty working together. They come to you, the project manager, for help resolving the issues. You immediately set up a meeting that includes the functional manager. After the meeting you and the functional manager discuss the issues and agree on a solution. This type of management probably indicates you are working in what type of organizational structure?

   ❑ A. Functional
   ❑ B. Weak matrix
   ❑ C. Balanced matrix
   ❑ D. Projectized

9. You have just completed the scope planning and scope definition. What should you do next?

   ❑ A. Scope verification
   ❑ B. Activity definition
   ❑ C. Create WBS
   ❑ D. Scope control

10. You have just completed the activity definition, activity resources estimating, and activity duration estimating processes. Which process have you left out?

   ❑ A. Activity sequencing
   ❑ B. Schedule development
   ❑ C. Schedule control
   ❑ D. Create WBS

Answers to Exam Prep Questions

1. Answer C is correct. As explained in this question, recurring security vulnerability assessments with no ending date cannot be considered a project. Projects must have time boundaries. Answer A is incorrect because the project product does not have to be directly related to an organization's main product(s). Answer B is incorrect because the lack of a specific start date in the question description would not automatically disqualify the assessment as a project. Answer D is incorrect because a security vulnerability assessment does create at least one product—the vulnerability assessment report.

2. Answer B is correct. In a strong matrix, the project manager has the preeminent position of authority. Because the functional manager does still have authority, a good project manager will keep the functional manager in the loop as much as possible. Answer A is incorrect because projectized organizations do not have functional managers. Answers C and D are incorrect because in a weak matrix and functional organization the project manager does not have greater authority than the functional manager. The project manager would have to defer to the functional manager, not just keep her in the loop.

3. Answer A is correct. Project scope management is mainly concerned with defining the work a project needs to accomplish. This definition is used to ensure all the necessary work is done and no unnecessary work is done. Answers B, C, and D are incorrect because these process groups focus on areas of a project other than scope.

4. Answer C is correct. The reason you decide to include the business analyst is because he possesses a superior knowledge of the application. Answers A and C are incorrect because his application knowledge is the focus, not general management or interpersonal skills. Answer D is incorrect because it is not a specified area of expertise in the PMBOK (it would fall under application knowledge and skills). This question is an example of too much information. You will find many questions on the PMP exam that contain more information than you need. Use only what is necessary to answer the question. Don't get confused with extraneous information.

5. Answer A is correct. Risk and uncertainty are the highest at the beginning or a project. These two factors make the probability of failure the highest at the beginning. The more you know about a project, the better chance you will have of completing it successfully. Answer B is incorrect because a lot is known about a project by the time you publish any plan. Risk and uncertainty are lower than at the beginning.

Answers C and D are incorrect for similar reasons. As you move closer to the end of a project, you gain a higher level of confidence in the project's outcome. This is largely due to the fact that, as more work is accomplished, you can view and evaluate more and more or the project's output.

6. Answer C is correct. Stakeholder influence is greatest at the beginning of the project. When the initial objectives are being developed, the stakeholders have a lot of input. After the main project parameters are agreed upon, the project manager and project team start working on those objectives and the stakeholder involvement decreases. Answer A is incorrect because the project manager directs project activities, not the stakeholders. Answers B and D are incorrect because they do not reflect the stakeholder involvement.

7. Answer B is correct. The question states that training is not meeting the schedule and the result is that the training is not getting people properly trained. That means both schedule and quality are suffering. Of all the solutions, answer B provides the best description of the effects on your project. Answer A is incorrect because it does not mention the impact on project quality. Answer C is incorrect for several reasons. The problem might be the responsibility of the organization that supplied the trainers, but the responsibility of the impact on the project is the project manager's. Answer C also ignores the quality issue. Answer D is incorrect because is implies that the project manager padded the schedule. This is not an ethical practice. Your estimates should be realistic. If you expect such problems to occur, you should address them in the beginning of the project, along with appropriate recovery methods. By padding the schedule, you hide a real risk to the project.

8. Answer C is correct. In a balanced matrix the project manager and functional manager share equal authority. Answers A and B are incorrect because the functional manager has greater authority and would likely handle problems directly in a functional or weak matrix structure. Answer D is incorrect because the project manager would handle such issues directly in a projectized organization.

9. Answer C is correct. Create the WBS is the process that follows scope planning and scope definition. Answers A, B, and D are incorrect because they do not follow the PMBOK process flow.

10. Answer A is correct. The PMBOK places activity sequencing between activity definition and activity resource estimating. Answers B, C, and D are incorrect because they do not follow the PMBOK flow. You will see questions similar to questions 9 and 10 in the PMP exam. Know your process flows.

Need to Know More?

 Kerzner, Harold. *Project Management: A Systems Approach to Planning, Scheduling, and Controlling, Eighth Edition*. Indianapolis: John Wiley and Sons, 2003.

 Project Management Institute. *A Guide to the Project Management Body of Knowledge, Third Edition*. Newton Square, PA: Project Management Institute, 2004.

Wysocki, Robert K. and Rudd McGary. *Effective Project Management, Third Edition*. Indianapolis: John Wiley and Sons, 2003.

Understanding Project Initiation

Terms you'll need to understand:

✓ Assumptions
✓ Constraints
✓ Go/No-go decision
✓ Management by objectives (MBO)
✓ Project boundaries
✓ Project charter
✓ Project initiation
✓ Project initiator
✓ Project scope
✓ Project selection
✓ Project sponsor

Techniques and concepts you'll need to master:

✓ Gathering initial project information
✓ Project authorization
✓ Understanding the importance of project initiation
✓ Assignment of project manager
✓ Shared project ownership
✓ Developing a project charter
✓ Developing a preliminary project scope statement
✓ Knowing the difference between initiating and planning process group activities

The first process group you will encounter in the project life cycle is *project initiation*. Although project initiation is a relatively small topic that represents less than 10% of the questions on the PMP exam, it is an important topic. In addition to being a small topic, it is also one with which most project managers have little experience. In spite of clear PMI definitions of activities that should be carried out during project initiation, many organizations approach the initial steps of projects differently. As a result, your firsthand experience might differ with the PMI recommendations in this process group. Don't trivialize the material in this chapter. Ensure that you understand project initiation before moving on to tackle some of the larger topics.

The Function of Project Initiation

The project initiation process group is the first step in the project life cycle. In fact, much of the work performed in this process group is actually outside the scope of the project. The main purpose of project initiation is to authorize a project to begin or continue.

Project initiation commonly occurs at the beginning of a project and can also be required at certain points throughout the project. For example, a large project with the goal of producing a prototype of a commercial jet will likely encounter several points along the project life cycle at which important decisions must be made. After the fuselage and airfoil have been produced and joined together, they must be tested to evaluate performance against project goals. If the performance does not meet certain standards, the components must be reworked to meet standards before continuing. Alternatively, the whole project could be terminated if the product is deemed to be unable to effectively meet the project standards. This point in the project is a crucial go/no-go decision point and would constitute activities in the project initiation process group.

It bears repeating that the project initiation process group activities can be required more than once in the project life cycle. Although the most common place for these activities is at the beginning of a project, don't overlook the fact that they can be called for during the project at any material point.

It is not uncommon for large projects to call for project initiation processes several times throughout the project life cycle. Anytime you need to assess the progress of a project, reevaluate its merit, and request approval to continue, project initiation processes are executed.

In all cases, project initiation processes require input from previous activities. The entities charged with deciding whether to proceed will require substantiating information on which to base a decision. When project initiation occurs at the beginning of a project, at least some of the input must be created in tasks that are not part of the project. This work predates the project initiation date and makes the project start point fuzzy at times. The points in time at which a project begins and ends are referred to as the *project boundaries*. Because a substantial amount of the inputs to the initiation process is created outside the scope of the project, the starting boundary can be unclear. A project always starts as a result of a business need, and the business need develops before the project commences. Likewise, any documentation of the need for the project is developed before the actual project starts.

You will need to know the inputs and outputs of each process defined in the PMBOK. That's 44 separate input and output sets! The exam will include several questions that require you to know process inputs, outputs, and general information flow. Start now by rationalizing the inputs and outputs of each process.

Think: "For this process, what information do I need before I start (inputs) and what information or deliverables will I produce (outputs)?"

Subsequent project initiations (within the project life cycle) will use inputs from preceding activities. It is important to understand that the activities in the project initiation process group always result in a critical project decision. The end of the project initiation process group is represented by a decision to continue the project, go back and redo some of the work, or terminate the project altogether.

In most projects, you should include any customers and other stakeholders in many of the activities in the initiation process group. Including as many stakeholders as possible in the early project activities fosters a sense of pride and shared ownership of the project. Any stakeholder who feels a sense of ownership will likely be more diligent to ensure the project succeeds. Stakeholder participation will increase the success of setting the project scope, gathering project requirements, and defining the overall criteria for project success.

Let's take a look at the various elements and activities of the project initiation process group.

The Project Charter and Its Purpose

The project initiation process group consists of two processes. The first process is the development of the project charter. The second process, developing the preliminary project scope statement, is discussed in a later section. The *project charter* is the initial document that describes the project at a high level and formally authorizes the project. PMI requires that a project charter be created and accepted before a project is considered official. As a PMP, you will be required to insist on a project charter before proceeding in the role of project manager.

 The PMBOK requires a project charter for every project. The lack of a project charter is a project stopper.

Authorization from the stakeholders is necessary for the project manager to allocate resources and actually perform the work of the project. Even before bestowing authorization, the stakeholders must assign the project manager to the project. The project charter provides the framework for carrying out these actions. It is also the first deliverable of the project and sets the stage for the whole project. Remembering the output of this process is easy because the only output is the project charter document. The inputs are more numerous, however. Table 2.1 lists the inputs, the tools and techniques, and the output for the develop project charter process.

Table 2.1	Develop Project Charter Process: Inputs, Tools and Techniques, and Output	
Inputs	**Tools and Techniques**	**Output**
Contract	Project selection methods	Project charter
Project statement of work	Project management methodology	
Enterprise environmental factors	Project management information systems	
Organizational process assets	Expert judgment	

As you study for the PMP exam, don't just memorize each of the inputs, tools, techniques, and outputs for each process. Really think about why PMI put them where they are. In the case of the develop project charter process, ask yourself what you need before you start. Each piece of information you need to start the process of creating the project charter is represented in the input section. You need some sort of document that specifies the need for the project (contract or statement of work). You also need to understand the policies and procedures governing projects for your organization. After you have all the necessary information to start, you can start the process of developing the project charter.

During the project charter development, you will use some, or all, of the tools and techniques listed in Table 2.1, which lists the various methods used

EXAM CRAM 2™

The PMP Cram Sheet

This Cram Sheet contains the distilled, key facts about the PMP Exam.

PROJECT MANAGEMENT FRAMEWORK

1. **Project**—Temporary endeavor undertaken to create a unique product, service, or result.
2. **Progressive elaboration**—Developing in steps and continuing by increments; it's a characteristic of projects.
3. **Project life cycle**—Phases that connect the beginning of project to its end; project life cycle phases are not the same as project management processes.
4. **Level of uncertainty**—This is highest, and risk of failure is greatest, at start of project.
5. **Ability of stakeholders to influence project**—This is highest at the start and gets progressively lower as the project continues.
6. **Cost of changes and correcting errors**—These increase as the project continues.

PROJECT MANAGEMENT PROCESS GROUPS

Not all project management processes apply to all projects or project phases. Process groups can overlap and interact. Forty-four project management processes are contained within the five project management process groups:

1. Initiating
2. Planning
3. Executing
4. Monitoring and controlling
5. Closing

INITIATING PROCESS GROUP

Formally authorizes new project or project phase. The two processes are

1. **Develop project charter**—Authorizing project or project phase. The *project charter* defines project's purpose, identifies objectives, and authorizes the project manager to start the project.
2. **Develop preliminary project scope statement**—Documents the project and the deliverable requirements, product requirements, project boundaries, methods of acceptance, and high-level scope control.

PLANNING PROCESS GROUP

Defines objectives and plans course of action required to meet objectives and project scope. Facilitates project planning across process groups. The 21 processes are

1. Develop project management plan
2. Scope planning
3. Scope definition
4. Create WBS
5. Activity definition
6. Activity sequencing
7. Activity resource estimating
8. Activity duration estimating
9. Schedule development
10. Cost estimating
11. Cost budgeting
12. Quality planning
13. Human resource planning
14. Communications planning
15. Risk management planning
16. Risk identification
17. Qualitative risk analysis
18. Quantitative risk analysis
19. Risk response planning
20. Plan purchases and acquisitions
21. Plan contracting

EXECUTING PROCESS GROUP

Integrates resources to carry out project management plan. These seven processes are

1. Direct and manage project execution
2. Perform quality assurance
3. Acquire project team
4. Develop project team
5. Information distribution
6. Request seller responses
7. Select sellers

MONITORING AND CONTROLLING PROCESS GROUP

Monitors progress to identify variances from the project management plan so corrective action can be taken to meet project objectives. The following 12 processes are included:

1. Monitor and control project work
2. Integrated change control
3. Scope verification
4. Scope control
5. Schedule control
6. Cost control
7. Perform quality control
8. Manage project team
9. Performance reporting
10. Manage stakeholders
11. Risk monitoring and control
12. Contract administration

CLOSING PROCESS GROUP

Formalizes acceptance of product, service, or result and brings project or project phase to an end. The following two processes are included:

1. **Close project**—Finalizing all activities across process groups to formally close project or project phase.
2. **Contract closure**—Completing each contract, including resolution of open items, and closing each contract relevant to project or project phase.

PROJECT MANAGEMENT KNOWLEDGE AREAS

Not all project management knowledge areas apply to all projects or project phases. Knowledge areas can interact and overlap. All 44 project management processes are contained within the 9 project management knowledge areas:

1. Integration
2. Scope
3. Time
4. Cost
5. Quality
6. Human resources
7. Communications
8. Risk
9. Procurement

PROJECT INTEGRATION MANAGEMENT

The seven processes occurring in every project management process group are

1. Develop project charter
2. Develop preliminary project scope statement
3. Develop project management plan
4. Direct and manage project execution
5. Monitor and control project work

6. Integrate change control
7. Close project

➤ **Project statement of work (SOW)**—A narrative description of products or services to be supplied by project.

➤ **Chartering project**—Links it to ongoing work of sponsoring organization.

➤ **Project selection methods**—The two categories are benefit measurement and mathematical models

➤ **Project management methodology**—A set of process groups, their processes, and control functions.

➤ **Project management information system (PMIS)**—Automated tools to support information creation and dissemination.

➤ **Configuration management system**—Subsystem of PMIS; process for submitting proposed changes, tracking systems for reviewing and approving changes, defining approval levels for changes, and validating approved changes.

➤ **Change control system**—Subsystem of configuration management system; documented procedures defining how project deliverables and documentation are controlled, changed, and approved.

➤ **Closure procedures**—The two types are administrative and contract.

➤ **Earned value technique (EVT)**—Measures project performance moving through project life cycle; a forecasting tool that uses past performance to predict future performance.

PROJECT SCOPE MANAGEMENT

The five processes occurring in two project management process groups (planning, and monitoring and controlling) are

1. Scope planning
2. Scope definition
3. Create WBS
4. Scope verification
5. Scope control

➤ **Decomposition**—Subdivision of project deliverables into small, more management components until work and deliverables are defined to work package level.

➤ **Work package**—Lowest level of WBS; cost and schedule can be reliably estimated.

➤ **Organizational breakdown structure (OBS)**—Hierarchical breakdown of project organization to depict work packages by performing organizational unit.

➤ **Risk breakdown structure (RBS)**—Hierarchical, organized depiction of identified risks by risk category.

➤ **Resource breakdown structure (RBS)**—Hierarchical, organized depiction of resources by type to be used.

to take input data and create output data. In the case of the project charter, the only output is the project charter itself. The main point to listing each of the inputs, tools, techniques, and outputs for each process is to understand each component of each process. Don't just memorize the tables! Really think through why each element is included.

Because the development of the project charter is the first project activity, much of the work to produce the input for this process occurs either before the project initiation or within the scope of another project. Most of the input for this process serves to define the project and the environment in which it exists.

After the input information has been collected, the project initiator compiles and issues the project charter. The initiator must be someone who holds the authority to fund the project. Although it is desirable to assign a project manager early in the process, the project manager is not absolutely necessary to issue the project charter. It is important that the stakeholders have a material role in the creation of the project charter. The project manager, if one has been assigned at this point, can be the one to actually do the work of compiling the stakeholders' needs, but the actual input for the project charter and the authority to issue it comes from the project initiator. The main reason so much emphasis is put on the project charter is that it provides the first and best opportunity for the stakeholders to really think through a project before the work begins and gives everyone a chance to consider the project before committing to it.

There is no standard format for a project charter, but each project charter should address these areas:

➤ Assumptions

➤ Constraints

➤ Deliverables and milestones

➤ Estimated budget

➤ Organization

➤ Project justification

➤ Project manager

➤ Requirements or business need (business case)

➤ Stakeholders

Each area of the project charter provides information on the business need and how the project will meet the need. It is important to have a general understanding of the project charter contents for the exam. Although you won't be asked specific questions about the project charter's contents, you will be asked questions about the project charter as a whole and its purpose.

 The PMP exam will ask a few questions about the roles of the project initiator, or sponsor, and the project manager. The project initiator starts the official project process. All of the project manager's authority comes from the project initiator and the stakeholders. For this reason, the project charter must be issued by someone with the authority to fund the project and assign resources to it. The project initiator's role is to describe and authorize the project, assign the project manager, and fund the project. The project manager's role is to plan and execute the project.

The Project Manager Assignment

PMI requires that the project manager be assigned prior to any project planning taking place. The project manager doesn't have to be assigned until the end of the project initiation process group. However, it makes sense to assign the project manager earlier. A project manager who helped create the project charter will be more comfortable with a project and have a generally easier time planning the project.

It is the responsibility of the project initiator, or project sponsor, to officially assign the project manager. Once assigned, the project charter identifies the project managers and provides the authority to carry out project management tasks.

Developing the Project Charter— Tools and Techniques

After a decision is made to enter the initiation process for a project, the collection of input information begins. This is where the project boundaries can be a little unclear, but it is generally accepted that activities starting with the collection of inputs for initiation are part of the project. Remember that the project has not yet been authorized, so all resources required for the initiation processes must be funded explicitly by the project initiator. In other words, someone has to pay for the time required to produce the project charter.

It is entirely possible that the organization decides not to pursue a project after it sees the project charter. The project charter might show that the project will not be worth the resource expenditures. In such a case, the resources already expended to produce the project charter have actually saved the organization from wasting many more resources. Therein lies part of the value of project initiation.

Project Selection Methods

PMI encourages organizations to employ formal methods to select projects. Formal methods make it possible to compare multiple projects and select the one(s) that will produce the most benefit for an organization without being persuaded by emotional ties to certain projects. Additionally, organizations can set specific standards that potential projects must meet to be accepted. There are two main selection method categories you will need to know for the PMP exam. It is not important that you have an in-depth knowledge of these methods, but you will need to be able to identify each type of method and understand their basic differences.

Benefit Measurement Methods

Benefit measurement methods document the relative benefits of completing each project. This approach enables organizations to compare projects by comparing their impact. Each specific method uses different measurements and results in different types of output. You don't need to understand how to assess the relative measurements for the exam. Just know that these methods produce relative output an organization can use to compare projects.

Mathematical Models

Mathematical models analyze project description data to result in a more standardized set of output values. Simply put, a mathematical model can rate a project on a scale from 1 to 100. The organization then decides how desirable a single project is based on its rating.

Project Management Methodology

The organization's standard practices when conducting project activities, along with the project management standards, make up the project management methodology. Any standards, guidelines, procedures, or just common practices all work together to form the general way of managing projects within any organization. The particular methodology you use depends on the culture of your organization, and all these factors affect the content of the project charter.

Project Management Information System

The project management information system (PMIS) is the collection of computerized tools used to collect, store, analyze, and interpret project information. Although most project managers use software to schedule projects, the PMIS often consists of far more than just project management software. When managing a project, learn which tools are available and use them to support the project throughout its life cycle.

Expert Judgment

One of the tools and techniques used in project initiation is tapping the expert judgment of others. Some technical or procedural details might require input from an expert in a specific area. Such experts can be stakeholders or customers of the project or be totally unrelated to the project. PMI encourages using any available source for project information input. When determining input sources for the project charter, or any needed expert input, consider any of these alternatives:

➤ Internal organization assets with specific expertise

➤ External consultants

➤ Stakeholders, including customers

➤ Professional or trade associations

➤ Industry or user groups

Using Management by Objectives

Many organizations use a common management technique called management by objectives (MBO). MBO is not covered directly in the PMBOK, but you will need to understand its general concept for the PMP exam. In very simple terms, MBO helps ensure that objectives within various areas or levels within an organization agree, or harmonize, with objectives from other areas and levels. In short, MBO gets everyone thinking with an enterprisewide perspective.

The project initiation process group is really a set of activities that directly support MBO techniques. The main purpose of project initiation is to ensure projects are understood, provide value to the organization, and are fully authorized by the organization.

MBO is closely related to solid project management practices for several reasons:

➤ MBO implements goal setting and recurring reviews and suggests activities similar to the project control process.

➤ MBO is concerned with ensuring that goals are consistent across an organization, and one task of the project charter is to state how the project supports an organization's overall goals.

➤ Both MBO and sound project management work only if management supports them at a high level.

Implementing MBO is relatively simple. Here are the basic MBO process steps:

1. Establish clear and achievable objectives.

2. Periodically check whether objectives are being met.

3. Take corrective actions on any discovered discrepancies.

Accounting Concepts Used with Project Initiation

It is important for project managers to have a good general understanding of the basic accounting principles that apply to their projects. Nearly all phases of the project life cycle require some type of accounting processes and valuation. Even initiation requires projects to be evaluated for the benefit to the organization. We discussed the two general categories of project selection methods earlier in this chapter. Both benefit measurement methods and constrained optimization methods require the application of some accounting methods.

You will need to understand several cost accounting concepts that are frequently used when performing the project selection process for the PMP exam. Of the two main project selection methods, the benefit measurement methods require more cost calculations. You are not expected to be an expert at cost methods for the PMP exam. However, you will have to understand all of these accounting concepts and know how to use them during the project selection activity. Table 2.2 lists the main accounting concepts you will need to know and how they relate to project selection.

Table 2.2 Project Selection Accounting Concepts

Accounting Concept	Description	Keys for Project Selection	Notes
Present value (PV)	The value today of future cash flow	The higher the PV, the better.	PV = FV/(1 + r)n
Net present value (NPV)	The present value of cash inflow less the present value of cash outflow	A negative NPV is unfavorable; the higher the NPV, the better.	Accounts for different project durations
Internal rate of return (IRR)	The interest rate that makes the net present value of all cash flow equal zero	The higher the IRR, the better.	The return that a company would earn if it invested in the project
Payback period	The number of time periods required until inflows equal, or exceed, costs	The lower the payback period, the better.	
Benefit cost ratio (BCR)	A ratio describing the relationship between the cost and benefits of a proposed project	A BCR less than 1 is unfavorable; the higher the BCR, the better.	
Opportunity cost	The difference in benefit received between a chosen project and a project that was not chosen		
Sunk costs	Money that has already been spent and cannot be recovered	This should not be a factor in project decisions.	

PMI also expects a project manager to understand other accounting concepts. Table 2.3 lists some of the most common accounting concepts you will need to know for the PMP exam.

Table 2.3 General Accounting Concepts

Accounting Concept	Description	Notes
Variable costs	Costs that change based on an organization's activity	For example, fuel costs
Fixed costs	Costs that remain constant, regardless of activity level	For example, rent and lease payments

(continued)

Table 2.3 General Accounting Concepts (continued)		
Accounting Concept	**Description**	**Notes**
Direct costs	Costs that can be directly associated with the production of specific goods or services	For example, labor and material costs
Indirect costs	Costs that cannot be directly associated with the production of specific goods or services	For example, legal costs, administration, and insurance
Working capital	Total assets less total liabilities	
Straight-line depreciation	A depreciation method that evenly divides the difference between an asset's cost and its expected salvage value by the number of years it is expected to be in service	The simplest method
Accumulated depreciation	A depreciation method that allows greater deductions in the earlier years of the life of an asset	Double declining balance (DDB)
Life cycle costing	Includes costs from each phase of a project's life cycle when total investment costs are calculated	

These accounting principles represent one area of project management (and general management) a project manager must understand. There will be several general management concepts on the PMP exam. Don't worry, though, because you will only be required to understand the basic concepts because they will affect projects.

Developing the Preliminary Project Scope Statement

The second process in project initiation is developing the preliminary project scope statement. The *project scope statement* states what the project will and will not accomplish. The reader of the project scope statement should understand what the project is expected to produce and when it completes without possessing any prior project knowledge. The project scope statement defines the actual boundaries of the project. This process does not develop the complete project scope statement—only the preliminary version. The development of the complete project scope statement occurs in the planning process group, which is discussed in the next chapter.

One change in the PMBOK, Third Edition is that the process to develop the preliminary scope statement has been added to the project initiation process group. You'll likely see a question that addresses this new process.

The preliminary project scope statement should include as much of the available information about the project as possible. Much of the information will come from the project initiator and other stakeholders. Although the amount of information included in this preliminary scope statement differs based on project complexity and environment, here are some common types of information it should include

➤ Approval and acceptance requirements

➤ Assumptions

➤ Constraints

➤ Deliverables

➤ Estimated budget

➤ Milestones

➤ Objectives

➤ Preliminary work breakdown structure (WBS)

➤ Project boundaries

➤ Project risks

➤ Quality requirements

Many of the items included in the preliminary project scope statement are similar, if not identical, to items in the project charter. The main differences between the two documents are their purpose and audience. Whereas the project charter's purpose is to formally authorize a project, the preliminary scope statement's main purpose is to provide a statement of overall project intent. The audience of the preliminary scope statement is anyone who wants to know about the project, whether internal or external to the project team.

The process to develop the preliminary project scope statement uses the project charter and its supporting data and inputs. The tools and techniques are the same as the project charter's tools and techniques; there is only one output; and the only output is the preliminary scope statement. Table 2.4 lists the inputs, the tools and techniques, and the output for the develop preliminary scope statement process.

Table 2.4   Develop Preliminary Project Scope Statement: Inputs, Tools and Techniques, and Output

Inputs	Tools and Techniques	Outputs
Project charter	Project management methodology	Preliminary project scope statement
Project statement of work	Project management information systems	
Enterprise environmental factors	Expert judgment	
Organizational process assets		

Remember to avoid just memorizing each of the process inputs, tools, techniques, and outputs. Think about why each element is needed. Notice that the inputs are the same for the develop preliminary project scope statement as for the develop project charter process (except that the project charter is included as an input for this process). The elements are similar, but the purpose of this process differs from creating the project charter in that the main purpose of this process is to start narrowing the focus of what the project will and will not do.

As with all processes defined in the PMBOK, think through why each element in Table 2.4 is needed to complete the develop preliminary project scope statement process.

Exam Prep Questions

1. You are a project manager newly assigned to a project to implement new manufacturing management software. The project sponsor tells you he has chosen you because he is impressed with your record of completing projects. He tells you that work must start immediately and there is not enough time to go through all the formal documentation process. He asks for a quick list of tasks to start now. What do you do?

   ❏ A. Put a quick list of the most important task together, per the sponsor's request.

   ❏ B. Start working on the project tasks and develop a general plan as soon as you can.

   ❏ C. Refuse to start on the project until you develop a project charter and get it approved.

   ❏ D. Explain the need for a project charter and project plan to the sponsor.

2. The main purpose of project initiation is to _____.

   ❏ A. Produce the project charter.

   ❏ B. Formally describe the project.

   ❏ C. Formally authorize the project.

   ❏ D. Assign the project manager to the project.

3. At what points in a project might you perform the processes of project initiation?

   ❏ A. Project initiation is the first process group and occurs only at the beginning of a project.

   ❏ B. Project initiation should actually be named "phase initiation" and really only occurs during execution between major project phases.

   ❏ C. Project initiation must occur at the beginning of a project and before any major milestone to authorize the project to continue toward the next milestone.

   ❏ D. Project initiation can occur at the beginning of a project and again at any point when authorization to continue the project is either required or desired.

4. Which document formally authorizes a project?

   ❏ A. The project sponsor/initiator charter

   ❏ B. The project charter

   ❏ C. The preliminary project scope statement

   ❏ D. The project contract

5. Which is the only process that must occur after a project manager has been assigned to the project?
   - ❑ A. Develop the project charter
   - ❑ B. Develop the preliminary project scope statement
   - ❑ C. Develop the project statement of work
   - ❑ D. Scope planning

6. You have just been assigned as the project manager for a new project. You have collected the necessary input information and delivered the project charter to the stakeholders. What should you do next?
   - ❑ A. Develop the preliminary project scope statement.
   - ❑ B. Get the project charter signed.
   - ❑ C. Start the initial project planning process.
   - ❑ D. Ask the stakeholders for resources.

7. Which accounting concept refers to the value today of future cash flow?
   - ❑ A. Present value (PV)
   - ❑ B. Net present value (NPV)
   - ❑ C. Opportunity cost
   - ❑ D. Sunk cost

8. Who is responsible for issuing the project charter?
   - ❑ A. The project manager
   - ❑ B. The project sponsor
   - ❑ C. The project team
   - ❑ D. The Project management office (PMO)

9. What is the main difference between the project charter and the preliminary scope statement?
   - ❑ A. The contents of the two differ substantially.
   - ❑ B. They are created during different process groups.
   - ❑ C. One is created by the project sponsor, and the other is produced by the project manager.
   - ❑ D. The purpose and audience of the documents differ.

10. Who applies project selection methods to decide whether to accept or reject a project?
    - ❑ A. The project sponsor
    - ❑ B. The project manager
    - ❑ C. The project team
    - ❑ D. The project accountant

Answers to Exam Prep Questions

1. Answer D is correct. Answers A and B ignore the PMBOK requirement that a project manager insist on proper project management techniques. It is crucial that a PMP candidate understand the need for properly obtaining authorization for a project (initiation) and then planning a project before starting actual work. Answer C is too extreme for the initial response. The sponsor might have made the request to immediately begin work out of a lack of understanding of project management. Always start by getting as much information as you can and educating others on the benefits of good project management.

2. Answer C is correct. Answer A does mention one of the outputs of a process in project initiation, but the project charter is not the main purpose of project initiation. Answer B is incorrect as well because describing the project is not the primary purpose of project initiation. Answer D is incorrect because assigning a project manager is a task carried out during project initiation but is not the primary purpose.

3. Answer D is correct. Project initiation generally occurs at the beginning of a project and can also be optionally included multiple times throughout the project. There are no absolute requirements for conducting initiation processes during a project. Because initiation can occur during a project but is not required, answers A, B, and C are incorrect.

4. Answer B is correct. Answer A mentions a document that is not defined in the PMBOK. The preliminary scope statement is an output in project initiation but does not authorize the project, so answer C is incorrect. The project contract is one of the inputs to both processes in the project initiation process group and does not convey project authorization so answer D is incorrect. The contract does commit the organization to perform action but does not authorize the project itself.

5. Answer D is correct. The scope planning process occurs during project planning. Answers A, B, and C all occur during project initiation. Even though a project manager should be assigned as early as possible, the project manager is not required until project planning.

6. Answer B is correct. Before continuing with any activity, you must have the authority to do so. Have the stakeholders sign the project charter and authorize the project. Answers A, C, and D constitute working on a project before it is authorized.

7. Answer A is correct. Answers B, C, and D each refer to other accounting concepts. Refer to Table 2.2 for more information.

8. Answer B is correct. The project sponsor creates and issues the project charter. Answers A, C, and D list groups that can assist in creating the project charter but do not have the responsibility to issue the project charter.

9. Answer D is correct. The purpose of the project charter is to authorize the project, and the audience is the stakeholders. The purpose of the preliminary scope statement is to describe the project, and its audience is the project team. Answer A is incorrect because the contents of the two documents are similar. Answer B is incorrect because both documents are created during project initiation. Answer C is incorrect because the project manager, if assigned, can work to create both documents (although the project sponsor formally issues the project charter).

10. Answer A is correct. All the other answers list project team members who lack the authority to select (or reject) a project. The project sponsor must have the authority to select and fund the project.

Need to Know More?

 Graves, Samuel B. and Jeffery L. Ringuest. *Models and Methods for Project Selection: Concepts from Management Science, Finance and Information Technology*. New York: Springer Publishing, 2002.

 Project Management Institute. *A Guide to the Project Management Body of Knowledge, Third Edition*. Newton Square, PA: Project Management Institute, 2004.

The Project Planning Process Group

Terms you'll need to understand:

- ✓ Activity
- ✓ Activity attributes
- ✓ Activity list
- ✓ Activity on arrow diagram (AOA)
- ✓ Activity on node diagram (AON)
- ✓ Activity sequence
- ✓ Analogous estimating
- ✓ Arrow diagramming method (ADM)
- ✓ Bottom-up estimating
- ✓ Critical path
- ✓ Dependency
- ✓ Milestone list
- ✓ Network diagram

- ✓ Parametric estimating
- ✓ Precedence diagramming method (PDM)
- ✓ Project management methodology
- ✓ Project management plan
- ✓ Project management processes
- ✓ Project scope
- ✓ Resource breakdown structure
- ✓ Rolling wave planning
- ✓ Slack
- ✓ Three-point estimates
- ✓ WBS dictionary
- ✓ Work breakdown structure (WBS)

Techniques and concepts you'll need to master:

- ✓ General project planning steps
- ✓ The importance of the WBS
- ✓ The relationships between scope, activities, and resources
- ✓ Estimating activity duration using three methods
- ✓ Creating PDM and ADM diagrams
- ✓ Reading and interpreting project network diagrams
- ✓ Understanding dependencies between project activities
- ✓ Identifying the critical path
- ✓ Estimating cost and creating a budget

In Chapter 1, "Project Management Framework Fundamentals," the PMI concepts of processes, process groups, and knowledge areas were introduced. Recall that PMI defines a total of 44 project processes that describe activities throughout a project's life cycle. These processes are organized into nine knowledge areas and represent five process groups. One of the most prominent of the process groups is project planning, evident in that nearly half of the processes occur in this group. This process group contains 21 of the 44 processes. In case you might think that planning processes are localized to a particular area of your project, note that processes in the planning group span all nine knowledge areas. Let's look at project planning in more detail.

Understanding PMI's Project Planning Process Group

After you are ready to plan your project, you have passed through the *initiation processes*. Remember what that means? It means that you possess formal authorization to conduct the work of the project. But what work will you do? What exactly are you trying to accomplish?

To answer these questions, start from what you know. There are two outputs from the initiation process group. Always start with the information necessary to proceed. Recall that PMI refers to this initial information for each process as the process's inputs. So, start with the project charter and preliminary scope statement and refine the project documents from there. Figure 3.1 shows how the processes in the planning group are related.

Think of the project initiation progress group as the processes that answer the what and why questions. The project planning processes answer the how questions. The planning processes result in outputs that explain how the project will progress toward reaching its goals.

Because planning includes so many processes, be prepared to answer many questions in this area on the exam. As with all other process groups, make sure you know the inputs, tools, techniques, and outputs of each process. It helps to draw your own process flow. Just the act of physically drawing the process flow in each process group helps you remember how the processes relate to one another.

PMI is very explicit in stressing the importance of planning. Far too many projects suffer from the poor practice of starting work before anyone really knows what needs to be done. This almost always results in wasted effort and lost time. Proper planning requires good communication among the team and sound leadership from the project manager. The result is a project team that is more informed and prepared to carry out the work required to meet the project's goals. You should expect to see several questions on the exam that require you to understand the importance of fully planning before starting work.

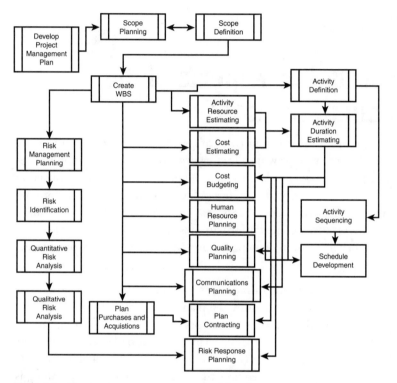

Figure 3.1 The planning process group process interactions.

Because planning is such a large process group, the material is divided into two separate chapters. This chapter covers the general concepts of planning and the processes that relate to the development of project baselines, including the following topics:

➤ Cost

➤ Schedule

➤ Scope

Chapter 4, "Elements of Project Planning," covers the remaining project planning processes that support project planning by applying more details to the baselines. Topics covered in Chapter 4 include these topics:

➤ Communications

➤ Human resources

➤ Procurement

➤ Quality

➤ Risk

Exploring Key Aspects of the Planning Processes

This chapter looks at the first four types of key planning processes. The main purpose of planning is to provide a framework to gather information to produce a project management plan. In fact, the plan itself is really a collection of other plans. The majority of activities in the planning group center around developing the supporting documents that comprise the final project management plan. As more detailed information is learned about the project, the overall plan becomes more complete and the confidence in the project increases.

Planning is an iterative group of processes as well. As the project progresses it often becomes necessary to modify the plan due to any number of reasons. Unexpected results, delays, outside factors, and internal factors can all require additional planning. Any scope changes will also likely require one or more planning processes to be revisited. Don't assume that planning is only accomplished once. The exam requires that you understand how planning is iterative throughout a project.

The following list details some fundamental planning process items you need to understand for the exam:

➤ **Project management plan**—One process in the planning group addresses the project management plan. The develop project management plan process is the high-level process that provides direction for developing subsidiary plans and compiling their information into the final project plan.

➤ **Scope**—Three processes address scope planning. These direct the refinement of the preliminary scope statement and break down the high-level goals of the project into smaller, more manageable chunks.

➤ **Activity**—Five processes deal with activity planning. After the work of the project is expressed in small, manageable chunks, the activity-related processes are oriented with defining the activity details, integrating with project resources, and sequencing the project activities.

➤ **Cost**—Two processes address cost planning. These processes collect estimates and organize them into a project budget.

Each of these processes is looked at individually in the next section.

Developing the Project Management Plan

The *project management plan process* covers all activities that identify and direct the actions of many other processes in the planning process group. Developing the project management plan includes coordinating the development of the subsidiary plans and incorporating them into the complete project plan. The main purpose of the project management plan is to define how the project is to progress from its beginning to completion.

In short, the project management plan provides the high-level gameplan for how the project moves through its life cycle. PMI defines many potential subsidiary plans that make up the overall project management plan. These subsidiary plans provide the specific details for managing each aspect of the project from initiation through closure. The subsidiary project management plans could include

➤ Communication management plan

➤ Cost management plan

➤ Process improvement plan

➤ Procurement management plan

➤ Project scope management plan

➤ Quality management plan

➤ Risk management plan

➤ Schedule management plan

➤ Staffing management plan

This list of subsidiary plans is a great outline of a project. Use the list as a table of contents when you consider what should be in a project management plan.

Onc of the more common mistakes inexperienced project managers make is to confuse a project plan with a project schedule. The output from many common project management software packages do not qualify as a project plan. They are a good start, but a true project plan is made up of much more information than just scheduling information. This process requires a focused effort to create a plan that incorporates all known information about a project. Table 3.1 shows the inputs, tools, techniques, and outputs for the develop project management plan process.

Table 3.1 Develop Project Management Plan Inputs, Tools, Techniques, and Outputs		
Inputs	**Tools and Techniques**	**Outputs**
Preliminary project scope statement	Project management methodology	Project management plan
Project management processes	Project management information system	
Enterprise environmental factors	Expert judgment	
Organizational process assets		

Scope Management

Scope management is the set of processes that ensures that the requirements of the customer are captured in a specification of work that ensures its delivery, that all the project work is done, and that only the work required to complete the project is done. In other words, scope management makes sure that the project is completed without expending any unnecessary effort.

Scope planning defines the document that states how the scope will be specified, controlled, and verified. The project team develops the scope management plan for each project. More complex projects require a more detailed scope planning process. Table 3.2 shows the inputs, tools, techniques, and outputs for the scope planning process.

Table 3.2 Scope Planning Inputs, Tools, Techniques, and Outputs

Inputs	Tools and Techniques	Outputs
Enterprise environmental factors	Expert judgment	Project scope management plan
Organizations process assets	Templates, forms, and standards	
Preliminary project scope statement		
Project management plan		

The next process, *scope definition*, is the process that refines the preliminary scope statement and clearly states what the project will and will not accomplish. The supporting documents are reviewed to ensure the project will satisfy the stated goals and the resulting scope should state the stakeholders' needs and clearly communicate the expectations for the performance of the project. Table 3.3 shows the inputs, tools, techniques, and outputs for the scope planning process.

Table 3.3 Scope Definition Inputs, Tools, Techniques, and Outputs

Inputs	Tools and Techniques	Outputs
Organizational process assets	Product analysis	Project scope statement
Project charter	Alternative identification	Requested changes
Preliminary project scope statement	Expert judgment	Project scope management plan (updates)
Project scope management plan	Stakeholder analysis	
Approved change requests		

Work Breakdown Structure: A Common and Dangerous Omission

Many inexperienced project managers move too quickly from the scope statement to the activity sequencing processes. This practice is a mistake and often leads to activity omissions and inaccurate plans. PMI stresses the importance of first creating a *work breakdown structure (WBS)*, and then moving to activity management processes.

The WBS provides the project manager and project team with the opportunity to decompose the high-level scope statement into much smaller, more manageable units of work, called *work packages*. The resulting WBS should provide a complete list of all work packages required to complete the project (and nothing more). Table 3.4 shows the inputs, tools, techniques, and outputs for the create WBS process.

Table 3.4 Create WBS Inputs, Tools, Techniques, and Outputs		
Inputs	**Tools and Techniques**	**Outputs**
Organizational process assets	Work breakdown structure templates	Project scope statement (updates)
Project scope statement	Decomposition	Work breakdown structure
Project scope management plan		WBS dictionary
Approved change requests		Scope baseline
		Project scope management plan (updates)
		Requested changes

 The *PMI Practice Standard for Work Breakdown Structures* is the guide you need to use for the PMP exam. This is an example of information on the exam that goes beyond the PMBOK. You can find the WBS Practice Standard in the publications section of the PMI website (www.pmi.org).

In creating the WBS, the project team repeatedly decomposes the work of the project into smaller and smaller units of work, resulting in a collection of small work packages. The process continues until the resulting work packages are simple enough to reliably estimate in terms of duration and required resources. Don't go overboard, though. When you have work packages that are manageable and represent a single work effort, stop the process. Each project is different, so this process results in different levels of detail for each project.

The last main feature of the WBS is that it is organized in a hierarchical fashion. The highest level is the project. Under the project, the children that represent project phases, divisions, or main deliverables are listed. Each child process or task is then divided into further levels of detail until the lowest level, the work package, is reached. Figure 3.2 depicts a sample WBS with multiple levels.

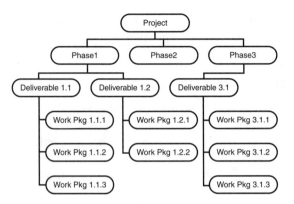

Figure 3.2 Sample work breakdown structure.

In addition to the WBS itself, another output of the create WBS process is the WBS dictionary. The *WBS dictionary* is a document that supports the WBS by providing detailed information for each work package. The WBS dictionary can contain many types of information, including

➤ Work package name or identifier

➤ Accounting control account

➤ Description of work

➤ Technical specifications

➤ Quality requirements

➤ Owner or responsible party assignment

➤ Required resources

Activity Planning—From WBS to Project Schedule

The next section of the planning processes address those steps required to develop the project schedule. This is the part of the project plan that might be most familiar to new project managers. Many automated project management tools help create schedules by keeping track of activities, resources, durations, sequencing, and constraints. Although the schedule is an integral part of the project plan, it is only one part. Don't start working on the schedule until you have a proper WBS. Starting to work before completing the WBS usually results in doing more work than is necessary. A good WBS reduces task redundancy and helps ensure all work performed is in the scope of the project. In fact, the WBS is a required input to activity planning.

Defining Activities

The first process in the activity planning section is *activity definition*. This process starts with the WBS and identifies the activities required to produce the various project deliverables. Activities are viewed from the perspective of the work packages. You ask the question, "What activities are required to satisfy this work package requirement?" The resulting information from this process is used next to organize the activities into a specific sequence. Table 3.5 shows the inputs, tools, techniques, and outputs for the activity definition process.

Table 3.5   Activity Definition Inputs, Tools, Techniques, and Outputs

Inputs	Tools and Techniques	Outputs
Enterprise environmental factors	Decomposition	Activity list
Organizational process assets	Templates	Activity attributes
Project scope statement	Rolling wave planning	Milestone list
Work breakdown structure	Expert judgment	Requested changes
WBS dictionary	Planning component	
Project management plan		

Sometimes it is difficult to know everything about a project during the planning stage. It is common to learn more about the project as you work through the project life cycle. This is called *progressive elaboration* and it affects the planning process. If you don't know everything about the project, you can't plan the whole project to the level of detail necessary. For large projects, it is common to plan the entire project at a high level. The project starts with detailed plans in place for the work packages that are near the beginning of the project. As the time draws near to begin additional work, the more detailed, low-level plans for those work packages are added to the project plan. The planning process is revisited multiple times to ensure that the detailed plans contain the latest information known about the project. This practice is called *rolling wave planning* because the planning wave always moves to stay ahead of the work execution wave.

Sequencing Activities

The next process is that of arranging the activities list from activity definition into a discrete sequence. Some activities can be accomplished at any time throughout the project. Other activities depend on input from another activity or are constrained by time or resources. Any requirement that restricts the start or end time of an activity is a *dependency*. This process identifies all relationships between activities and notes restrictions imposed by these relationships.

For example, when building a car you cannot install the engine until the engine has been built and delivered to the main assembly line. This is just one simple example of how activities may be dependent on one another. This process is one that can benefit from the use of computer software to assist in noting and keeping track of inter-activity dependencies. Table 3.6 shows the inputs, tools, techniques, and outputs for the activity sequencing process.

Table 3.6　Activity Sequencing Inputs, Tools, Techniques, and Outputs		
Inputs	**Tools and Techniques**	**Outputs**
Project scope statement	Precedence diagramming method (PDM)	Project schedule network diagrams
Activity list	Arrow diagramming method (ADM)	Activity list (updates)
Activity attributes	Schedule network templates	Activity attributes (updates)
Approved change requests	Dependency determination	Requested changes
	Applying leads and lags	

Network Diagrams

One of the more important topics to understand when planning project activities is creating network diagrams. *Network diagrams* provide a graphical view of activities and how they relate to one another. The PMP exam tests your ability to recognize and understand two types of network diagrams: the *precedence diagramming method (PDM)* and the *arrow diagramming method (ADM)*. Make sure you can read each type of diagram and use the information it presents.

Precedence Diagramming Method

The PDM shows nodes, representing activities, connected by arrows that represent dependencies. To represent that activity B is dependent on activity A (in other words, activity A must be complete before activity B starts), simply draw an arrow from A to B. PDM diagrams are also referred to as activity-on-node (AON) diagrams because the nodes contain the activity duration information. (You don't have enough information yet to complete all the information presented here. You'll fill in the duration information during activity duration estimating.) In fact, nodes generally contain several pieces of information, including

➤ **Early start**—The earliest date the activity can start

➤ **Duration**—The duration of the activity

➤ **Early finish**—The earliest date the activity can finish

➤ **Late start**—The latest date the activity can start

➤ **Late finish**—The latest date the activity can finish

➤ **Slack**—Difference between the early start and the late start dates

Figure 3.3 shows an example of a PDM diagram.

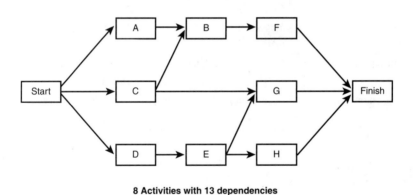

Precedence Diagramming Method (PDM)

8 Activities with 13 dependencies

Figure 3.3 The precedence diagramming method.

The PDM diagram in Figure 3.3 shows eight activities, labeled A–H. The arrows show how some activities are dependent on other activities. For example, activity B cannot start until activities A and C are complete. To show this dual dependency, you draw an arrow from A to B and another arrow from C to B.

You can represent four types of dependencies with a PDM diagram:

➤ **Finish-to-start (the most common dependency type)**—The successor activity's start depends on the completions of the successor activity.

➤ **Finish-to-finish**—The completion of the successor activity depends on the completion of the predecessor activity.

➤ **Start-to-start**—The start of the successor activity depends on the start of the predecessor activity.

➤ **Start-to-finish**—The completion of the successor activity depends on the start of the predecessor activity.

Carefully consider the various types of dependencies. Some can be confusing (especially start-to-finish). On the exam, you will be asked to evaluate the scheduling impact to changes in start or end dates. The overall impact to the project depends on the type of relationship between activities. Don't skip over the dependencies too quickly. Take the time to really read the question before you construct your diagrams.

Arrow Diagramming Method

The arrow diagramming method (ADM) is similar to the PDM, except that all dependencies are finish-to-start. Also, durations are generally depicted on the arrows. For this reason, the ADM diagram is also called the activity-on-arrow (AOA) diagram. Figure 3.4 shows an example of an ADM diagram.

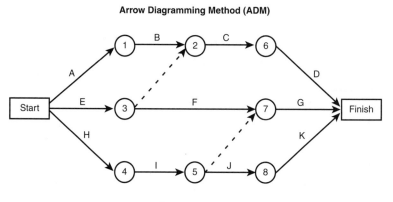

11 Activities and 2 dummy activities

Figure 3.4 The arrow diagramming method.

The ADM diagram in Figure 3.4 shows 11 activities, labeled A–K. Unlike the PDM diagram, activities are labeled on the arrow, not the nodes.

Dependencies are noted in a similar fashion to the PDM diagram, but there is another type of activity in ADM diagrams. Look at the dependency between node 3 and node 2. The arrow has a dotted line, which means the activity has no duration and is called a *dummy* activity. The purpose of dummy activities is simply to allow you to depict dependencies. In Figure 3.4 activity C cannot start until activity E has completed. Likewise, activity G cannot start until activity I has completed.

After you are comfortable with the main types of network diagrams, you need to understand how to use them. Let's talk about a few basic scheduling concepts and look at how network diagrams help you understand project schedules, starting with a few project tasks. Table 3.7 lists the tasks for a project along with the predecessors, duration, and earliest start date.

Table 3.7	Project Task Information		
Activity	Predecessor	Duration	Earliest Start Date
A	None	5	9/5/05
B	A	2	9/10/05
C	A	3	9/10/05
D	B	7	9/12/05
E	C	4	9/13/05
F	D	1	9/19/05
G	E, F	2	9/20/05

Now use the sample PDM node template to create a PDM diagram for the project. Figure 3.5 shows the sample PDM node template.

Early Start	Duration	Early Finish
	Task name	
Late Start	Slack	Late Finish

Figure 3.5 The sample PDM node template.

The completed network diagram should look like the diagram in Figure 3.6.

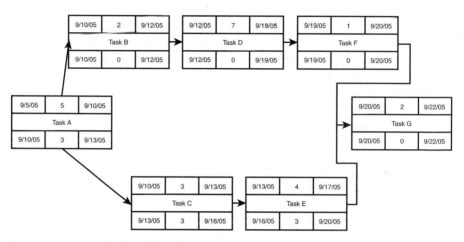

Figure 3.6 The completed sample PDM diagram.

Estimating Activity Resources

Now you have a list of activities and their relative dependencies. The next process associates activities with the resources required to accomplish the work. This process lists each type and amount, or quantity, of each required resource. Every activity requires resources of some sort. Activity resources can include

➤ Equipment

➤ Money

➤ Materials and supplies

➤ People

Table 3.8 shows the inputs, tools, techniques, and outputs for the activity resource estimating process.

Table 3.8 Activity Resource Estimating Inputs, Tools, Techniques, and Outputs		
Inputs	**Tools and Techniques**	**Outputs**
Enterprise environmental factors	Expert judgment	Activity resource requirements
Organizational process assets	Alternatives analysis	Activity attributes (updates)
Activity list	Published estimating data	Resource breakdown structure
Activity attributes	Project management software	Resource calendar (updates)
Resource availability	Bottom-up estimating	Requested changes
Project management plan		

Two of the tools and techniques warrant further discussion. One of the techniques you use when estimating activity resources is *alternative analysis*. Analyzing the various alternatives provides an opportunity to consider other sources or ways to achieve the desired result for an activity. Alternatives might be more desirable than the initial expected approach due to cost savings, higher quality, or earlier completion. Another important outcome of alternative analysis is that in case the primary source becomes unavailable, you might have already identified a replacement method to complete the work. Suppose your main supplier of industrial fittings suffers a catastrophic fire. If your alternative analysis identified another source, you might be able to continue the project with minimal disruption.

The second item is bottom-up estimating. Recall that one of the purposes of creating the WBS is to decompose project work into work packages that are small enough to reliably estimate for duration and resource requirements. Using the WBS, you can provide estimates for mid- and high-level work by aggregating the estimates for the work packages that make up the desired work. Because this process starts at the lowest level of work (the work package) to create the estimate, it is called *bottom-up estimating*. This type of estimating tends to be fairly accurate because the estimates come from the people doing the actual work. The alternative is *top-down estimating*. Top-down estimates generally come from management or a source that is higher up than the people actually doing the work. The estimates are really educated guesses on the amount of resources required for a collection of work packages and tend to be less reliable than bottom-up estimates.

Estimating Activity Durations

After the resource estimates are established for each of the activities, it's time to assign duration estimates. The *activity duration estimating process* assigns the number of work periods that are needed to complete schedule activities. Each estimate assumes that the necessary resources are available to be applied to the work package when needed. Table 3.9 shows the inputs, tools, techniques, and outputs for the activity duration estimating process.

Table 3.9 Activity Duration Estimating Inputs, Tools, Techniques, and Outputs		
Inputs	**Tools and Techniques**	**Outputs**
Enterprise environmental factors	Expert judgment	Activity duration estimates
Organizational process assets	Analogous estimating	Activity attributes (updates)

(continued)

Table 3.9 Activity Duration Estimating Inputs, Tools, Techniques, and Outputs (continued)

Inputs	Tools and Techniques	Outputs
Project scope statement	Parametric estimating	
Activity list	Three-point estimates	
Activity attributes	Reserve analysis	
Activity resource requirements		
Resource calendar		
Project management plan		

In addition to expert judgment, three main techniques are used for project activity duration estimation. In many cases, using multiple techniques provides more accurate estimates. The three estimation techniques are

➤ **Analogous estimating**—This uses actual duration figures from similar activities. These activities can be from the same project or another project.

➤ **Parametric estimating**—This calculates duration estimates by multiplying the quantity of work by the productivity rate. This type of estimate works best for standardized, and often repetitive, activities.

➤ **Three-point estimates**—This uses three estimate values for each activity:

   ➤ **Most likely**—The duration most likely to occur.

   ➤ **Optimistic**—The duration of the activity if everything goes as planned, or better.

   ➤ **Pessimistic**—The duration of the activity in a worst-case scenario.

Developing the Project Schedule

The next step is to develop the actual project schedule. The *schedule development process* pulls all of the activity information together and results in the project's initial (baseline) schedule. As work is iteratively planned and accomplished and the project moves through its life cycle, changes to the schedule will likely occur. The schedule is a dynamic document and requires constant attention on the part of the project manager to ensure the project stays on track. Table 3.10 shows the inputs, tools, techniques, and outputs for the schedule development process.

Table 3.10 Schedule Development Inputs, Tools, Techniques, and Outputs

Inputs	Tools and Techniques	Outputs
Organizational process assets	Schedule network analysis	Project schedule
Project scope statement	Critical path method	Schedule model data
Activity list	Schedule compression	Schedule baseline
Activity attributes	What-if scenario analysis	Resource requirements (updates)
Project schedule network diagrams	Resource leveling	Activity attributes (updates)
Activity resource requirements	Critical chain method	Project calendar (updates)
Resource calendar	Project management software	Requested changes
Activity duration estimates	Applying calendars	Project management plan (updates)
Project management plan	Adjusting leads and lags	
	Schedule model	

An important topic to understand with respect to project schedules is the critical path. Look back at the AON diagram in Figure 3.3. The critical path is the longest path from start to finish. It is calculated by adding up all of the durations along each path from start to finish. The reason it is called the critical path is that any delay (or increase in duration) of any activity on the critical path causes a delay in the project. It is critical that all activities on this path be completed on schedule.

Critical Path

Using the network diagram in Figure 3.6, you can calculate the project critical path. The *critical path* is the route with the longest total duration. This example shows two routes from task A to task G:

➤ Path A-B-D-F-G takes 17 days to complete. (Just add up all the durations: 5 + 2 + 7 + 1 + 2 = 17)

➤ Path A-C-E-G takes 14 days to complete.

From this diagram you can see that the longest path is A-B-D-F-G, and that is your critical path. Any delays in any of these tasks will delay the project.

Float

Take another look at Figure 3.6. This PDM diagram has several pieces of information filled in for each node that we have not discussed yet. The task name and duration are self-explanatory. What about the rest of the information, though? The main task of developing the project schedule is to relate each of the tasks and combine duration, resource requirements, and dependencies. You will need to make several passes through the network diagram to calculate the values necessary to create a project schedule.

In general, you will make two main passes through each path in your network diagram. The first pass starts with the initial project task (the project start task). The starting date of the initial task is its early start date. A task's *early start date* is the earliest you can start working on that task. In Figure 3.6, the early start date for task A is 9/5/05. The duration for task A is 5 days, so the earliest task A can finish is 9/10/05. To get the early finish date, just add the duration to the early start date. Now, the early finish date for task A becomes the early start date for any tasks that are dependent on task A (namely, task B and task C). Then, continue to follow each path until you reach the final task, calculating the new early end dates by adding the duration to the early start dates.

 Be sure you follow every path from the starting task to the ending task. There will likely be several paths that will get you there.

Now it's time for the second pass through your project to calculate the late start and late ending dates. This pass starts at the end and moves backward through the same paths you just followed in the forward pass. The first step in the backward pass is to record the late ending date. It is the same as the early ending date for the last task in the project. Then, subtract the duration to get the late start date. In Figure 3.6, the late ending date for task G is 9/22/05 and the late start date is 9/20/05. Next, move backward to each task on which your current task depends (for example, each task that has an arrow pointing to your current task). The late ending date for this predecessor task is the same as the late start date of the dependent task. In other words, the late ending date for task F and task E would be 9/20/05 (the late start date for task G). Continue backward through the project, subtracting the duration to calculate a new late start date.

After completing both the forward and backward passes, you should have all the early start times (ESTs), early finish times (EFTs), late start times (LSTs), and late finish times (LFTs) filled in. To complete the network diagram entries, calculate the float for each task by subtracting the early start date from the late start date. The *float* represents the amount of time each task can be delayed without delaying the project.

Finally, add up the durations for each path from the start task to the finish task. The smallest total represents the critical path of your project—there could be more than one critical path. Remember that tasks on the critical path all have a float of 0 and any delay of a task on the critical path results in an overall project delay.

Critical Cost Estimating Factors

The *cost estimating process* associates an expected cost of performing work to each activity. Cost estimates can include labor, materials, equipment, and any other direct costs for project activities. Based on the activity resource and duration estimates, the cost estimates express the cost, normally in monetary amounts, of completing the work of the project. As with all project documents, the cost estimates can change throughout the project as conditions change. Different events can cause the cost for any activity to go up or down and require the cost estimates for the project to change. Table 3.11 shows the inputs, tools, techniques, and outputs for the cost estimating process.

Table 3.11 Cost Estimating Inputs, Tools, Techniques, and Outputs		
Inputs	**Tools and Techniques**	**Outputs**
Enterprise environmental factors	Analogous estimating	Activity cost estimates
Organizational process assets	Determine resource cost rates	Activity cost estimates supporting detail
Project scope statement	Bottom-up estimating	Requested changes
Work breakdown structure	Parametric estimating	Cost management plan (updates)
WBS dictionary	Project management software	
Project management plan	Vendor bid analysis	
	Reserve analysis	
	Cost of quality	

Cost estimates are compiled into the project budget. The *cost budgeting process* aggregates the activity cost estimates into a single document for the project. The resulting project budget expands on the preliminary budget from the project charter and provides far more detail. Table 3.12 shows the inputs, tools, techniques, and outputs for the cost budgeting process.

Table 3.12 Cost Budgeting Inputs, Tools, Techniques, and Outputs		
Inputs	**Tools and Techniques**	**Outputs**
Project scope statement	Cost aggregation	Cost baseline
Work breakdown structure	Reserve analysis	Project funding requirements
WBS dictionary	Parametric estimating	Cost management plan (updates)
Activity cost estimates	Funding limit reconciliation	Requested changes
Activity cost estimates supporting detail		
Project schedule		
Resource calendars		
Contract		
Cost management plan		

Exam Prep Questions

1. You are a project manager newly assigned to a large project for your organization. The project charter has been signed and the preliminary scope statement has been accepted. What should you do next?
   - ❑ A. Ask appropriate team members to submit WBS input.
   - ❑ B. Initiate the scope planning process.
   - ❑ C. Initiate the develop project management plan process.
   - ❑ D. Begin the activity definition process.

2. As project manager, you are about to start the scope definition process. You have the project charter, the organizational process assets list, and the project scope management plan. Since there are no change requests in your project at this point, what must you have before you begin?
   - ❑ A. Product analysis
   - ❑ B. Preliminary project scope statement
   - ❑ C. Updates to project scope management plan
   - ❑ D. WBS

3. You are creating your WBS and find that you keep decomposing tasks into smaller and smaller units. How can you tell when you are done?
   - ❑ A. Keep decomposing tasks until you reach an amount of work that is small enough to reliably estimate required resources and duration.
   - ❑ B. Keep decomposing tasks until you reach an amount of work that can be accomplished in one hour.
   - ❑ C. Keep decomposing work until you reach an amount of work that can be accomplished in your organization's basic work unit.
   - ❑ D. Keep decomposing work until you reach a predetermined number of hierarchy levels to keep the WBS balanced.

4. What term is defined as the practice of planning activities based on how soon the tasks are scheduled to start, such that activities that are close to their start date are planned at a more detailed level than those farther in the future? This term also implies that as activities near their start date more detailed plans will be required.
   - ❑ A. Progressive elaboration
   - ❑ B. Rolling wave planning
   - ❑ C. Planning component elaboration
   - ❑ D. Milestone detail planning

5. Which type of network diagram allows you to depict four types of dependencies?
   - ❑ A. Precedence diagramming method (PDM)
   - ❑ B. Arrow diagramming method (ADM)
   - ❑ C. Dependency diagramming method (DDM)
   - ❑ D. Gannt chart diagram (GCD)

6. Which type of network diagram is also referred to a activity-on-arrow (AOA) diagrams?
   - ❑ A. Precedence diagramming method (PDM)
   - ❑ B. Arrow diagramming method (ADM)
   - ❑ C. Dependency diagramming method (DDM)
   - ❑ D. Gannt chart diagram (GCD)

Use Figure 3.7 for questions 7, 8, and 9.

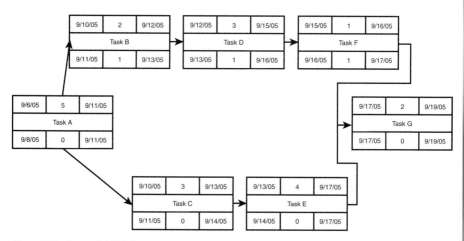

Figure 3.7   A sample PDM diagram.

7. What is the critical path for this project, and what is the duration of the critical path?
   - ❑ A. A-B-D-F-G, 13 days
   - ❑ B. A-C-E-G, 14 days
   - ❑ C. A-B-D-F-G, 14 days
   - ❑ D. A-C-E-G, 13 days

8. How many days can task D be late in starting without affecting the project completion date?
   - ❑ A. One day
   - ❑ B. Two days
   - ❑ C. Zero days
   - ❑ D. Three days

9. If task C starts two days late, what is the effect on the project end date?

- ❑ A. The project ends one day late because there is slack of one day.
- ❑ B. The project is still two days early because tasks B, D, and F each have one day of slack.
- ❑ C. The project is one day late because task C is on the critical path.
- ❑ D. There is no effect on the project end date.

10. When developing the estimates for project phases, you choose to add the individual estimates for the activities that comprise each phase. What type of estimation method are you using?

- ❑ A. Parametric estimating
- ❑ B. Bottom-up estimating
- ❑ C. Top-down estimating
- ❑ D. Analogous estimating

Answers to Exam Prep Questions

1. Answer C is correct. The first process in the planning group is develop project management plan. Answers A, B, and D skip the first process and start subsequent processes prematurely.

2. Answer B is correct. The preliminary scope statement is an input you need before starting the scope definition process. Answer A is incorrect because product analysis is a tool and technique of scope definition, not an input. Answer C is incorrect because project management plan updates are an output, not an input. Answer D is incorrect because the WBS is an output of a subsequent process and would not be available at this point. Know your inputs, tools, techniques, and outputs of all processes.

3. Answer A is correct. A properly sized work package is one that is small enough to allow for reliable estimates for required resources and duration. Answers B, C, and D are incorrect because they assume you are working toward some artificial target that does not contribute to well-sized work packages.

4. Answer B is correct. Rolling wave planning is providing detailed plans for tasks that are about to start in the near future using the most current information and revisiting future activities when they near their starting dates. Answer A is incorrect because progressive elaboration is the reason many project details might not be known up front, not the practice of providing detailed plans as project activities near their start date. Answers C and D are incorrect because they are not valid project planning terms.

5. Answer A is correct. The precedence diagramming method (PDM) supports finish-to-start, finish-to-finish, start-to-start, and start-to-finish dependencies. Answer B is incorrect because the arrow diagramming method (ADM) only allows for finish-to-start dependencies. Answers C and D are incorrect because they are both nonexistent diagramming methods.

6. Answer B is correct. The arrow diagramming method (ADM) is also referred to as activity-on-arrow (AOA) diagramming method. Answer A is incorrect because the precedence diagramming method (ADM) is also referred to as activity-on-node (AON) diagramming method. Answers C and D are incorrect because they are both non-existent diagramming methods.

7. Answer B is correct. The path A-C-E-G is the longest direct path from start to finish. All other answers are incorrect because they either state the incorrect path or project duration.

8. Answer A is correct. Because task D is not on the critical path and has a slack of one day, it can start one day late (at most) without affecting the project end date.

9. Answer C is correct. Because task C is on the critical path, any delay of the task delays the project.

10. Answer B is correct. Bottom-up estimating is the process of calculating estimates by aggregating the individual estimates of activities that make up the desired activity group. Answer A is incorrect because parametric estimating uses a process of multiplying quantity of work by the productivity rate. Answer C is incorrect because top-down estimating starts with an estimate and decomposes the estimate into smaller units to apply to the individual work packages. Answer D is incorrect because analogous estimating uses similar work packages, not estimate aggregation.

Need to Know More?

 Kerzner, Harold. *Project Management: A Systems Approach to Planning, Scheduling, and Controlling, Eighth Edition.* Indianapolis: John Wiley and Sons, 2003.

Project Management Institute. *A Guide to the Project Management Body of Knowledge, Third Edition.* Newton Square, PA: Project Management Institute, 2004.

Wysocki, Robert K. and McGary, Rudd. *Effective Project Management, Third Edition.* Indianapolis: John Wiley and Sons, 2003.

Elements of Project Planning

Terms you'll need to understand:

- ✓ Acceptance
- ✓ Avoidance
- ✓ Enhance
- ✓ Expected monetary value
- ✓ Exploit
- ✓ Mitigation
- ✓ Process improvement planning
- ✓ Procurement management plan
- ✓ Procurement planning
- ✓ Qualitative risk analysis
- ✓ Quality management
- ✓ Quantitative risk analysis
- ✓ RACI
- ✓ RAM
- ✓ Responsibility matrix
- ✓ Risk event
- ✓ Risk factor
- ✓ Risk identification
- ✓ Risk management
- ✓ Risk register
- ✓ Risk response planning
- ✓ Share
- ✓ Staff acquisition
- ✓ Subsidiary plans
- ✓ Transfer
- ✓ Utility theory

Techniques and concepts you'll need to master:

- ✓ The difference between risk management planning and risk response planning
- ✓ The purpose and elements of each subsidiary management plan
- ✓ Human resource principles and PMI's human resource management philosophy
- ✓ Human resource responsibilities of the project manager
- ✓ Quality management principles and PMI's quality management approach
- ✓ Cost of quality
- ✓ Difference among quality planning, quality assurance, and quality control
- ✓ The various responses to risks
- ✓ Understanding key procurement management principles and PMI's procurement management philosophy
- ✓ Contract types and risk/benefits to sellers and buyers

Additional Project Management Plan Components

The main components of the plan are the primary drivers that establish the key project baselines (scope, schedule, and cost). The supporting planning processes are equally important and establish the mechanisms to apply quality, reality (risk), stakeholder assignment, contract assignment, and project information management (communication) to those baselines. These plans include items such as the following:

➤ **Risk management plan**—This plan describes how risk management activities will be performed, including methodology, responsibility, cost, timing, and definitions for risk categories, probabilities, and impacts.

➤ **Staffing management plan**—Describes when and how HR requirements will be met, including acquisition approach, timing, training, and recognition.

➤ **Quality management plan**—This plan describes how the team will implement the quality policy. It addresses quality control, quality assurance, and continuous improvement.

➤ **Process improvement plan**—This plan describes how the team will analyze processes for improvement. It includes determining process boundaries, interfaces, metrics, and improvement targets.

➤ **Procurement management plan**—This plan describes how procurement activities will be performed, including contract types and responsibilities.

➤ **Communication management plan**—Describes how communication requirements will be met, including stakeholder communication, communication responsibility, communication timing, and techniques.

Risk Management Planning

Risk management planning is the first step in the risk management process. During this step the project manager plans how to effectively manage any risks posed to the project. This is obviously a critical step to follow in order to offset any problems that can derail the project and to ensure the other five steps in the risk management process will be carried out effectively. Planning meetings are an effective tool for identifying potential risks and developing the risk management plan. More on risk management planning is covered in the section "Understanding Key Risk Management Principles and PMI's Risk Management Philosophy."

Human Resource Planning

Human resource (HR) planning is the process for determining what HR resources are needed for the project, when they are needed, and how they will be obtained. The planning includes determining roles and responsibilities, developing project organization charts, and creating the staffing management plan.

Quality Management Planning

Quality planning is the first step of the project quality management process. During planning the project manager must identify which quality standards apply to the project. In parallel with other planning activities, the project manager documents how the quality standards will be achieved. This is identified in the quality management plan and is one of the subsidiary management plans included in the project management plan.

Process Improvement Plan

The *process improvement plan* is used to plan out details for analyzing and improving processes. The analysis includes process boundaries, configuration, metrics, and improvement targets. The process improvement plan is included as a subsidiary management plan in the project management plan.

Procurement Management Planning

Procurement management planning is the set of steps used to determine how best to bring in outside resources when they are needed to complete the project. The make/buy decision is the point where it is determined to use outside resources. An analysis is done to determine if the product or service can be produced by the project team or if it should be purchased. This analysis might also include buying versus renting/leasing a product.

Communication Management Plan

The *communication management plan* describes how the team will communicate with one another. Components to the plan include communication requirements with respect to medium and content, as well as mandatory versus discretionary communication.

Other Significant Items Found in Project Management Plans

The plans discussed previously, plus other components, can be either at a summary or detailed level, depending on the scope of the project. Other components of the project management plan include items such as the following:

➤ Milestone list

➤ Resource calendar

➤ Schedule baseline

➤ Cost baseline

➤ Scope baseline

➤ Quality baseline

➤ Risk register

Table 4.1 details these important components further.

Table 4.1 Other Significant Items Found in a Project Management Plan	
Component	Explanation
Milestone list	A list of all project milestones. Indicates mandatory and optional milestones.
Resource calendar	A composite calendar showing working time of all resources. Indicates holidays and other nonworking time for each resource.
Schedule baseline	The accepted and approved schedule for the project.
Cost baseline	The accepted and approved budget for the project.
Scope baseline	The accepted and approved scope for the project.
Quality baseline	The quality objectives for the project.
Risk register	The output from risk identification, containing a list of identified risks with supporting detail.

Each subsidiary plan should be considered when preparing the project management plan. The formality and detail vary depending on the scope of the project, amount of risk, and organizational policies.

The inputs, tools, techniques, and outputs for each of the processes discussed in this chapter should be memorized.

Understanding Key Risk Management Principles and PMI's Risk Management Philosophy

PMI's risk management philosophy is based on a proactive approach to preventing negative risks and enhancing positive risks. Key points to remember about risk include

➤ Risk can be either positive or negative. Positive risks are opportunities, negative risks are threats.

➤ A risk breakdown structure (RBS) is used to organize risk in a hierarchical structure.

➤ Monte Carlo analysis is a technique using simulations and probability in determining quantitative risk analysis.

➤ Risk categories are important in classifying risk.

➤ Probability and impact are both needed to assess risks.

➤ Quantitative analysis is generally reserved for high-probability, high-impact risk.

➤ Risk management planning and risk response planning are not the same activities.

➤ Risk identification is an iterative process that is performed throughout the project, not just during planning.

➤ Decision tree analysis is a technique using probabilities and costs for structured decision making.

➤ Five of the six risk management processes are conducted during the planning process group.

➤ The risk register is an important tool for capturing and tracking risks.

Risk register is a term introduced by PMI for the document detailing information on risks.

A risk can have either a negative or positive impact on the project.

The Risk Methodology

The *risk methodology* is a definition of how risk will be managed. It includes the approach, tools, and techniques to be used for the project. The approach details how the steps of the risk process will be conducted. For example, the approach could specify that risk analysis will be conducted at the end of each planning meeting. The tools can include the risk register, the risk breakdown structure, the probability and impact matrix, and checklists.

Risk Management Planning and Risk Response Planning

The *risk management plan* includes the risk methodology, roles/responsibilities, budget, execution timing, and definitions for risk categories, probabilities, and impacts. It is a summation of how the project team will carry out the remainder of the risk management activities for the project. The risk management plan should not be confused with the risk response plan, which is where the project manager captures responses to specific risks that have been identified during the risk identification process.

The risk management plan is not the same as the risk response plan.

Risk Breakdown Structure

A *risk breakdown structure (RBS)* is a tool that can be used to organize risks in a hierarchical fashion. The structure is defined using the risk categories. Even if an RBS is not used, risk categories are still defined in risk management planning. Risk categories can include

➤ **Technical**—Risk associated with using new technology.

➤ **Organizational**—Risk associated with either the organization running the project or the organization where the project will be implemented.

➤ **Cost**—Risk associated with project costs. This could include uncertainty in costs for materials or human resources.

➤ **Schedule**—Risk associated with time estimates for completing tasks.

➤ **Resource**—Risk associated with obtaining the necessary resources for the project.

Risk Probability and Impact

Probability can be defined as the likelihood that a risk will occur. It can be expressed mathematically (.2) or as a relative scale (low, medium, high). The definition for probability is developed during risk management planning.

Impact is the effect a risk has if it does occur. It can also be defined on a relative scale or mathematically. The definition for impact is developed during risk management planning.

The team documents in the project management plan detail how probabilities and impacts are measured. For example, a red/yellow/green scale might be used, where high-probability, high-impact risks are red; low-probability, low-impact risks are green; and so forth. A probability and impact matrix can also be used; for an example, refer to PMBOK Figure 11.8.

Both probability and impact are necessary for evaluating risks.

Risk Identification, Analysis, Response Planning, and Monitoring/Controlling

In the risk management process, completing the risk management plan is the first step. After the plan is in place, according to PMI the next steps in the risk management process are

➤ Identification

➤ Analysis (qualitative and quantitative)

➤ Response planning

➤ Monitoring/controlling (discussed in Chapter 6, "Project Control")

Understand the difference between qualitative and quantitative risk analysis. Qualitative evaluation is a prioritization based on probability and impact. Quantitative evaluation uses techniques to further advance the specific probabilities and impacts of project risks. For instance, modeling techniques such as Monte Carlo determine the overall effect of risks on project objectives and are typically used for high-probability, high-impact risks.

Risk Identification

Risk identification is determining the risk that might affect the project and characterizing those risks. The inputs for risk identification include

➤ Commercial databases

➤ Industry/academic/benchmarking studies

➤ Information from internal database (lessons learned)

➤ Scope statement, including WBS

➤ Risk management plan

➤ Project management plan including schedule, budget, and network diagrams

 The WBS is an important input to risk planning. Each element of the WBS can be reviewed to determine if there is an associated risk.

Obviously, the ability to identify risks is key in an effective risk management process. Keep in mind that risk identification is not just the project manager's responsibility; team members, subject matter experts, customers, stakeholders, and others are involved in this process. Table 4.2 summarizes tools used for risk identification.

Table 4.2 Risk Identification Tools	
Tool	**Application**
Documentation reviews	Review key project documents including the lessons learned from previous projects, commercial databases, the scope statement, risk management plan, and project management plan.
Brainstorming	Team members and experts outside the team participate in a facilitated session to develop a comprehensive list of risks, which are then categorized.
Delphi technique	A consensus-gathering technique that relies on experts in an anonymous process. A questionnaire is used to gather input, the results are summarized, and then distributed.
Interviews	Interviews are a main source of data gathering. They target the same audience as brainstorming or Delphi, but do so in a more personal setting.
Root cause analysis	This tool is also used in quality management. By addressing the causes of risks, the project manager can classify and effectively plan responses to the risks.
SWOT analysis (strength, weakness, opportunity, threat)	Analyzing the project across these perspectives can broaden the results of the risk analysis.

The Risk Register

The *risk register* is the output of risk identification. The risk register contains the following fields:

➤ Risk description

➤ Date identified

➤ Category

➤ Potential responses

➤ Current status

NOTE Risk identification is not a one-time event occurring during the planning process. It should be conducted throughout the project, including during major milestones and when a risk occurs.

Qualitative and Quantitative Risk Analysis

Qualitative risk analysis provides further definition to the identified risks in order to determine responses to them. The key terms are *probability* and *impact*. Probability is important because it measures how likely it is that a risk will occur. A high-probability risk deserves more attention than a low-probability risk. Likewise, impact is a measure of how the risk will affect the project should it occur. A risk with low impact has a different response than one with a high impact.

Qualitative risk analysis quickly prioritizes risks in order to conduct response planning and quantitative risk analysis, if used. Using the probability and the impact and a probability impact matrix, the project manager develops a prioritized list of risks. The output to this step is captured in the risk register.

Quantitative risk analysis looks at those risks that are prioritized high during qualitative risk analysis. The goal of this process is to quantify possible outcomes for the project, determine probabilities of outcomes, further identify high-impact risks, and develop realistic scope, schedule, and cost targets based on risks.

A key tool used in quantitative risk analysis is decision tree analysis. Using a decision tree diagram (see Figure 4.1), the impact of different scenarios is captured. Both probability and cost are used, resulting in an expected monetary value (EMV).

For this example, there are two vendors for a software package; Acme and WebCo. The details of the two options are presented in Table 4.3.

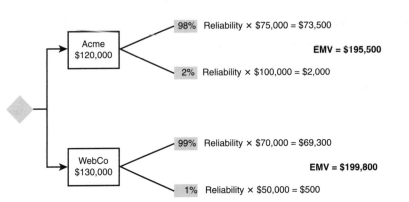

98% Reliability × $75,000 = $73,500

Acme $120,000

EMV = $195,500

2% Reliability × $100,000 = $2,000

99% Reliability × $70,000 = $69,300

WebCo $130,000

EMV = $199,800

1% Reliability × $50,000 = $500

Figure 4.1 An example of a decision tree analysis.

Table 4.3 Decision Tree Analysis Sample Data		
	Acme	**WebCo**
Purchase cost	$120,000	$130,000
Maintenance	$75,000/year (98% reliability)	$70,000/year (99% reliability)
Failure cost	$100,000 (2% probability)	$50,000 (1% probability)

Responses to Positive and Negative Risk

After all risks are identified, options to deal with the risks must be identified. Each risk is assigned to one or more owners to carry out the planned response. The responses are documented in the risk register.

There are four responses to negative risks:

➤ Avoid

➤ Mitigate

➤ Transfer

➤ Accept

For positive risks, responses include

➤ Exploit

➤ Enhance

➤ Share

➤ Accept

They are summarized in Table 4.4.

Table 4.4 Summary of Risk Responses

Response	Description	Risk Type
Avoid	Eliminating the threat by changing the project management plan.	Negative
Transfer	Shifting the risk to a third party.	Negative
Mitigate	Reducing either the probability or impact of the risk.	Negative
Exploit	Taking steps to make the opportunity happen.	Positive
Share	Using a third party to help capture the opportunity.	Positive
Enhance	Increasing the probability or positive impact of the risk.	Positive
Accept	Taking no steps in the project because of the risk. Contingency reserves might be established.	Positive and negative

Risk Monitoring and Controlling

The risk process is not just performed once during the planning process. Throughout the project, risks must be continually monitored, with additional analysis and risk response development taking place as new risks are identified. *Risk monitoring and controlling* focuses both on identification and analysis of new risks, as well as tracking previously identified risks and risk triggers.

Risk triggers are indications that risks have occurred or are about to occur. They are identified during risk identification and monitored throughout the project.

Risks should be reevaluated when the following events occur:

➤ A risk trigger is identified.

➤ A change request is approved.

➤ Key project milestones.

➤ End of project phases.

➤ Deviations detected in variance and trend analysis.

➤ Corrective or preventive actions are implemented.

Activity Resource Estimating, Cost Estimating, and Organizational Planning

As part of the project time management knowledge area, the activity resource estimating activity was completed. Resources can refer to either people (human resources) or other resources, such as equipment, office space, and so forth. You will see more on HR planning in the following sections.

Activity resource estimating is closely tied to cost estimating, where costs of resources are estimated. Organizational planning is concerned with roles, responsibilities, and reporting structure. Table 4.5 illustrates the differences among the three activities.

Table 4.5	Differences Among Activity Resources Estimating, Cost Estimating, and Organizational Planning		
Category	Activity Resource Estimating	Cost Estimating	Organizational Planning
Purpose	Determining what resources and how many are needed for the project.	Developing approximate cost of resources.	Determining the roles, responsibilities, and reporting relationships.
Knowledge area	Time.	Cost.	Human resources.
Why	Used to develop the project schedule.	Used to develop the project budget.	Focus is specific to the roles of human resources.
Notes	Resources include people, equipment, and so on.	Decisions about the type of resources used affect the cost.	Initiated during activity resource estimating.

The Project Manager's HR Responsibilities

The project manager must fulfill the role of manager and leader of the project team. Using the same skills and techniques a line manager uses, the project manager has the following responsibilities:

➤ Determine the HR needs of the project.

➤ Develop job descriptions.

➤ Negotiate with line managers for internal resources.

➤ Acquire external resources through the procurement process.

➤ Determine training needs.

➤ Identify/plan team-building activities.

➤ Determine the performance review approach for a project's human resources.

➤ Determine the reward and recognition approach for motivational purposes.

➤ Document the team structure and each team's responsibilities.

➤ Create a project organization chart.

➤ Develop a staffing management plan.

Key Human Resource Principles

Project human resource management is the set of processes used to organize and manage the project team, also referred to as the project staff. A subset of the project team is the project management team, composed of the project manager, project sponsor, and others responsible for project management activities such as planning, controlling, and closing the project.

HR planning has a number of key deliverables, including project organization charts, the staffing management plan, and determining the roles and responsibilities of each human resource.

Table 4.6 summarizes the tools used in human resource planning.

Table 4.6 Human Resource Planning Tools		
Name	**Description**	**Use**
Organizational breakdown structure (OBS)	Graphically displays work packages according to departments.	Each department can easily identify the work assigned to it.
Resource breakdown structure (RBS)	Graphically displays resources by type.	Effective in tracking costs. Groups resources even if they are working on different deliverables.
Responsibility assignment matrix (RAM)	A chart displaying resources and for which assignments they are responsible.	Allows easy identification of all responsibilities for a given resource.

(continued)

Table 4.6	Human Resource Planning Tools *(continued)*	
Name	**Description**	**Use**
RACI matrix	A specific type of RAM that shows the resources that are responsible, accountable, consulted, and informed in project activities.	Provides additional detail than RAM.
Position description	Text-based description of responsibilities.	Provides a high level of detail for a given position.

An organizational breakdown structure (OBS) is a graphical representation of the project team arranged according to an organization's existing structure. A resource breakdown structure (RBS) is also a graphical representation but is organized according to resource type. An RBS can contain resources other than human resources, such as equipment, and can be used to track costs.

In addition to graphical representations, resources might be documented in matrix-based documents such as a responsibility assignment (RACI) matrix. These documents are effective communication tools to ensure team members understand which assignments they are responsible for. Table 4.7 offers you an example of an RACI matrix.

RACI stands for responsible, accountable, consult, inform.

Table 4.7	RACI Matrix		
Activity	**Person**		
	Bill	**Mary**	**John**
Design	Responsible	Consult	Accountable
Build	Accountable	Responsible	Consult
Test	Inform	Accountable	Consult

The Staffing Management Plan

The *staffing management plan* is used to document the type of resources needed and the timing for those resources. The plan includes how the resources will be acquired, start and end dates, training requirements, policies and procedures for the team, and the team recognition approach and budget.

Resource leveling is a technique to determine the workload for resources over a given time; hours per week, for example. If resources are over-allocated, they are scheduled for more hours than are available. Resource leveling is reducing the number of hours worked to match the available hours, which results in extending the schedule or the need for additional resources.

Understanding Key Quality Management Principles and PMI's Management Philosophy

Although the project manager has overall responsibility for quality, the entire project team plays a role in quality management. Every member of the project team must understand the importance of her contributions, accept ownership for problems, be committed to monitoring and improving her performance, and openly discuss issues among team members.

Although specific techniques and measures apply to the product being produced, the overall project quality management approach applies to any project, and is relevant to the project as well as the product being produced.

 Understand the difference between *quality* and *grade*. Quality is a measure of how well the characteristics match requirements. Grade is assigned based on the characteristics that a product or service might have. So a product might be of low grade, meaning it has limited features, but might still be acceptable. Low quality is never acceptable.

The quality planning process has a number of key inputs, including the project management plan, the scope statement, organizational policies, lessons learned from other project, government/industry standards, and even company culture. The following list highlights important key concepts in PMI's quality management:

➤ The cost of preventing mistakes is generally less than the cost of repairing them.

➤ In order to be successful, management support for the quality program must exist.

➤ Quality is tied closely to the scope-cost-time triangle; without quality these objectives cannot be met successfully.

➤ The cost of quality refers to the cost to implement a quality program.

➤ Understanding and managing customer expectations is important to a successful quality program.

➤ The quality program should emphasize continuous improvement.

➤ There is a close alignment between the quality approach and the overall project management approach on a project.

 Memorize PMI's definition of quality: The degree to which a set of inherent characteristics fulfill requirements.

Quality Theories and PMI Quality Management Approach

The quality management approach presented in the PMBOK is intended to be compatible with other standards, including the International Organization for Standardization (ISO), Total Quality Management (TQM), Six Sigma, and others.

Exam questions on this topic are frequently taken from sources other than the PMBOK. Table 4.8 identifies some of the more popular quality theories. Additional references can be found in the "Need to Know More?" section at the end of the chapter.

Table 4.8 Common Quality Theories

Theory Name	Pioneers	Description
Continuous Improvement or Kaizen	Masaaki Imai, F.W. Taylor, and others	Processes are improved, mastered, and then further improvement is identified. Includes quality circles as a group oriented means of developing ideas.
The Deming Cycle or Plan-Do-Check-Act	Dr. W. Edward Deming	Similar to Kaizen, an improvement is planned, completed, measured, and then further improvement acted upon.
Six Sigma	Based on statistical work by Joseph Juran	A statistical measure of quality equating to 3.4 defects per million items. If defects can be measured, a process can be put into place to eliminate them.
Total Quality Management (TQM)	Dr. W. Edward Deming	Fourteen points of management that call for awareness of quality in all processes.

(continued)

Table 4.8 Common Quality Theories *(continued)*		
Theory Name	**Pioneers**	**Description**
Malcolm Baldrige Award	Howard Malcolm Baldrige	An award established by the U.S. Congress to promote quality awareness.
CMM (capability maturity model)	Software Engineering Institute (SEI)	Five levels of capability exist: initial, repeatable, defined, managed, and optimized.

The Plan-Do-Check-Act Cycle

PMI identifies the Plan-Do-Check-Act (PDCA) cycle, also referred to as the Deming Cycle, as both a quality tool and the underlying concept for interaction among project management processes. First, an improvement is planned. Next, the improvement is carried out and measured. The results are checked and finally acted upon. Acting upon the improvement might mean making the improvement a standard, further modification to the improvement, or abandoning the improvement. Figure 4.2 demonstrates the PDCA cycle.

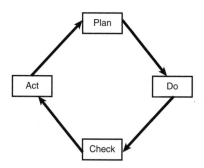

Figure 4.2   The Plan-Do-Check-Act cycle.

Quality Approaches and Project Management

Quality approaches align with project management approaches in a number of areas, including achieving customer satisfaction, preventing defects instead of inspecting for them, management support for quality, and continuous improvement. Table 4.9 provides additional detail.

Table 4.9 Principles Common to Quality Management and Project Management

Alignment Area	Description
Customer satisfaction	Customer requirements are met through a thorough understanding and management of expectations.
Prevention over inspection	It is cheaper to prevent defects than repair ones that are identified in inspections.
Management responsibility	Management must provide the support and resources for a quality program to be successful.
Continuous improvement	Processes are improved, mastered, and then further improvement is identified. Includes quality circles as a group-oriented means of developing ideas.

The Cost of Quality

The *cost of quality* is a term that refers to the cost to produce a product or service that meets requirements. Part of the cost is rework when requirements aren't met. An effective quality program reduces cost from rework.

The three primary types of cost associated with the cost of quality are

➤ Prevention costs

➤ Inspection costs

➤ Failure costs (internal and external)

Addressing prevention and inspection can be viewed as addressing the cost of conformance. This includes training, prototyping, design reviews, and testing. Failure costs (the cost of nonconformance) includes bug fixes, rework, cost of late delivery, and customer complaints.

Differences Among Quality Planning, Quality Assurance, and Quality Control

One area of confusion, especially among project managers without a background in quality, is the difference between the three processes in quality management. Table 4.10 helps clarify these concepts.

Table 4.10   Summary of Quality Management Processes

	Quality Planning	Quality Assurance	Quality Control
Process group	Planning	Executing	Monitoring/controlling
Emphasis	Planning	Implementing	Measuring and adjusting
Key activities	➤ Determining relevant quality standards ➤ Determining how to apply standards	➤ Applying planned activities ➤ Ensuring continuous improvement	➤ Monitoring results ➤ Identifying ways to eliminate unwanted results
Key outputs	➤ Quality management plan ➤ Quality improvement plan ➤ Quality metrics ➤ Quality checklist	➤ Requested changes ➤ Recommended corrective action	➤ QC measurements ➤ Validated defect repair ➤ Recommended corrective and preventive actions ➤ Requested changes ➤ Recommended defect repair ➤ Validated deliverables

Understanding Key Procurement Management Principles and PMI's Procurement Management Philosophy

Procurement management involves the relationship between the buyer and the seller when products, services, or other results are being purchased by the project team in order to complete the project. Key PMI principles for procurement management include

➤ The contract statement of work (SOW) is a key document that defines the work in order to allow buyers the ability to evaluate and bid on the work.

➤ There are three primary contract types:

  ➤ Fixed price

  ➤ Time and material

  ➤ Cost reimbursement

➤ The risk to both the buyer and seller depends on the type of contract chosen.

➤ The contract is a formal, written document and any changes are submitted in writing.

The Make/Buy Decision

The first step in procurement is resolving the make/buy decision. This decision is made during the plan purchases and acquisition process. An analysis is done to determine if the product or service can be produced by the project team or if it should be purchased. This analysis might also include buying versus renting/leasing a product.

The Contract Statement of Work

In addition to making the make/buy decision during the plan purchases and acquisition process, it is during this step that the contract statement of work (SOW) is developed and the type of contract to be used is determined. The SOW is a document that defines the work to be performed. A contract SOW is work performed under contract. The contract SOW is developed from the scope statement and WBS and should be sufficiently detailed to allow the potential sellers to determine their ability to perform the work. A project can have multiple SOWs.

Contract Types

A number of contract types are used in the procurement process. In order to be prepared for the exam, understand the benefit of each type, as summarize in Table 4.11

Table 4.11   Contract Types

Name	Description	Pro/Con
Firm fixed price (FFP) (or lump sum)	The work is completed for a predetermined price.	Benefits the buyer. Seller at risk if item isn't clearly defined. Seller must manage changes closely.
Fixed price incentive (FPI)	Similar to fixed price but an incentive is offered for early completion.	More administrative effort for buyer and seller.
Purchase order	A form of fixed price, usually for off-the-shelf items.	Optimal for both parties when item is a commodity (such as computers).
Cost reimbursement, includes CPF, CPPC, CPFF, and CPIF (see the following exam alert)	The seller is reimbursed for his costs, plus an additional fee.	Benefits the seller because his cost is covered. Risk to buyer if costs are higher than anticipated; the budget is affected.
Time and material (T&M)	Hybrid arrangement between fixed price and cost reimbursement where elements of both are used; a fixed unit rate can be set for certain elements of work while other components are completely reimbursable. For example, a programmer might be acquired at $125 per hour without defining how long they will be used.	Seller benefits if amount of work can be extended, which affects the buyer's budget.

PMI identifies four types of cost-reimbursement contracts that only vary in how the fee is calculated: cost plus fee (CPF), cost plus percentage of cost (CPPC), cost plus fixed fee (CPFF), and cost plus incentive fee (CPIF). Be familiar with all four variations of cost-reimbursement contracts, found on page 278 of the PMBOK.

Figure 4.3 illustrates the risk to buyer and seller for the contract types.

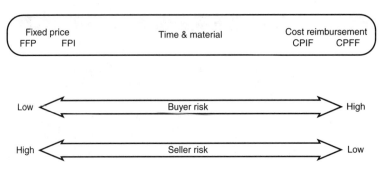

Figure 4.3 The buyer and seller risk for contract types.

The Procurement Management Plan

The procurement management plan is developed to plan out how procurement activities will be carried out. Evaluation criteria are a key output of plan contracting. Criteria can include

➤ Costs

➤ Quality

➤ Capabilities of the sellers, including technical, financial, capacity, and so on

➤ Technical approach

➤ References

The steps of the procurement process are only necessary if the decision is made to buy outside resources.

Building a Communication Plan

The first process covered in this chapter is the development of the communication plan. This plan is important to set the expectations of how the project team should communicate in an effective and timely manner. It also sets the expectations of the stakeholders and makes their need for information a part of the overall project plan. Most communication issues start with a lack of clear directives as to how and when to communicate. Most people are reluctant to initiate unsolicited communication. That's why a communication plan is crucial to good project team interaction. The plan actually tells team members what is expected of them throughout the project. Table 4.12 shows the inputs, tools, techniques, and outputs for the communication planning process.

Table 4.12 Communication Planning Inputs, Tools and Techniques, and Outputs		
Inputs	**Tools and Techniques**	**Outputs**
Enterprise environmental factors	Communication requirements analysis	Communication management plan
Organizational process assets	Communication technology	
Project scope statement		
Project management plan		

Exam Prep Questions

1. Who has overall responsibility for quality planning?
   - ❏ A. Project manager
   - ❏ B. Quality manager
   - ❏ C. Senior management
   - ❏ D. Project planner

2. Which input is not used for risk identification?
   - ❏ A. Project charter
   - ❏ B. Scope statement
   - ❏ C. Project management plan
   - ❏ D. Academic studies

3. Which risk response is most likely to involve contingency reserves?
   - ❏ A. Transfer
   - ❏ B. Mitigate
   - ❏ C. Acceptance
   - ❏ D. Share

4. Which contract type would be best for the seller if the scope of work is not well defined?
   - ❏ A. Fixed price
   - ❏ B. Purchase order
   - ❏ C. Time and material
   - ❏ D. Cost plus incentive fee

5. Which of the following activities is not part of risk management planning?
   - ❏ A. Developing a risk management plan
   - ❏ B. Identifying risk categories
   - ❏ C. Updating risk register
   - ❏ D. Determining risk roles and responsibilities

6. Which of the following is not a responsibility of the project manager?
   - ❏ A. Acquiring HR resources for the project team
   - ❏ B. Managing overall responsibility for quality in the organization
   - ❏ C. Overall responsibility for risk on the project
   - ❏ D. Overall responsibility for customer satisfaction on the project

7. Which project document is best suited for tracking costs of resources?

   ❑ A. Resource breakdown structure
   ❑ B. Organizational breakdown structure
   ❑ C. Work breakdown structure
   ❑ D. Risk breakdown structure

8. Which document is best suited for tracking the assignment of all resources to specific tasks?

   ❑ A. Staffing management plan
   ❑ B. Organizational breakdown structure
   ❑ C. Position description
   ❑ D. RACI matrix

9. Which subsidiary plan/component documents the quality objectives for the project?

   ❑ A. Quality management plan
   ❑ B. Quality baseline
   ❑ C. Process improvement plan
   ❑ D. Quality control checklist

10. Which quality theory outlines 14 points and calls for quality awareness at all levels of the organization?

   ❑ A. CMM
   ❑ B. Kaizen
   ❑ C. TQM
   ❑ D. Malcolm-Baldrige

Answers to Exam Prep Questions

1. Answer A is correct. The project manager has overall responsibility. All other members of the project team assist in the process.

2. Answer A is correct. The project charter is not used. The scope statement and project management plan are used. Academic studies are part of enterprise environmental factors that also include commercial databases, benchmarking, or other industry studies.

3. Answer C is correct. Acceptance is when no change to the project is made for a risk. A contingency can be set aside to offset the impact of the risk. Transferring moves the risk to a third party and there most likely would be an upfront cost associated with this response. Mitigate is taking steps to reduce the probability or impact. Sharing is similar to transferring for a positive risk.

4. Answer D is correct. Cost plus incentive fee is always the lowest risk for the buyer. Fixed price and purchase order are the best choice when the item is well defined. Time and materials balances the risk between buyer and seller.

5. Answer C is correct. Updating the risk register first happens in risk identification. All other activities occur during risk management planning.

6. Answer B is correct. Senior management is responsible for quality in the organization. The project manager is responsible for product quality on the project.

7. Answer A is correct. The resource breakdown structure organizes all resources in a hierarchical structure, allowing for cost tracking. An organizational breakdown structure is used to document the project organization (human resources). A work breakdown structure shows deliverables, but is not a detail of cost. A risk breakdown structure is used for risk analysis.

8. Answer D is correct. The RACI matrix list responsibilities of all resources. The staffing management plan only lists types of resources and timing. The organizational breakdown structure lists resources according to the organization to which they belong. A position description only lists responsibilities for a specific position.

9. Answer B is correct. The quality baseline documents the quality objectives for the project. The quality management plan lists which quality policies apply to the project. The process improvement plan documents how processes will be analyzed for improvement. A quality control checklist is used to ensure steps of a process are completed.

10. Answer C is correct. Total Quality Management (TQM) uses 14 points and calls for quality awareness from everyone involved. CMM outlines five levels of process maturity. Kaizen, or continuous improvement, calls for a cycle of improvements to processes. Malcolm-Balrige is an award for quality awareness.

Need to Know More?

 Ireland, Lewis. *Quality Management for Projects and Programs*. Newtown Square, PA: Project Management Institute, 1991.

 Pritchard, Carl (ed). *Risk Management Concepts and Guidelines*. Arlington, VA: ESI International, 1997.

 International Organization for Standardization. "Quality Management Principles." http://www.iso.org/iso/en/iso9000-14000/understand/qmp.html.

 Value Based Management.net. "Management Methods, Management Models, Management Theories." http://www.valuebasedmanagement.net/.

Project Management Executing Processes

Terms you'll need to understand:

- ✓ Arbitration/litigation
- ✓ Bidder conference
- ✓ Claims/disputes/appeals
- ✓ Co-location
- ✓ Continuous improvement
- ✓ Contract
- ✓ Contract management plan
- ✓ Contract negotiations
- ✓ Corrective action
- ✓ Defect repair
- ✓ Evaluation criteria
- ✓ Organizational process asset
- ✓ Payment system
- ✓ Preventive action
- ✓ Project management information system
- ✓ Project management methodology
- ✓ Quality audit
- ✓ Root cause analysis
- ✓ Weighted system

Techniques and concepts you'll need to master:

- ✓ Change control system
- ✓ Considerations when selecting team members
- ✓ Virtual teams
- ✓ Team performance assessment
- ✓ Process analysis
- ✓ General management skills
- ✓ Tools for team acquisition
- ✓ Types of power
- ✓ Theories of motivation
- ✓ Steps in team development
- ✓ Information gathering and retrieval tools
- ✓ Information distribution techniques
- ✓ Lessons learned process
- ✓ Use of a weighted evaluation system

Executing a Project Management Plan

In the executing process group, the work of the project takes place. The activities of the executing process group overlap with the monitoring and controlling process group (as well as the other process groups, to some extent). The specific activities that PMI identifies as part of executing are

➤ Direct and manage project execution

➤ Perform quality assurance

➤ Acquire the project team

➤ Develop the project team

➤ Information distribution

➤ Request seller responses

➤ Select sellers

 Memorize which processes belong to the project executing process group (there are seven):
- ➤ Direct and manage project execution
- ➤ Perform quality assurance
- ➤ Acquire project team
- ➤ Develop project team
- ➤ Information distribution
- ➤ Request seller response
- ➤ Select sellers

Project Execution

PMI includes the *direct and manage project execution process* within the integration knowledge area and defines the process as "executing the work defined in the project management plan to achieve the project's requirements defined in the project scope statement."

The PMBOK includes a list of activities that are included in the direct and manage project execution process. The purpose of these activities is to produce the deliverables that are defined within the project's scope. The work also includes completed approved changes, corrective action, preventive action, and defect repair. Finally, work performance information is produced. This information is used to monitor and control activities against the project plan baseline.

The key output of this activity is the set of deliverables. They might be tangible deliverables, such as a road or computer software, or intangible deliverables such as training.

The project manager executes the project using the organization's project management methodology and project management information system. The methodology is the tools, templates, and procedures for executing projects. For example, it would include the change management process or status reporting process.

The project management information system (PMIS) includes the scheduling tool (such as Microsoft Project), tools for reporting, document repositories, and any other systems used in project execution. The PMIS also includes the techniques used for gathering, integrating, and disseminating process outputs. The PMIS can be both manual and automated.

As a result of monitoring/controlling activities, additional work might be required in execution. For example, a quality control activity might indicate that a deliverable does not meet the quality standards, which would cause rework. A summary of the controlling activities, potential impacts, and resulting work is found in Table 5.1.

 NOTE Understand the difference between corrective action and preventive action. *Preventive action* is anything done to prevent, or avoid, a specific situation. *Corrective action* is anything done "after the fact" to fix an issue after it has occurred.

Table 5.1 Impact of Monitoring/Controlling Activities on Project Execution

Monitoring/Controlling Process	Potential Output	Resulting Work in Execution
Monitor/control project work	Corrective action to bring actual results in line with planned activities	Implementation of corrective action
Integrated change control	Change request	Implementation of approved change request
Scope verification	Change request	Implementation of approved change request
Scope/schedule/ cost control	Change request	Implementation of approved change request
Perform quality control	Identification of deliverables not meeting quality standards	Rework to bring deliverable up to quality standards, preventive action to eliminate cause of problem

(continued)

Table 5.1 Impact of Monitoring/Controlling Activities on Project Execution *(continued)*		
Monitoring/Controlling Process	Potential Output	Resulting Work in Execution
Manage project team	Team member not completing work activities per project management plan	Corrective or preventive action to align team member performance with plans
Performance reporting	Forecast indicating project is behind schedule	Corrective action to bring performance in line with plans
Manage stakeholders	Issue raised by stakeholder	Corrective action to resolve issue
Risk monitoring/ controlling	Planned risk emerges	Application of risk response, risk reassesment
Contract administration	Seller's deliverables completed	Payment to seller

Ensure you have a clear understanding of the activities and the interfaces that are part of the direct and manage project execution and the monitoring and controlling project work processes.

Ensuring Quality

Quality assurance is the planned, systematic, quality activities that are used to ensure the project will employ all processes needed to meet requirements. It differs from quality control, which is monitoring specific project results to ensure they meet quality standards.

Understand the difference between quality assurance and quality control.

PMI stresses the importance of continuous improvement, which is an iterative process for improving quality. Continuous improvement is an ongoing cycle of process analysis leading to process improvements at which point further process analysis is undertaken. Process analysis is an in-depth look at what processes are being executed, how they are executed, by whom they are being executed, and related processes.

The benefits of continuous improvement include reduced waste and reduction in non–value-added processes, leading to increased efficiency and effectiveness.

Work performance information is an important input to quality assurance. *Work performance information* is defined as data on the status of project schedule activities. This information can be used in audits, quality reviews, and process analysis. Other important inputs to quality assurance include approved change requests and quality control measurements. *Approved change requests* are any change requests that have been processed through the change management process and approved by the proper authority. Quality control measurements are the results of quality control activities.

Memorize all the inputs to quality assurance.

The tools used in quality planning and quality control can also be used in quality assurance. Refer to Chapter 4, "Elements of Project Planning," and Chapter 6, "Project Control," for more details.

Along with the tools used in quality planning and quality control, two other tools in quality assurance are quality audits and process analysis. *Quality audits* are independent reviews to verify compliance with quality standards. For example, a review team would look at control charts to determine if the processes were being controlled properly and if proper actions were taken when processes fell outside control limits. *Process analysis* supports continuous improvement, as explained in the previous section.

Root cause analysis is a technique to examine a problem, determine the underlying cause of the problem, and implement corrective action to prevent further occurrence.

The application of quality assurance might result in changes to the project, which take the form of change requests or recommended corrective action. Updates are made to the project management plan and/or organizational process assets.

Acquiring and Developing the Project Team

The project cannot be completed without people. Using the procedures defined during planning, the project manager acquires the necessary resources. Note, however, that the project manager may not have direct control over what resources are assigned to the project. When the project manager does have the ability to influence or direct staff assignments, the following should be considered:

➤ **Availability**—Does the person's schedule allow him to support the project?

➤ **Ability**—Does the person have the proper skill set?

➤ **Experience**—Will the project require an individual with significant experience?

➤ **Interest**—An important factor in motivation. Will the person want to work on the project?

➤ **Cost**—How much will the person cost? This can be in terms of hiring a contractor. If the resource is internal, other factors might be considered, including the impact on another project that the individual might support.

A number of tools may be used in acquiring human resources; they are summarized in Table 5.2.

Table 5.2 Summary of Human Resource Acquisition Tools	
Tool	**Description**
Preassignment	Assignments made prior to beginning of execution. They might be named in the proposal, contract, or charter; or assigned because of a specific skill.
Negotiation	The project manager/team negotiates with functional managers or other managers for the resources they want. Organizational politics might be a factor in obtaining the desired resources.
Acquisition	Outside resources, such as consultants or contractors, are brought in through the acquisition process.
Virtual team	A team that is not located together and relies on electronic tools (email, conference calls, and so forth) for communication. With decreasing communication costs and improved reliability, virtual teams have become more prevalent. This can also include off-shoring, where some of the project work is done in a separate country.

The use of virtual teams requires additional work during the communication planning process to ensure all the communication needs of the virtual team are met.

Team Development

Team development has two facets: increasing the competency of the team and improving the interaction among team members. Although team development should occur throughout the project, it is most effective when conducted early in the project life cycle.

PMI lists a number of tools for team development, including general management skills, training, teambuilding activities, ground rules, co-location, and recognition and rewards:

➤ **General management skills**—These skills are sometimes referred to as soft skills and include empathy, creativity, influence, and group facilitation skills.

➤ **Training**—This is used for increasing competency, might be formal or informal, and includes classroom training, computer-based training, and coaching/mentoring.

➤ **Team building**—This is any activity used to improve team cohesiveness. Team building can encompass anything from a short activity at the beginning of a meeting to an offsite event. Even team participation in a project activity such as risk identification can serve to build team cohesiveness.

➤ **Ground rules**—These dictate the expected behavior of the team. Having the team develop the ground rules can serve as a team building activity.

➤ **Co-location**—This is the opposite of virtual teams. PMI uses the team war room to describe a room where the team activities take place. Critical projects might use co-location to improve communication among team members.

➤ **Recognition and rewards**—These are used to motivate the team and reinforce positive behavior. The approach should be developed during planning and take into account the culture of team members, the type of behavior to be rewarded, and the budget.

Power is an important concept within the team environment. Although the project manager is in charge, he might not have legitimate power over all team members. Other team members must also rely on some power to accomplish their tasks. A summary of the types of power is presented in Table 5.3.

Table 5.3 Summary of Types of Power	
Type of Power	**Description**
Legitimate	Power based on position or title, such as senior executives.
Referent	Power transferred from someone with legitimate power. A project charter approved by a vice-president assigning the project manager gives the project manager referent power.
Expert	Power based on knowledge. A team leader might have expert power because of her knowledge in a programming language.
Reward	Power based on the ability to give or hold back rewards. A project manager who can award performance bonuses has this type of power.
Coercive	Power based on force or intimidation.

Referent power is important for project managers. Often their authority does not equal their responsibilities on the project. This is especially true in a matrix environment when they don't have direct authority over team members.

Team Motivation

As mentioned previously, recognition and rewards are used to motivate the team. Knowledge of motivation theories is often tested in the PMP exam. A summary of the leading theories is presented in Table 5.4.

Table 5.4 Summary of Motivation Theories		
Theory	**Developer**	**Description**
Hierarchy of needs	Abraham Maslow	People have a hierarchy of needs, described as a pyramid. When one level is satisfied, they move onto the higher level needs. The base is physical needs (food, shelter), and then progress through safety and security, social needs (love, friendship), esteem, and finally self-actualization. On a project team, a worker would very likely be motivated by esteem, which can be self-esteem for mastery of a task or the esteem that comes from recognition by others for accomplishments.

(continued)

Table 5.4   Summary of Motivation Theories *(continued)*

Theory	Developer	Description
Motivation-hygiene theory (or the two factor theory)	Fredrick Herzberg	There are motivators and hygiene factors. Hygiene factors (pay, adequate supplies) prevent dissatisfaction but otherwise don't motivate. Motivation comes from factors such as learning new skills or being promoted. A project manager must ensure hygiene factors are present and create the motivators as part of the assignment.
Expectancy theory	Victor Vroom	People are motivated by the expectation of being rewarded for their work. In addition, if a team is told they are high performing, they will act that way, with the corollary for low performance also being true.
Achievement theory	David McClelland	The three motivators for people are power, affiliation, and achievement. A person might not have one of these factors, and therefore is not motivated in his job.
X and Y theories Theory Z	Douglas McGregor William Ouchi	Theory X states people are lazy and need autocratic leadership. Theory Y states people are generally hard workers and do not require constant supervision. Theory Z is not related to McGregor's work. It states people are not only self-motivated to do their work, but also have a desire to help the company succeed.
Contingency theory	Fred Fiedler	The most effective leadership style is contingent on the situation. It is influenced by the leader's relationship with the team, the task to be completed, and the positional power of the leader.
Situational leadership	Ken Blanchard	Individuals move through four stages of development, and leaders need to apply the correct leadership style. The progression of leadership styles is directing, coaching, supporting, and delegating.

Understand how the project manager would use the theories of motivation to influence team members.

Expectancy theory believes motivation is a factor of valence (the value of the reward), expectancy (belief in the ability to complete a task), and instrumentality (belief you will receive the reward if you complete the task).

Team Formation

The theories presented in Table 5.4 focus primarily on development of individuals. PMI also discusses how the team forms as a cohesive unit. A leading theory in team development was developed by Bruce Tuckman. His theory states that teams go through stages; forming, storming, norming, and performing. He later added a fifth stage, adjourning. His model is summarized in Table 5.5.

Table 5.5 Tuckman's Model on Team Formation	
Stage	**Description**
Forming	Initial stage when team is first brought together. Team goals and individual roles are unclear. High dependence on the project manager for direction.
Storming	Team members attempt to establish themselves within the team. Cliques might form. Still some uncertainty in goals.
Norming	Roles are accepted. Consensus exists. May be social interactions outside the project.
Performing	Very clear focus. Little direction is needed from the project manager.
Adjourning	Break up of the team after completion of the project. Feelings of insecurity might exist.

Blanchard's situational leadership model, seen in Table 5.4, can also apply to teams. The four leadership styles can be used in Tuckman's four stages of development. Figure 5.1 compares these two theories.

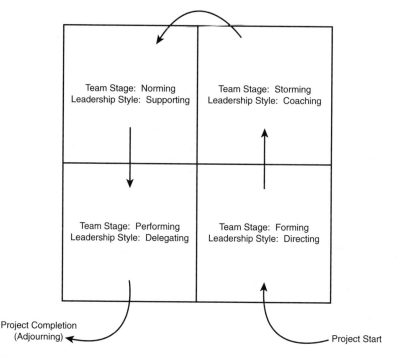

Team Stage: Norming
Leadership Style: Supporting

Team Stage: Storming
Leadership Style: Coaching

Team Stage: Performing
Leadership Style: Delegating

Team Stage: Forming
Leadership Style: Directing

Project Completion
(Adjourning)

Project Start

Figure 5.1 Comparison of situational leadership and team formation.

Distributing Information

Information distribution is the task of keeping stakeholders informed. This includes communication outlined in the communication plan as well as responding to ad-hoc requests. The communication must be both timely and accurate. A project manager spends a large portion of his time communicating.

The number of communication channels is an exponential relationship. See Figure 5.2 for the formula and examples for calculating communication channels. In the example, the first team has three people (N=3), so the formula is

$3 \times (3 - 1)/2 = 3$

In the second figure, there are six team members, so the formula is

$6 \times (6 - 1)/2 = 15$

Number of Channels = n(n-1)/2

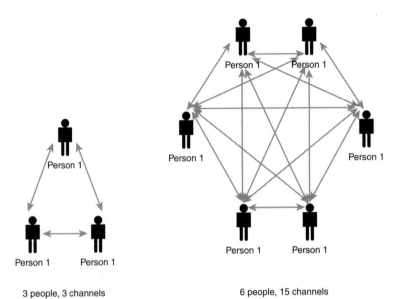

3 people, 3 channels

6 people, 15 channels

Figure 5.2 Communication channels.

Be able to calculate the number of communication channels given the number of team members.

Tools and Techniques for Information Distribution

The tools and techniques for information distribution include communication skills, information gathering and retrieval systems, information distribution methods, and lessons learned process.

Communication Skills

Communication skills are a part of general management skills. *Communication* is comprised of a sender, a receiver, and the communication channel. The sender is responsible for making the message clear and accurate. The receiver is responsible for understanding the message. Communication can include the following:

➤ Written and oral

➤ Listening and speaking

➤ Internal and external

➤ Formal and informal

➤ Vertical and horizontal

Issues can result if communication is not managed effectively on the project. For example, because email cannot easily convey emotions, an email could be sent with a comment meant to be sarcastic, but the receiver doesn't understand that and is upset based on the content of the email. The project manager should plan out communication to avoid these types of issues, including the best method for delivering messages based on the audience and content.

Information Gathering and Retrieval

If there are unique needs for information gathering and retrieval systems, they should be identified during planning. As an example, a project that involves subcontractors might need a document repository that exists outside the company's computer network. These tools allow anyone with permission to access documents through a common web browser, even from remote locations. A summary of possible tools is provided in Table 5.6.

Table 5.6 Information Gathering and Retrieval Tools	
Tool	**Description**
Manual filing system	When printed documents exist, they must be filed so team members have access to them. If a war room is used, they would be stored in the war room.
Project management tools	Enterprise level project management tools store project information on servers that team members can access and update. For example, a team member can update the status of her tasks and have it automatically available to the project manager.
Electronic databases	Often databases are used to track issues and risks. The information from these databases can be used in status reporting.
Document repository	Project documents such as reports, design documents, other technical documents, and other project deliverables can be stored electronically in a document repository. The repository may be web based or use other computer filing conventions and exist on a company server or intranet, or on an extranet accessible by remote users.

Information Distribution

The project manager must ensure that information is effectively collected and distributed to project stakeholders. There are a number of methods to accomplish this:

➤ Face-to-face project meetings

➤ Virtual meetings using conference bridges, web conferencing, or video conferencing

➤ Distribution and filing of printed documents

➤ Shared access to electronically filed documents and document repository tools

➤ Email and fax

➤ Telephone and voice mail

➤ Access to project scheduling and other project management tools

Lessons Learned

Lessons learned are specific items captured throughout the project that can help improve either the current project or future projects. An effective lessons learned process helps the project manager and team with continuous improvement. Lessons learned sessions should be conducted throughout the project, not just at the conclusion. The end of project phases or the completion of key milestones are opportunities to conduct lessons learned meetings.

The focus of lessons learned meetings should be on both the positive and negative aspects of the project. Processes that went well should be documented as best practices. Improvements to processes that didn't go well should also be documented.

In order to be effective, the lessons learned sessions cannot be a blame session. The focus has to be on process improvement, not identifying whose fault an issue might have been.

Capturing the lessons learned is not the final step. The information has to be stored in a way that perpetuates the information. This might include a lessons learned database or other knowledge management system within the organization. The results might also result in changes to corporate policies and procedures.

Managing Project Procurement

During planning, the procurement approach was mapped out. PMI identifies two steps to be completed during execution: *requesting seller responses* and *selecting sellers*. In addition, *contract administration*, discussed in Chapter 6, is performed as a monitoring/controlling activity.

Request Seller Responses and Selecting Sellers

Using the procurement management plan and other procurement documents (such as the invitation for a bid, a statement of work, or a request for quotation) developed during planning, the project team seeks out potential sellers for the items being procured. request might be made via a bidder conference, advertising, or through use of a qualified seller list. The most important output from this process are proposals from potential sellers.

 The bidder conference is also known as the contractor conference, vendor conference, or pre-bid conference. Understand that these terms are interchangeable.

With proposals in hand, the project team must select the seller(s) that are best able to deliver the product or service. In addition to the proposals, evaluation criteria were identified during planning that are used to evaluate the proposals.

The evaluation criteria used can include any of the following:

➤ Seller's overall understanding of the need

➤ Price

➤ Overall life cycle cost

➤ History of seller with the company

➤ Seller capabilities and approach including technical, managerial, and financial

➤ Seller's production capacity, business size, and interest in the product/service

➤ Seller's desire to assert intellectual property or proprietary rights on the product or service

➤ References

PMI lists other inputs with which you should be familiar, including the procurement management plan, procurement policies, the procurement document package, proposals, qualified seller list, and the project management plan.

There are a number of tools used during seller selection, which are summarized in Table 5.7.

Table 5.7 Seller Selection Tools

Tool	Description
Weighting system	A weighting system is used to quantify the importance to each evaluation criteria. Some criteria might be more important than others and therefore be weighted more. For example, if reliability is more important than cost, a seller with better reliability would score higher then one with better cost.
Independent estimates	Independent estimates are prepared by outside organizations or the procurement department as a check against the proposal pricing. These estimates are compared to proposals to determine if the proposals are within reason.
Screening system	A screening system is a way to set up minimum performance levels that must be achieved. Any proposals that don't meet the minimum are not considered further. This tool is effective to easily screen out some of the bids when there are a large number of bids to evaluate.
Contract negotiation	Contract negotiations are used to provide clarification on the proposals. This can become a process on its own in large procurement situations. Negotiations cover technical details, financing, pricing, payment schedules, responsibilities of both parties, change and conflict resolution processes, and rights to intellectual or proprietary property. The result of contract negotiation is the signed contract. These negotiations may be lead by someone other than the project manager.
Seller rating system	A seller rating system is used by an organization to track seller performance based on past contracts.
Expert judgment	A review team with expertise in the items being contracted use their expert judgment to evaluate the proposals.
Proposal evaluation techniques	Proposal evaluation techniques can incorporate the other tools, such as a weighting system or expert judgment, as well as the process that will be used to evaluate proposals. Often scorecards are used as part of the process. The technique includes the overall process for comparing results of screening processes, weighting results from multiple contributors, or using expert judgment to make the final decision.

The proposal evaluation technique should be able to take into account both objective and subjective criteria. The technique incorporates the weighting system for the evaluation criteria. The proposal evaluation is conducted by multiple reviewers. An example of a proposal evaluation scorecard is shown in Table 5.8. In this example, Vendor Two had the higher score and would be selected as the seller.

Table 5.8   Sample of Proposal Evaluation Scorecard

	Vendor One			Vendor Two		
Criteria	Raw Score	Weight	Weighted Score	Raw Score	Weight	Weighted Score
Price	4	.7	2.8	5	.7	3.5
Delivery Schedule	3	.5	1.5	4	.5	2.0
Technical Knowledge	3	.5	1.5	2	.5	1.0
Experience	1	.3	0.3	3	.3	0.9
Total			6.2			7.4

 Understand the concept of using a source selection weighting system for the exam.

The weighting system is developed based on the criteria that the organization determined was important for the project. In Table 5.8, price received the highest weight, while experience received the lowest weight. Using that scorecard, a vendor with a lower price receives a higher weighted score than a vendor with significant experience. The raw scores are determined by the individuals or team reviewing the proposals.

The weighting system can be used to either select a final seller or to prioritize the list of sellers for contract negotiations. If a satisfactory contract cannot be arranged with the seller receiving the top score, contract negotiations could begin with the next seller.

The process for selecting a seller can be repeated. An initial proposal can be evaluated to reduce the number of vendors. The vendors selected for the next round of evaluation can then be given a more detailed request for proposal (RFP) and evaluated on more criteria.

Exam Prep Questions

1. Which activity is not performed as part of the direct and manage project execution process?
   - ❏ A. Staff, train, and manage the project team.
   - ❏ B. Create and validate deliverables.
   - ❏ C. Manage risks and implement risk responses.
   - ❏ D. Monitor implementation of approved changes.

2. Which of the following monitoring/controlling activities would not result in preventive action being applied?
   - ❏ A. Integrated change control
   - ❏ B. Scope control
   - ❏ C. Manage project team
   - ❏ D. Quality control

3. The technique to identify the underlying cause of a problem and take steps to prevent further occurrence is called what?
   - ❏ A. Continuous improvement
   - ❏ B. Root cause analysis
   - ❏ C. Quality audits
   - ❏ D. Ishikawa analysis

4. As part of the team acquisition process, the project manager hires a new employee and assigns her to the project team. According to Maslow's hierarchy of needs, what need level is she most likely at?
   - ❏ A. Self acquisition
   - ❏ B. Safety and security
   - ❏ C. Social need
   - ❏ D. Physical need

5. The project manager has budgeted money to provide cash awards to team members that exceed expectations. A project team member that is motivated by the chance to earn a cash reward can most accurately be explained by which theory?
   - ❏ A. Hierarchy of needs
   - ❏ B. Theory X
   - ❏ C. Achievement theory
   - ❏ D. Expectancy theory

6. The project is a month into the executing phase. There are some cliques forming among the team members. Which leadership style is most appropriate?

   ❑ A. Directing
   ❑ B. Delegating
   ❑ C. Coaching
   ❑ D. Supporting

7. How many communication channels exist in a team of 20 members?

   ❑ A. 20
   ❑ B. 80
   ❑ C. 190
   ❑ D. 230

8. The project team is composed of team members in two countries plus a contractor team in a third country. What tool would optimize communication?

   ❑ A. Project schedule tool
   ❑ B. War room
   ❑ C. Manual filing system
   ❑ D. Extranet-based electronic document repository

9. A lessons learned session should be held at what point in a project?

   ❑ A. At the project conclusion
   ❑ B. When something goes wrong
   ❑ C. At key milestones
   ❑ D. When risk events occur

10. During the process of selecting the sellers, the project manager rejects one vendor because it doesn't have the manufacturing capability. This is an example of which selection tool?

   ❑ A. Weighting system
   ❑ B. Expert judgement
   ❑ C. Seller rating system
   ❑ D. Screening system

Answers to Exam Prep Questions

1. Answer D is correct. During the direct and manage project execution process, approved changes are implemented but monitoring of those changes is part of monitoring/controlling project work. All other activities are performed as part of direct and manage project execution.

2. Answer B is correct. Scope, schedule, and cost control can all result in corrective action, but not preventive action. All other choices do have preventive action as a possible output.

3. Answer B is correct. Root cause analysis looks at the underlying causes of an issue and applies corrective action to prevent further occurrence.

4. Answer C is correct. Because she is new to the company, she is most likely looking for acceptance and friendship. She needs to achieve this and self-esteem before being able to move to self-actualization. Since she has a job, you can assume she does not need safety and security or physical needs.

5. Answer D is correct. The person is working hard because he expects to be rewarded. The other theories do not talk about rewards as motivators.

6. Answer C is correct. The formation of cliques occurs during the storming stage of team development. During this stage, the correct situational leadership style is coaching.

7. Answer C is correct. Using the formula $(N)(N-1)/2$, the calculation is $(20 \times 19)/2$.

8. Answer D is correct. An electronic document repository allows all team members access to the documents, regardless of location. Manual filing and war rooms are optimal for a project team in one location. A project scheduling tool might allow team members on a shared network to share data, but would not be helpful for a third party team.

9. Answer C is correct. Although lessons learned should be held at project conclusion, they should be held throughout the project, so answer C is most correct.

10. Answer D is correct. A screening system rejects sellers that don't meet minimum requirements.

Need to Know More?

 http://www.valuebasedmanagement.net/index.html

http://www.businessballs.com/

Project Control

Terms you'll need to understand:

- ✓ Actual cost
- ✓ Approved defect repair
- ✓ Contract and vendor management
- ✓ Control charts
- ✓ Cost performance index
- ✓ Cost variance
- ✓ Earned value analysis
- ✓ Feasibility study
- ✓ Holistic project management

- ✓ Project charter
- ✓ Project objectives
- ✓ Project scope
- ✓ Qualitative and quantitative risk
- ✓ Quality assurance
- ✓ Scheduled performance index
- ✓ Stakeholders
- ✓ Validated deliverables

Techniques and concepts you'll need to master:

- ✓ Corrective or preventive actions
- ✓ Effective controls
- ✓ Project management plan
- ✓ Alternative planning
- ✓ Project life cycle
- ✓ Work breakdown structure
- ✓ Cost constraints
- ✓ Change control process
- ✓ Rebaselining
- ✓ Quality control
- ✓ Project team management
- ✓ Performance reporting
- ✓ Contingencies
- ✓ Reserves
- ✓ Statistical sampling
- ✓ Cause and effect

- ✓ Conflict management
- ✓ Project performance appraisals
- ✓ Communication methods
- ✓ Trend analysis
- ✓ Reserve analysis
- ✓ Observation: conversation
- ✓ Inspection (scope and quality)
- ✓ Variance analysis (scope, schedule, and management)
- ✓ Configuration control
- ✓ Performance measurement (technical and commercial)
- ✓ Progress reporting
- ✓ Project performance reviews
- ✓ Forecasting

What Is Project Control?

Project control refers to all the activities and processes available to successfully manage project risks. For the PMP test, project control entails a total of 12 distinctive processes out of the 44 project management processes in the body of work.

In essence, *project control* is all the effective activities that the project manager performs to keep project performance and resource utilization at optimal levels. The magnitude and frequency of these activities are dictated by the size and organizational impact of the project. No matter the size of the project, there are three core elements of effective project control:

➤ Effective definition of project baseline and milestones

➤ Effective tracking of your project activities and resource utilization

➤ Effective risk definition for proposed corrective or preventive actions

You could think of this as having a

➤ Good, flexible plan

➤ Good management plan

➤ Good tracking and risk management

All these elements help to prescribe a measured and controlled execution environment.

 Why is project control important? In general, all project failures and cancellations can be tracked back to the lack of effective controls in one or more of these areas: scope, cost, quality, and risk management.

Figure 6.1 depicts how the process groups of the project management methodology are related, and that all of them must be monitored and controlled for effective project completion.

Monitoring and Controlling

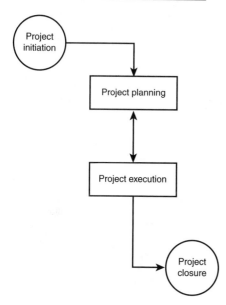

Figure 6.1 The project control framework.

Factors That Cause Project Change

In order to effectively control a project, the project manager must prepare organizational processes that work like sentinels on the fence. These sentinels help the project manager identify events (people, cultural, or strategic) that might force a change to the project or the environment where the project is executing. In other words your project is influenced by elements outside of its normal execution and identified risks. These processes can include elements, such as

➤ Execution trend analysis

➤ Risk trigger management

➤ Forecast reports (just like the weather)

➤ Work package progress status and variances reports

➤ Lessons learned from similar projects

➤ Best practices

➤ Corporate strategy committee resolutions

Some examples of project control processes and their elements are

➤ You could use earned value analysis to determine how your project is performing against the planned activities, schedule, and cost.

➤ You can prescribe corrective or preventive actions after performing trend analysis in work package variances.

➤ You can identify a potential project change request after evaluating defect and frequency control charts.

➤ When executing enterprise projects, you can arrange a monthly meeting with the company CEO to discuss progress and new corporate initiatives.

 Project control is an iterative process. Milestones tend to have a compilation of work packages and deliverables under them, so if you only do project control activities at their completion, you might learn of problems late in the project. Like the autopilot in an airplane, the main function of project control is to make frequent minor course corrections instead of waiting until you are several degrees and miles off the flight plan.

Approving Project Changes

When an opportunity for change is identified, you must make the time to acknowledge the request for change, evaluate its associated risks, and consider its potential—not for just the timeline but also scope, cost, staff, quality, make/buy, and communication. This process helps you to identify if the change is gold plating or if it has direct impact to the project deliverables and its return on investment.

 What is *gold plating*? Gold plating is a change to the project or a work package within the project that has not gone through an adequate change control management process.

After you have determined that a proposed change has merit and supports the project objectives, the change request is submitted to the project control team for final determinations. For the most part, the interaction with the control board is defined in the planning stage and can remain in place until the completion of the project. In the event that your organization has a project management office, the members of the change control board can change to accommodate strategic impact or affected areas in your organization.

What is a *change control board*? A change control board is an enterprise decision body tasked with approving the changes to projects or their impact in strategic initiatives.

In addition, you should monitor any trends that might point to an inadequate requirements definition in the planning stage of your project.

The Project Feedback Loop

You know that projects have five distinctive processes: initiate, plan, execute, control, closure (IPECC). But what of the external changes that occur during the execution of your project? This is where iterative information gathering and dissemination processes serve as information feedback loops.

One of the challenges of the traditional waterfall methodology approaches is that they do not provide for methods to incorporate organizational changes midstream and do not verify their range to target impacts. In other words, a project without feedback loops makes the assumption that nothing will change throughout the life of project; the requirements will not change or are frozen.

 What is *waterfall methodology*? With the waterfall methodology first comes the analysis, then design, then implementation, and then testing completes the process; each phase flows naturally into the next phase, like water over a series of falls, without going upstream.

 A project with frozen structure and processes is bound to fail because it does not take into account any discoveries or organizational changes that might occur during its execution.

Remember that sometimes enterprise changes have a direct effect on the viability of the project. Some examples of events that you might want to be made aware of in advance are

➤ A hostile takeover

➤ A divestment of a business unit

➤ Personnel or resource availability reduction

➤ A corporate relocation

Providing Corrective Action for a Project

After evaluating your work package progress reports and the earned value analysis calculation, you have come to the realization your project has fallen behind and is beyond recovery under its current execution and control framework.

 What is *earned value analysis*? Earned value analysis in its simplest form is the value of the work performed to date against the project baseline expectations. The steps to calculating earned value (and other project-related values) are covered in the "Identifying Variance with Earned Value Management" section.

Your recourse is to implement corrective or preventive actions or a change request to align the project execution with its expected results and timelines.

 A *corrective* or *preventive action control* is a control that is implemented in order to bring future project events and tasks into alignment with the project plan and its baseline.

Some options available at this time could be to

➤ Update the project baseline to reflect your current situation.

➤ Crash the schedule. Add people (internal/external) or resources to the tasks that have fallen behind and have a direct impact on the critical path; the down side is that this might cause unscheduled expenses.

➤ Fast track. Rearrange your activities in order to perform activities in parallel.

➤ Outsource the project or the affected part.

➤ Reduce the scope of the project.

Remember that the whole idea behind a corrective or preventive control is to help preserve the healthy execution of your project and maximize its resource utilizations.

Some of the items used to measure and keep control of the schedule and cost variances are seen in Table 6.1.

Table 6.1   Items Used to Measure and Keep Control of Schedule and Cost Variances

Item	Description
Planned value or budgeted cost of work scheduled (BCWS)	The budgeted cost of the work according to the schedule.
Budgeted at completion	The project baseline cost.
Earned value	The value of the work performed to date against the project schedule. Use the formula % completed × budgeted at completion.
Actual cost or actual cost of work performed (ACWP)	Cost of the work performed to date.
Scheduled variance	The difference between the earned value less the planned value.
Cost variance	The difference between the earned value less the actual cost.
Cost performance index	The result from dividing the earned value by the actual cost. A result less than one suggests that the project is at budget risk.
Scheduled performance index	The result of dividing the earned value by the planned value. A result less than one suggests that the project is at schedule risk.
Estimate at completion	The result of dividing the budget at completion into the cost performance index.
Estimated to completion	The result of subtracting the estimate at completion from the actual cost.
Variance at completion	The result of subtracting the estimated at completion from the budget at completion.

Using the WBS to Control the Project Scope

The *scope control process* is the process tasked with effective control of the scope and deliverables of the project. Its main component is the *scope baseline*. The scope baseline defines the project scope and its associated deliverables and documents the acceptance parameters of the final product. This baseline helps in clarifying any details that might have been left in a to-be-determined (TBD) mode during the project initiation phase or items that require further clarification with the project sponsor of its stakeholders. Your project process indicators in this process are

➤ The work breakdown structure

➤ Work package progress reports

What is a *work breakdown structure*? A work breakdown structure (WBS) decomposes the project work into manageable chunks or work packages.

What is a *work package*? A work package is the lowest descriptive level in a WBS.

The idea behind effectively defining the work breakdown structure is to create the roadmap that defines all the activities that will be executed in order to accomplish the project goal.

The WBS is one of those elements that morphs and changes as time and resource utilization passes. Why? As you perform the tasks outlined in your baseline, the recorded changes accommodate any differences between the planned theory and the actual execution.

An effective WBS assists the stakeholder to understand the activities and events that help in delivering the project promise, as well as outlining internal and external resource use. The entire project execution looks at the WBS to inquire about present, past, and future deliverables and their effectiveness.

Due to its nature and importance, the creation of the WBS should not be taken lightly. It should be viewed as the one element that all project participants must consider when formulating an opinion.

Identifying Variance with Earned Value Management

Earned value analysis is a tool used to help in identifying how well the team is performing and where the project might end up in comparison to the project plan. It was initially conceived by the United States Department of Defense (DoD) as a tool to standardize the way contractors report on the progress of their assigned projects.

The three key variables involved in the project earned value analysis are

➤ Budgeted cost for work scheduled (BCWS)

➤ Budgeted cost for work performed (BCWP)

➤ Actual cost for work performed (ACWP)

 BCWS is also referred to as planned value. The total BCWS or planned value for a project can be called the *budget at completion (BAC)*.

ACWP is also referred to as *actual cost (AC)*.

BCWP is also referred to as *earned value (EV)*.

In order to successfully report on earned value management, your project must have a well-defined WBS and an effective task planned versus actual performance reporting system.

A basic utilization example is as follows:

The budgeted cost for work scheduled (BCWS), or PV, is the planned value of the work according to the project budget. The BCWS of a 12 milestone/ 144 work packages project is $200,000, and the cost for every three milestones has been estimated at $50,000.

The actual cost for work performed (ACWP) is how much you really have incurred in the project. In this example, you are at milestone 6 and the project has used $80,000; therefore, your ACWP is $80,000.

The budgeted cost for work performed (BCWP), or EV, is the value of how much work has been completed. So while your ACWP is $80,000, your BCWP is $100,000.

Armed with this information, you can determine derivative calculations such as the schedule performance index (SPI) and the cost performance index (CPI).

In this example, the calculations are

SPI = EV/PV or BCWP/BCWS

    = 100000/200000

    = .5; your project is behind schedule

CPI = EV/AC or BCWP/ACWP

    = 100000/80000

    = 1.25; your project is using less money than expected

Measuring Quality Control

In the project context, quality is not only defined as delivering the right thing at the right time and at the right cost, but also delivering to customer expectations. As such, you, the project manager, have to ensure that the required metrics, tolerances, reports, and checklists are in place to ensure a quality prone execution and delivery sandbox is in place.

Some of the tools available to the project manager in controlling quality are

➤ The Ishikawa (also called the fishbone or cause and effect) diagram

➤ Control charts, such as the ones available using Three or Six Sigma

   ➤ Six Sigma—99.99% defect free or about 0.002 defective parts per million

   ➤ Three Sigma—99.73% defect free or about 2,700 defective parts per million

➤ Pareto chart (the 80/20 rule)

➤ Statistical sampling, such as the ones used in the standard audit processes

Diagrams and Charts Used to Measure Quality Control

The three diagrams that follow are typical diagrams or charts used to help monitor quality control:

➤ **Ishikawa diagram**—This diagram type can be easily identified because it resembles fish bones. It is used to determine the root cause of a defect (see Figure 6.2).

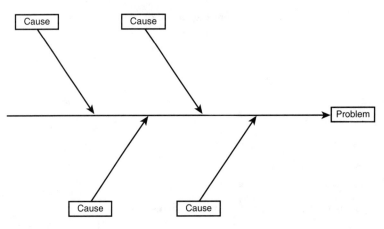

Figure 6.2 A root cause diagram.

Remember that a product or task defect is the symptom, but not the cause of the problem. This is why the Ishikawa diagram is effective in graphically displaying what might be causing a problem at the end of the production line.

➤ **Control charts**—Control charts are a statistical tool used to identify process points that are outside of the normal flow of a process. They help to graphically display process execution boundaries, its trending, and its overall performance over time (see Figure 6.3).

Figure 6.3 A trending and performance control chart.

➤ **Pareto charts**—Also know as the *80/20 rule*. Vilfredo Pareto postulated that the distribution of income and wealth follows a regular logarithmic pattern where 20% of the population controls 80% of the wealth. Subsequently in 1937 Dr. Joseph M. Juran adapted Pareto's economic observations to business applications, which he called the "vital few and trivial many." Translated to project terms, 80% of the problems are caused by 20% of the activities (see Figure 6.4).

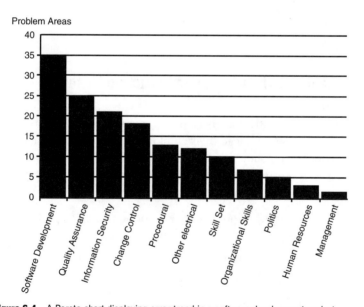

Figure 6.4 A Pareto chart displaying error trend in a software development project.

Managing Your Project Team

You can not manage what you do not measure. Team performance entails tracking team performance against the expectations of the project and its deliverables. No matter what type of organization you work for, the project resources need to be recognized as temporal and shared by functional or project managers.

Because of the realities of project environments, the project manager must be aware of

➤ Staff acquisition practices in his organization

➤ Negotiation techniques

➤ The ways that power influences behavior

➤ How people tend to deal with conflict

➤ How people participate in a team environment

 Because individuals tend to work and react differently in groups versus individually, you need to keep track of the tone of the team and the individual. For the individual you can use behavioral theories such as

➤ MacGregor's Theory Y
➤ MacGregor's Theory X
➤ Maslow's Hierarchy of Needs
➤ Ouchi's Theory Z

Popular Behavioral Theories Used in Human Resource Management

Managers manage differently, but there has been a sizable body of research on the ways managers see and lead their employees. This section touches on some of the theories you should understand for project team management and for the exam. In essence, the following theories speak to the way individuals are motivated and might behave by themselves or in a group:

➤ **MacGregor's Theory X**—Individuals can not be trusted to perform on their own, avoid responsibility, and need to be directed at all times.

➤ **MacGregor's Theory Y**—Individuals are willing to work unsupervised and have an inherent desire to achieve.

➤ **Maslow's Hierarchy of Needs**—All individuals are motivated by a basic set of needs that must be satisfied before they can perform their job:

➤ Physiological (lowest)   ➤ Esteem

➤ Safety   ➤ Self-actualization (highest)

➤ Social

➤ **Ouchi's Theory Z**—Individuals tend to be more participative and are capable of performing many and varied tasks. It emphasizes practices such as job rotation, succession planning, generalists versus specialists, and the need for continuous training.

Communicating How Your Project Is Performing

Communicating with the world is one of your primary jobs. As a communicator, you must understand the mechanics involved in sending a message. There has to be an initiator, who encodes and sends the message, and the receiver who decodes, acknowledges, and, last but not least, confirms that he received the message.

In the normal exchange of information with your entire project team you will find methods and techniques that help you with formal and informal communication. Formal methods include items such as contracts, status reports, public speeches, and performance appraisals. Informal methods are those such as "The Scuttlebutt," email, and telephone conversations.

One way to determine how complex communication will be in a project is to determine its communication channels by using the formula $(n \times (n - 1))/2$, where n represents the number of participants in a project. For example, a project with 10 participants requires 45 communication channels.

With this in mind, you need to understand that you might have to adjust the message and its delivery method based on the audience and the level of impact the project might have on the individuals with whom you are communicating. For example, consider the adjustments in communication that might have to occur between a board member and the person doing the work. For the worker, getting information about revenue projections and return on investment might be of little or no consequence in her daily duties. Giving the worker figures on how many additional widgets can be made in an hour, however, would definitely have an impact on her duties and equipment maintenance cycles.

In addition, you must be cognitive that when delivering a message, nonverbal communication and physical appearance have a direct effect on the message being delivered. For example, you are tasked with delivering a message to a construction team. First, you need to make sure that you use language and colloquialism appropriate to the construction group. This approach might not work the same way when giving a project update to the company senior team. At the same time, you need to make sure that the message and intentions are clearly understood by the audience to whom you are delivering the message.

Examples of common tools used to communicate are a budget, a contract, a teleconference, and a chart.

Risk Monitoring and Risk Control

Project risk control and monitoring is where you keep track of how your qualitative or quantitative risk responses are performing against the plan, as well as the place where new risks to the project are managed.

There could be cases in which risk might be identified as having a material impact to the enterprise but not to your project. For these risk types, your project must allow an alternate communication path that forwards alerts to the enterprise risk management functions. In addition, you must remember that risks can have negative and positive impacts. For example, you are leading a project for a bridge that will interconnect two roads with a maximum traffic flow of 10,000 cars and 300 tons, but a weather event forces a traffic change from other roads, doubling the capacity requirements for your bridge for at least 18 months after you complete the project. Although it has nothing to do with your deliverable, you must account for it and make recommendations on how to address the matter.

Remember that to determine how much of an affect a risk will have, you need to multiply its probability times its material impact. As the probability of risk materialization increases, your risk register should make resource (money, equipment, people, and time) allocations ahead of time, thus increasing your reserves. You must also have as part of your risk management plan the processes that would replenish these reserves before they become depleted.

The purpose of project risk control is to

➤ Identify the events that can have a direct effect in the project deliverables

➤ Assign qualitative and quantitative weight—the probability and consequences of those events that might affect the project deliverables

➤ Produce alternate paths of execution for events that are out of your control or can not be mitigated

➤ Implement a continuous process for identifying, qualifying, quantifying, and responding to new risks

The utility theory assigns subjective value to a management decision in risk mitigation strategies in uncertain conditions.

In the risk register, you account for positive and negative risks. A positive risk is a risk taken by the project because its potential benefits outweigh the traditional approach. A negative risk is one that could negatively influence the cost of the project or its schedule.

Some of the techniques you can implement to evaluate your risk control and monitoring effectiveness is to compare actual risk resolution practices versus those that were planned at the time the risk was identified. If you identify any deviations (negative or positive), you could implement a corrective action in your risk management plan.

Risk triggers are those events that will cause the threat of a risk to become a reality. For example, you have identified the fact that you only have one water pump station available and the replacement takes six weeks to arrive. In the middle of your irrigation and recycling process tests, you discover that water pressure tends to fluctuate beyond pump tolerance levels. If you do not find a way to solve this problem, your risk will become a reality.

Remember that for each identified risk, you must provide a response plan. It is not much help to you if the risk becomes a reality and you do not have an alternate execution path or an emergency procurement plan.

Business risks and pure risks are different because a pure risk takes into account impacts on loss of financial profits. Business risk concentrates on events that might cause a company to lose position with its investors or have financial difficulty.

In addition, your risk reserves must be evaluated in order to determine the best way to replenish them. Some examples of events that could have a negative impact in your risk mitigation and control strategies are

➤ Resource shortage

➤ Scope creep

➤ Contractual issues

➤ Lack of key resource availability

Contract Administration

Contract administration is when the vendor or service performance is compared to the contractual service level agreements (SLA). Due to its implications and its potential impact across several sections of your project or the enterprise, all team members must be aware of the legal ramifications of any change in the contractual relationship. In addition, project-vendor disbursements tend to tie the SLAs and deliverables to direct cash expenditures.

 At all cost, you must avoid any undocumented or unapproved cash disbursements or change that might go against your project deliverables.

In general, the project contract administrator is from the contract management office and/or your legal department and has the authority to issue change requests or early terminations.

Remember that all communications pertaining to contract administration must follow formal channels and be logged in your project log.

Your contract administration process should include mechanisms that allow for contract renegotiation, management response, and payment terms definitions.

Exam Prep Questions

1. What is a corrective action?
   - ❑ A. An action to correct something in the project
   - ❑ B. An action that fixes the requisition process
   - ❑ C. An action that brings future project events into alignment with the project plan
   - ❑ D. Both B and C

2. What is the communication channel delta if the stakeholders are increased from 4 to 11?
   - ❑ A. 6
   - ❑ B. 49
   - ❑ C. 55
   - ❑ D. 109

3. What can you tell of a project with a CPI of 1.6?
   - ❑ A. A critical path index of 1.6 means the project is falling behind.
   - ❑ B. A central performance index of 1.6 means the project is running ahead of schedule.
   - ❑ C. A control performance index of 1.6 means the project is using fewer resources than anticipated.
   - ❑ D. A cost performance index of 1.6 means the project is consuming fewer resources than anticipated.

4. What does an SPI of 1.6 mean?
   - ❑ A. All resources assigned to the project cost 1.6 units.
   - ❑ B. A scope performance index of 1.6 suggests that the project is running ahead of the schedule.
   - ❑ C. A schedule performance index of 1.6 suggests that the project is running ahead of the schedule.
   - ❑ D. None of the above.

5. What is the lowest level in a work breakdown structure?
   - ❑ A. Project task
   - ❑ B. Work package
   - ❑ C. Responsibility assignment matrix
   - ❑ D. Contract negotiations

6. The activity that is most concerned with the current status of the project schedule is
   - ❑ A. Project time management
   - ❑ B. Project risk management
   - ❑ C. Monitoring and controlling
   - ❑ D. Schedule control
   - ❑ E. Both C and D

7. The Ishikawa diagram, control charts, Pareto chart, and statistical sampling are examples of
   - ❑ A. Quality assurance
   - ❑ B. Quality control
   - ❑ C. Six Sigma
   - ❑ D. None of the above

8. _____ is not a form a leadership power.
   - ❑ A. Compromise
   - ❑ B. Coercive
   - ❑ C. Formal
   - ❑ D. Smoothing

9. In general, performance reporting takes into account information from the following areas except
   - ❑ A. Scope
   - ❑ B. Schedule
   - ❑ C. Execution
   - ❑ D. Cost
   - ❑ E. Quality

10. Before risk mitigation can occur, _____ and _____ must be accomplished.
    - ❑ A. Acceptance, delivery requirements
    - ❑ B. Identification, trigger recognition
    - ❑ C. Phasing, interactions
    - ❑ D. Quantitative, qualitative analysis
    - ❑ E. None of the above

11. Who is ultimately responsible for project quality control?
    - ❑ A. The project quality officer
    - ❑ B. The company quality group
    - ❑ C. The plant manager
    - ❑ D. The project manager
    - ❑ E. None of the above
    - ❑ F. All of the above

12. The ultimate way to ensure successful quality control is
    - ❑ A. By outsourcing the quality function
    - ❑ B. Making the quality department report to facilities
    - ❑ C. Making quality a priority at the organizational level
    - ❑ D. Playing a movie about quality in the auditorium
    - ❑ E. None of the above
    - ❑ F. All of the above

Answers to Exam Prep Questions

1. Answer C is correct. Remember that for the test you are looking for the best possible answer. As per the PMBOK, Third Edition, the best possible answer is C. A is accurate, but it is not the best possible answer. Answer B is the result of a corrective action but it is not the definition of what a corrective action is.

2. Answer B is correct. The communication channels calculation is $(n \times (n - 1))/2$. In this case the initial number of communication channels is 6 and the second is 55. $55 - 6 = 49$.

3. Answer D is correct. A cost performance index of 1 or greater suggests that project in delivering more with less money.

4. Answer C is correct. A schedule performance index of 1 or greater suggests that the project is ahead of schedule.

5. Answer B is correct. A work package is located at the lowest level of a work breakdown structure.

6. Answer D is correct. One of the schedule control deliverables is to determine the current status of the project schedule.

7. Answer B is correct. The Ishikawa diagram, the control charts, Pareto chart, and statistical sampling are examples of basic tools of quality control.

8. Answer D is correct. With exception of smoothing, which is a conflict resolution technique, the rest are forms of leadership power.

9. Answer C is correct. Project performance reporting takes into account trending and exceptions in the project scope, schedule, cost, and quality.

10. Answer B is correct. Before risks can be mitigated, you need to know how probable it is that they will occur and what their triggering events are.

11. Answer D is correct. The project manager is assigned to achieve the project objectives.

12. Answer C is correct. A successful enterprise program starts with the tone at the top and the enterprise governance of your organization.

Need to Know More?

 Bell, D. E., H. Raiffa, and A. Tversky, eds. *Decision Making: Descriptive, Normative, and Prescriptive Interactions*. New York: Cambridge University Press, 1988.

Cartwright, D., ed. *The Bases of Social Power*. Evanston, IL: Row, Peterson Publishers, 1960.

 Keeney, R. L. and H. Raiffa. *Decisions with Multiple Objectives: Preferences and Value Tradeoffs*. New York: Cambridge University Press, 1993.

 Kerzner, Harold. *Conflicts in Project Management: A Systems Approach to Planning, Scheduling, and Controlling*. New York: John Wiley and Sons, 2001.

Kliem, Ralph, Irwin Ludin, and Ken Robertson. *Project Management Methodology*. New York: Marcel Dekker Inc., 1997.

Project Management Institute. *A Guide to the Project Management Body of Knowledge, Third Edition*. Newton Square, PA: Project Management Institute, 2004.

Stuckenbruck, Linn C. *Team building for Project Managers*. Newton Square, PA: Project Management Institute, 1985.

Verzuh, Eric. *The Portable MBA in Project Management*. Hoboken, NJ: John Wiley and Sons, Inc., 2003.

Weiss, Joseph W. and Robert K. Wysocki. *5 Phase Project Management*. Boston: Addison-Wesley Publishing Company, 1992.

Project Closing

Terms you'll need to understand:

✓ Administrative closure

✓ Contract closure

✓ Lessons learned

✓ Post-implementation review

✓ Project archives

✓ Project/phase acceptance

Techniques and concepts you'll need to master:

✓ Documenting project results to date

✓ Cost benefit review

✓ Project resource release

✓ Contract agreement fulfillment

✓ Work performance indicators and compliance

✓ Resource utilization audits

The Project Closing Process Group

The project closing process group entails 7%, or 14 questions, of the PMP exam. *Project closing* is where you officially end a project phase or the project itself, release all the resources that were assigned to your project, and build reference material for coming projects. In addition, this is the process group where you get to organize and document all plans versus actual performance data. The road to this point has been about keeping focus, control, and processes optimization. Project closing ensures that the other side of the bell curve of execution looks the same way as when you started the process. Simply put, this is where you wrap up the project and tie up all the loose ends.

Look at is from this perspective; if you would have known everything that you know today about your project(s) when you started, would you have done things the same way? Would you have used the same resources?

Of course, probably by now you are thinking, "What a crock! We are not born as experts. How am I supposed to know when to do what and how to avoid execution problems?" This is where trusted consultants and experienced project manager come into play; they help in identifying what pitfalls to avoid.

One of the key recurring messages of the PMI methodology is to leverage expert resources and to use the project archives; executing the proper closure process ensures that the groundwork for your own internal expert resource and knowledge base is built combining knowledge and experience of your people, culture, and enterprise.

This process takes into account the needs for documentation and the understanding of the associated risks, the risks analysis techniques, and the decision-making process.

Figure 7.1 depicts the general project closing process flow.

 What is a *project deliverable*? A project deliverable is that specific, quantifiable product or service that will be attained after the completion of a project phase or the project.

The key input elements for project closing are

➤ Project plan ➤ Project deliverables

➤ Project contracts ➤ Trends and performance analysis

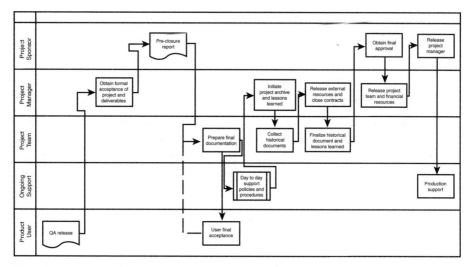

Figure 7.1 The project closure process flow.

For test purposes, you must remember that project close and contract closure are processes of the closing process group and that contract closure happens before project close.

Why have these been designated as key input elements? The intent is to take this time to verify that all of the project deliverables are met. Use the work breakdown structure (WBS), the work packages, and the packages' resource assignments as a roadmap to identify any remaining critical work elements to be completed and ensure the proper transitions.

A *work package* is the lowest descriptive level of work in a WBS.

If there are any unfinished tasks, you need to make arrangements to prepare their termination plan and measure their combined risk materiality to the long term viability of the project, services, and deliverables.

For example, one of the contracts calls for the return of all graphite composite containers to the lease company within 30 days of project completion. Your job as project manager is to issue all the proper closeout work orders and see that these containers are returned to the provider on time. Does this task have anything to do with the long-term functionality of your project?

Probably not; however, if not addressed by the deadline, it has the potential of impacting your company at a cost of 10 million pounds a year.

This process must be repeated throughout the entire work package dictionary to ensure that deliverables are in line with the project and the performance metrics that you assigned to the service provider.

One of the most important realizations of the project management process should be that the project does not stop when the end is on sight or the product or services are delivered. If anything, this is where you need to concentrate and make sure that all tasks and their peripheral activities are completed. Examples of some of these activities are

➤ Client or user final acceptance

➤ Updates to all pertaining historical records

➤ Transitions to ongoing support

➤ Release all project resources

➤ Get final signoff and release from the project sponsor

As per the PMI methodology, the formal outputs of the closing contract process are

➤ Administrative closure procedure

➤ Contract closure procedure

➤ Final product, service, or result

➤ Organizational process assets (updates)

➤ Administrative closure procedure (formal acceptance documentation, project files, project closure documents, historical information)

Closing Out a Contract

At project build-up, you might have been faced with the need to have extra capacity by bringing in external resources. The contract close out process is the place where you accept delivery of the product and close the corresponding contract agreements.

One thing to remember is that this process also applies to any company internal contract or agreements that might have been arranged in order to leverage internal business expertise or processes.

For example, you work for a multinational company that decides to leverage its internal expertise in building bridges over long water bodies by combining the resources from the steel and cement business units with its engineering unit. In addition to coordinating the building of the bridge, you are now faced with the challenge of having to orchestrate all the intercompany contracts, expenses, and revenue-generating models in order to ensure the proper level of synergies.

Not that this is any different that using external resources; however, you need to place close attention to the *human factor*. The human factor refers to any cultural and personal differences between your culture and the inbound resources.

Another example for contract management might include a combination of internal, external, and outsourced relationships. This relationship might call for a different set of closing instructions that depends on the relationship class.

Of course, this also means that you are part of the contract negotiation and interpretation, thus requiring a special dose of leadership and management techniques in an environment with multiple moving parts.

For closing a contract you need to be well aware of your vendor's or provider's

➤ Performance metrics

➤ Assigned work packages

➤ Deliverables

➤ Schedule performance

➤ Quality control metrics

➤ If applicable, inspection reports pertaining to regulatory requirements

In addition, you will need to address items such as

➤ Considerations to perform product or service verification that ensures all work was completed in accordance to the service level agreements (SLA) and the deliverables specified in the contract

➤ Review of contract terms and conditions in the event that the product is not delivered to specifications

➤ Enabling of early termination clauses and remediation due to the vendor's inability to deliver the product, agreed budget being exceeded, or failure to assign the required resources

When it comes to contracts, you must be aware that in the PMI world there are several types of contracts: *cost reimbursable*, *fixed price* or *lump sum*, *time and material*, and *unit price*.

Early contract terminations can be a result of a mutual agreement or due to a failure to fulfill the contract deliverables.

What does it mean to be faced with an early termination? It all goes back to your contract, the execution clauses that were stipulated at the beginning of the business relationship, and the parameters for contract termination and vendor replacement plan.

The *vendor replacement plan* refers to the implementation of an alternate path for future project fulfillment needs. If you don't have an alternate path, a good place to start is to consider second and third runner-up in your original selection process.

A way to effectively measure how well a contract might have served your project is to take into account the following:

➤ Activities to be performed in a project or a project phase

➤ Supporting schedules for time, deliverables, and cost

➤ Issue log and issue management plan

➤ Project delivery metrics

➤ Invoice and payment register

Procurement audits are a structured review of the processes and practices involved in the resource planning and acquisition. They can also be used to identify and evaluate deviations in regards to materiality and risk analysis of future procurement activities.

After all contractual agreement clauses are satisfied and you have delivered the provider execution report card, a company representative executes the stipulated documents to signify that the contract was completed and executed according to agreed specifications.

Project Closure Criteria

Everyone hopes for a successful project completion, but the cold hard reality is that on occasion some projects are presented with challenges from their inception up to their ultimate demise. Some of the outside reasons that can trigger an early termination could be linked to elements such as

➤ **Market conditions**—Where the company or client is forced to discontinue a project simply because the initiative is no longer in line with their long-term market share or presence objectives.

➤ **Customer requirements**—Your client decided to implement changes that are well beyond the capabilities of the current initiative, making it cost prohibitive to tackle the project at this time.

➤ **Insufficient resources**—You do not have the people, money, facilities, supplies, and so on to complete a project.

➤ **Technical problems**—In the project management arena, technical problems go beyond the computer. We could be talking about items such as variances in the density of the material used in a building to the inability to devise a way to hold the insulation on the space shuttle main fuel tank.

➤ **Enterprise culture**—The project and its product or services contradict the culture of the company. For example, a company is known for its face-to-face customer service practices and, after implementing a test of self-service point-of-sale checkout lines, discovers that implementing this initiative has a direct impact on the customer perception.

➤ **Bankruptcy**—Your client or company will not gain a cash position or additional market share by implementing your project, so it gets cancelled.

Even in these instances you must ensure a successful transition by leading your project towards project closure criteria elements, which include

➤ The formal acceptance of the project results or product by your customer

➤ Documentation and forms resulting from organizational requirements

➤ Project performance metrics and reports

➤ Budget expenditures

➤ Cost benefit metrics and verifications

➤ Lessons learned

Think of the project closure criteria as those elements that give reasonable assurance that your project took into account the initial deliverables, the client, and the sponsor approval.

In addition, this process works closely with the communication management and the procurement management plans to formalize the ending of your project.

Some of the key participants of this process are

➤ **Project sponsor**—This is who gives final validation that the project's services and products are inline with the original objectives and deliverables of the project before the official hand-off to the client and the operational support team takes place.

➤ **Project manager**—This is who keeps coordinating the execution of the communication, procurement, human resources, cost management, and quality plans until such time that the project is officially closed and who turns over all the archives.

➤ **Team members**—These are the people who assist the project manager in performing the aforementioned tasks, plus assist in transitioning the new product or service to operational support.

➤ **Quality assurance team**—These are the people who ensure that all work adheres to agreed project quality expectations and deliverables.

Formal acceptance is the binding process between the customer and the seller (provider) of the product or services which signifies that the product or service has been accepted. Its form and contents are predicated by the service agreement or negotiated in the contract.

Why is formal acceptance important? If during the execution and control processes the project acceptance criteria changed but the documentation did not, this could be the place where you update all your records to represent the final product.

The key item to remember when preparing for the project closure is that the actual project criteria plan and requirement definition began the day that the project charter and the project scope were defined and agreed upon by the client, sponsor, and the entire project team.

You are just making sure that there is an effective transition between what was agreed upon at the beginning of the project and what was delivered and accepted by the client.

Lessons Learned

Contrary to popular practice, lessons learned should be part of all phases of your project and recorded as they occur; do not get this confused with the post-mortem connotation used by some project managers. If you follow this approach, you might miss the opportunity to write down important elements that might prove essential in future projects.

Why make lessons learned throughout the project? An out-of-context example would be not writing down the license plate and color of a car involved in a hit and run; the more time that passes, the less clarity you have about the details.

The main intent of the lessons learned is to help build an information store that allows anyone in your company to look back in time and understand the decisions made and the circumstances that surrounded the decision-making process.

Some of the triggering events for lessons learned records are

➤ Significant course corrections are implemented.

➤ Corrective or preventive actions are taken.

➤ Scope changing events occurs.

➤ Root cause for variances between planned and actual project events.

It is incumbent upon you to make every effort to be extremely honest and include items that performed well and those that did not. You must highlight individuals involved in the process and the risk factors considered at the time of making the decision. Some of the elements this report might have are

➤ Executive summary

➤ Project phase

➤ Related work package

➤ Event description

➤ Event duration

➤ Action taken

➤ Decision makers

➤ Results

➤ Areas of improvement

➤ Time stamp

Do not make the mistake of confusing a project execution satisfaction survey with a lessons learned document—they have different functions.

In addition to recording lessons learned, you must make every effort to collect any evidence and include it as part of the project archive.

 Ideally, lessons learned are included as part of the enterprise risk repository to assist with the risk identification, best practices, and mitigation strategies in future projects.

Ending a Contract or Project

Ending a contract is not the same as ending the project. There might be cases where they coincide but that is not to be expected as the normal behavior. You could have a case where a contract for a service ends but the project continues with another provider or project phase.

In contract execution there are two actors: the buyer of goods and services and the seller of those goods and services. During the life of the project, contracts might end for one of the following reasons:

➤ **Successful completion**—Successful completion occurs when goods and services have been delivered in accordance with the contract specifications. At this point no further action is required with exception of formal acceptance of the product or services and final payment.

➤ **Collective agreement**—This occurs when both parties agree to end the contract—its specification and obligations for both parties. A collective agreement or mutual consent termination allows you to present and negotiate contract closing terms, such as a no-cost settlement, payment of all fees and charges accrued prior to the effectiveness of the cancellation, and payment at a reduced cost by settlement.

For the most part, the parameters of what is available as recourse will be specified in the contract by the paragraph that reads something like, "This agreement may be terminated by either party at the renewal/anniversary date by giving the other party notice at least 15 days prior to the renewal/anniversary date of the Term. This Agreement may also be suspended or terminated by…"

And you must issue your collective agreement notice for cancellation of services, such as "Pursuant to the termination section of the professional services agreement between client and provider, this contract is hereby terminated effective on dd-mm-yy. You are directed to cease all work upon presentment of this notice and start the contract closure criteria process" (which you need to have defined by now).

➤ **When there is a breach**—A breach of contract states that one of the parties is not complying with the terms and specifications of the contract. A breach of contract or contract default situation requires immediate and special attention from the legal counsel. Remember that the actions to take are as varied as the different clauses stipulated in the contract.

In addition, because good providers are difficult to find, executing a breach of contract procedure should be viewed as the last resort. Of course, it all depends on your long-term objectives with the relationship and the provider's willingness to solve the problem that caused the breach. For example, if the default occurs at the service level agreement (SLA) level, your contract might allow you to consider mitigating factors and make adjustments to the SLA. Or, you might be able to outsource, supplement, or augment the function in question at the provider's expense in order to deliver according to the SLAs.

Another key element to consider is a cure or remediation period. Basically, this is a cooling-off period that allows the provider a pre-ordinate amount of time to remediate the problem before taking any actions.

For contracts where the deliverables, products, and services go according the plan, the next step is to ensure that

➤ All issues have been resolved.

➤ All contract deliverables have been delivered and accepted by the client and the sponsor.

➤ The project manager gives final approval.

➤ All assets have been accounted for.

➤ Final payment has been issued.

Project contracts rarely go beyond the actual life of the project; project phases may end several times throughout the project but there is only *one* project closure.

Some of the reasons a project may conclude are

➤ The company loses interest in the project and its deliverables.

➤ The company, project, or group is replaced or displaced.

➤ The project comes to a normal end after all the products and services are delivered.

➤ The project becomes its own organization living beyond the end date as an organizational process.

➤ The project is replaced by another initiative.

 For test purposes you need to be familiar with project conclusion states such as *extinction, inclusion, integration, starvation, addition, collapse, absorption,* and *deterioration.*

Another element to consider when processing a project closing is what to do with the team that was assigned to your project.

➤ A project that ends in *integration mode* is the type of project whose resources are assigned to other areas and integrated into the normal operations of the business. Most often they are reintegrated into the department or group from which they came from.

One challenge to this project ending mode is that the responsibilities of the position could have been reassigned or replaced by new processes. This gives the returning team member the special opportunity to flex her muscles and take on new and more demanding responsibilities.

➤ A project that ends in *extinction* or *collapsed mode* is a project that has ended before meeting its stated objectives. Simply stated, in this situation people do not have a place to which to return.

➤ A project that ends in *inclusion, absorption,* or *addition mode* is a project that has been accepted and has transitioned to be part of the organization. In this type of project ending, your team keeps performing their assigned project functions as their new day-to-day responsibilities, maintaining the project performance in accordance to specifications.

➤ A project that ends in *starvation* or *deterioration mode* is a project whose resources have been cut. You just have an empty shell.

 From the process group perspective, closing a contract is part of the project procurement management processes, while closing the project is part of the project integration.

Final Review Meetings

At this point, you have received final approval from the client and the sponsor, compiled the final set of reports, released all your team members, and delivered the project products and services. Your next task is to meet with the project sponsor for the final review meeting. This meeting is where the project manager gets final release, receives project performance reports, and is able to return to the bench to wait for the next assignment.

The bench could be going back to your regular job or actually sitting in your company's project management office overseeing the final archiving steps and getting a new assignment all together.

Exam Prep Questions

1. One of your project deliverables is to perform a post-implementation review of the water treatment plant you just delivered. You have been asked to do what?
   - ❑ A. Present all the lessons learned.
   - ❑ B. Meet with the project sponsor to discuss what could have been improved in your project.
   - ❑ C. Investigate and report on the plan performance and maintenance requirements.
   - ❑ D. Meet with your project team and discuss plant support options.
   - ❑ E. None of the above.

2. Part of the project closure process is to gain formal acceptance. From whom do you need to gain this formal acceptance?
   - ❑ A. The qualify director
   - ❑ B. The head of the project management office
   - ❑ C. The project sponsor
   - ❑ D. The customer
   - ❑ E. C and D

3. You are the project manager of a project that just went into integration mode. This means that your project
   - ❑ A. Is still running but missing resources
   - ❑ B. Will be closed due to lack of resources
   - ❑ C. Resources are being assigned to other areas of the business
   - ❑ D. Has been accepted by the sponsor and the client
   - ❑ E. A and C

4. You are the project manager of a project that just went into extinction. This means that your project
   - ❑ A. Is still running but missing resources
   - ❑ B. Will be closed due to lack of resources
   - ❑ C. Resources are being assigned to other areas of the business
   - ❑ D. Has ended before its stated objective
   - ❑ E. B and D

5. You are the project manager of a project that just went into inclusion mode. This means that your project
   - ❑ A. Is still running but missing resources
   - ❑ B. Will be closed due to lack of resources
   - ❑ C. Has become part of the business processes
   - ❑ D. Has been accepted by the sponsor and the client
   - ❑ E. A and C

6. Which one of these is not an input to the close project process?
   - ❑ A. Project management plan
   - ❑ B. Project management information system
   - ❑ C. Contract documentation
   - ❑ D. Work performance information
   - ❑ E. Deliverables

7. Administrative closure is the process that
   - ❑ A. Includes all the activities needed to validate the project products and services
   - ❑ B. Collects user acceptance of the project product or service
   - ❑ C. Closes all activities pertaining to a specific project
   - ❑ D. None of the above

8. The primary output of the project closing process is
   - ❑ A. To formalize and distribute all information pertaining to the project closing
   - ❑ B. Lessons learned
   - ❑ C. To release all personnel assigned to the project
   - ❑ D. To get customer and sponsor approval
   - ❑ E. B and D

9. Which one of these is not an output of contract closure?
   - ❑ A. Close contracts
   - ❑ B. Contract file
   - ❑ C. Lessons learned documentation
   - ❑ D. Deliverable acceptance
   - ❑ E. Procurement audits

10. Lessons learned are
    - ❑ A. Best collected at the end of the project
    - ❑ B. Collected for the historical knowledge base
    - ❑ C. Only necessary at the end of the project
    - ❑ D. A store of historical information
    - ❑ E. Used to collect information about good and bad outcomes throughout the project

11. Product verification pertains to
    - ❑ A. All the activities that verify that the products and services delivered are in line with quality requirements
    - ❑ B. All the activities that verify that the products and services delivered are in line with project deliverables and sponsor and client satisfaction
    - ❑ C. All activities that verify tangible assets
    - ❑ D. A and C
    - ❑ E. None of the above

12. The main goal of having lessons learned is to
    - ❑ A. Keep the names of the team for prosperity
    - ❑ B. Close all open contracts
    - ❑ C. Record variances and the mental state behind corrective and preventive actions taken
    - ❑ D. Record all the qualitative reasoning behind corrective and preventive actions taken in the project

13. What is the main reason to make sure all contracts are closed at the end of the project?
    - ❑ A. Contracted materials must be returned.
    - ❑ B. Contractors need to return all excess materials.
    - ❑ C. Contracts are legally binding.
    - ❑ D. You would like to avoid any penalties.
    - ❑ E. None of the above.

14. Work performance information is considered as
    - ❑ A. A necessary process to enter a contract
    - ❑ B. Required as part of the vendor performance evaluation
    - ❑ C. Only needed for contracts in distress
    - ❑ D. A tool and technique for the contract administration process
    - ❑ E. None of the above

Answers to Exam Prep Questions

1. Answer C is correct. A post implementation review is a product or service performance review after the implementation has taken place.

2. Answer E is correct. Formal acceptance is the formal confirmation from the sponsor or the customer that the product or service delivered by the project meets the project deliverables. Remember that in the PMI realm, all of the project's products and services must comply with the project objectives and deliverables and must be accepted by the project client and the project sponsor.

3. Answer C is correct. A project that ends in integration mode is the type of project where its resources are being assigned to other areas. The other project modes are extinction and inclusion. A project that ends in extinction is a project that has ended before meeting its stated objectives, and a project that ends in inclusion mode is a project that has been accepted and has transitioned to be part of the organization.

4. Answer D is correct. A project that ends in extinction mode is a project that has ended before meeting its stated objectives. The other project modes are integration and inclusion mode. A project that ends in integration mode is a project which its resources are being assigned to other areas, and a project that ends in inclusion mode is a project that has been accepted and has transitioned to be part of the organization.

5. Answer C is correct. A project that ends in inclusion mode is a project that has transitioned to be part of the organization and its support infrastructure. The other project modes are extinction and integration mode. A project that ends in integration mode is the type of project which its resources are being assigned to other areas, and a project that ends in extinction mode is a project that has ended before meeting its stated objectives.

6. Answer B is correct. The inputs for the project close process are the project management plan, contract documentation, work performance information, and project deliverables. Answer B pertains to the tools and techniques of the project close process, which include project management methodology, project management information systems, and expert judgment.

7. Answer C is correct. Administrative closure pertains to all the processes involved in closing all the activities pertaining to a specific project. Other outputs of the close project process are contract closure procedure, final product, service, or result and organizational process assets (updates).

8. Answer A is correct. The primary output of the project closing process is to formalize and distribute all the information pertaining to the closing of the project. This coordinated message is distributed by administrative closure, contract closure procedure, final product, service, or result and organizational process assets (updates).

9. Answer E is correct. The actual outputs of the contract closure are closed contracts, organizational process assets (updates), contract file, deliverable acceptance, and lessons learned documentation.

10. Answer E is correct. Lessons learned are used to collect information pertaining good and bad outcomes throughout the project execution. If you look at the output sections of the Project Management Institute methodology, lessons learned are a part of virtually all the execution processes.

11. Answer B is correct. Product verification pertains to all activities that verify that the products and services delivered by the project are in line with project deliverables and sponsor and client expectations.

12. Answer C is correct. Remember that for the PMP test, you must select the most appropriate answer. In this case, you can argue that all of them could be correct at one time or another; however, the intent of the lessons learned is to record all the course corrections that might have affected the project baseline and the reasoning behind the preventive or corrective actions.

13. Answer C is correct. The contract closure process refers to all contracts initiated during the lifetime of the project. Due to their legal nature, contracts have to be evaluated and follow formal legal dissolution or fulfillment.

14. Answer D is correct. Contract performance reporting is one of the tools and techniques described by PMI for the contract administration process.

Need to Know More?

 Cooper, Cary L. *The Concise Blackwell Encyclopedia of Management.* Blackwell Business, 1998.

DePaoli, Dr. Tom. *Common Sense Purchasing: Hard Knock Lessons Learned From a Purchasing Pro.* BookSurge Publishing, 2004.

Frame, J. Davidson. *The New Project Management.* Jossey-Bass, 1994.

Kliem, Ralph, Irwin Ludin and Ken Robertson. *Project Management Methodology.* Marcel Dekker, 1997.

Project Management Institute. *A Guide to the Project Management Body of Knowledge, Third Edition.* Newton Square, PA: Project Management Institute, 2004.

Verzuh, Eric. *The Portable MBA in Project Management.* Hoboken, NJ: John Wiley and Sons, Inc., 2003.

Weiss, Joseph W. and Robert K. Wysocki. *5 Phase Project Management.* Boston: Addison-Wesley Publishing Company, 2003.

 Project Auditors. "Project Auditors Online Dictionary." http://www.projectauditors.com/Dictionary/DictionaryHome.html.

 Wideman, Max R. "Projectnet Glossary." Project Manager Today. http://www.maxwideman.com/pmglossary/PMGloss_Sources.htm.

Professional Responsibility

Terms you'll need to understand:

✓ Appearance of impropriety
✓ Confidentiality
✓ Conflict of interest
✓ Ethical standards
✓ Inappropriate compensation
✓ Intellectual property
✓ Personal gain
✓ PMI code of professional conduct
✓ Professional judgment
✓ Truthful representation

Techniques and concepts you'll need to master:

✓ What a conflict of interest is
✓ What constitutes the appearance of impropriety in vendor, client, and stakeholder relationships
✓ What ethical standards apply to project management professionals
✓ How to recognize and respect intellectual property
✓ How to maintain confidentiality of sensitive information
✓ What are inappropriate payments, gifts, or other forms of compensation

PMI PMP Code of Professional Conduct

In March 2002, the PMP Certification Examination changed to include an additional performance requirement specific to professional responsibility in the practice of project management. With the news media routinely reporting ethical lapses and abuses of professional judgment in various industries and companies, the PMI PMP Code of Professional Conduct clearly establishes what is and is not appropriate in the performance of professional project management services.

The PMI PMP Code of Professional Conduct focuses on conflicts of interest, truthful representation, and your responsibility to the profession, the customers, and the public. Most of the information contained in the PMI PMP Code of Professional Conduct will seem obvious and intuitive upon your initial read, but it ensures that all PMP-certified practitioners have an equal understanding of the responsibilities for honesty and integrity in the profession.

The PMI PMP Code of Professional Conduct is not a component of the PMBOK; rather it is a one-page stand-alone document available on the PMI website. It should be read carefully and thoroughly.

Of the six knowledge areas tested, professional responsibility accounts for 14.5% of the PMP Certification Examination. This means 29 of the 200 multiple-choice questions concentrate on professional responsibility. The inclusion of professional responsibility in the PMP Certification Examination is a testament to the value placed on ethical standards and integrity in the profession.

Where Do I Find the PMI PMP Code of Professional Conduct?

The PMI PMP Code of Professional Conduct is available on the PMI website, www.pmi.org/info/PDC_PMPCodeOfConductFile.asp.

If this URL is inactive or no longer works, visit the PMI website, select Professional Development and Careers from the available headings across the top of your screen, and a drop-down menu appears.

Select Certifications from the drop-down menu. The certifications menu appears on a new screen page with menu options on the left of the screen.

Select Project Management Professional. A new screen page appears with Code of Professional Conduct as a menu option on the left of the screen.

Select Code of Professional Conduct. A new screen page appears with an Adobe file of the document.

The PMI PMP Code of Professional Conduct accounts for one out of every seven questions on the PMP Certification Examination. This is only a one-page document but is the basis for a significant number of exam questions.

The PMI PMP Code of Professional Conduct is comprised of two sections: Responsibilities to the Profession, and Responsibilities to Customers and the Public. Both sections ask you to apply ethical standards to your work, acting in an accurate, trustworthy, honest manner while acknowledging and minimizing conflicts of interest.

In the first section, these responsibilities are concentrated in your obligation to the profession, while the later section applies these requirements in light of your accountability to customers. You are asked by PMI to support and adhere to all of these responsibilities.

Read through this chapter and become familiar with the terminology, specifically understanding how each concept is used in reference to the PMI PMP Code of Professional Conduct. After you have developed a frame of reference for these terms in conjunction with the Code, memorize the outline provided in Table 8.1. The outline allows you to recall the information connected with each area in detail during your examination.

Table 8.1   Outline of the PMI PMP Code of Professional Conduct

Professional Responsibilities	Summary
To the profession	A. Compliance with all organizational rules and policies
	B. Candidate/certificant professional practice
	C. Advancement of the profession
To the customers and the public	A. Qualifications, experience, and performance of professional services
	B. Conflict of interest situations and other prohibited professional conduct

Understanding Responsibilities to the Profession

The PMI PMP Code of Professional Conduct places the greater emphasis on responsibilities to the profession of project management. This section is comprised as follows:

➤ Compliance with all organizational rules and policies

➤ Candidate/certificant professional practice

➤ Advancement of the profession

Compliance with All Organizational Rules and Policies

This area outlines your duty to be accurate and truthful with representations to the PMI. The majority of this component entails your compliance with the PMI certification process, although you are also asked to report violations of the PMI PMP code of professional conduct and cooperation with PMI investigations of ethical breaches. There is also a professional obligation to fully disclose conflicts of interest to business associates.

Accurate and Truthful Representations

You are responsible for accurately representing yourself and your professional work experience throughout the PMI certification process as well as in your continued reporting to PMI when recertification is necessary. The information you submit to PMI should be truthful and complete. This requirement applies to all aspects of the PMI Certification Program, including

➤ Application for membership and certification

➤ Test preparation and test item banks

➤ Examinations and answers

➤ Candidate information

➤ PMI Continuing Certification Requirements Program reporting forms

Violation of the PMI PMP Code of Professional Conduct, particularly the falsification of applicant information, can result in disciplinary action, including certification and membership revocation.

Violations of PMI PMP Code of Professional Conduct

As a project management professional and PMI member, you have a personal responsibility to report possible violations of professional conduct within the project management professional community. This is a self-policing provision.

Cooperation with PMI Investigations

In accordance with your charge to report professional conduct violations, you are also required to cooperate with PMI in their investigation of ethics violations and the collection of pertinent information. An investigation requiring your cooperation might arise independent of you actually reporting a possible ethics violation.

Disclosure of Conflict of Interest

Full disclosure of any conflicts of interest, either real or perceived, to all stakeholders is crucial to comply with the PMI PMP Code of Professional Conduct. You are responsible for informing clients, customers, owners, contractors, and/or vendors of even the appearance of impropriety.

Conflicts of interest can arise if you are related to a vendor performing services for your company or have previous unacknowledged relationships with contractors bidding on work you are responsible for managing. This applies to your entire project team. It is ideal to address any potential conflicts of interest prior to project initiation.

This is a best practice for all business transactions and assures all business associates are acting in good faith. If an actual conflict of interest is determined, all stakeholders can decide the best course of action for resolution of the conflict. By disclosing any perceived conflicts of interest, you avoid the appearance of impropriety.

As a project manager with decision-making responsibility that affects a project, you must take the high moral ground. Your judgments and decisions must appear beyond reproach. If a conflict of interest arises that is not disclosed, this potential conflict can impair your ability to successfully lead the project. Your client, your fellow team members, and your professional colleagues might question your choices regarding any conflict of interest as well as all other decisions you are responsible for making.

Your truthfulness, reputation, and integrity are paramount as a project manager. PMI believes this is an obligation to the profession as well as to the customer. The concept of a conflict of interest being tied to your responsibilities as a project management professional is set forth in both sections of the PMI PMP Code of Professional Conduct. This first section stresses conflict of interest in relation to your profession. In the later section, conflict of interest is discussed with emphasis on your obligations to your customer and the public.

Conflict of interest is a key concept. It appears in both sections of the PMI PMP Code of Professional Conduct. Expect the exam to ask questions related to this responsibility.

Candidate/Certificant Professional Practice

This area extends the previous admonishment to be accurate and truthful in your representations to PMI to a greater purview—your professional practice of project management. You are directed to exhibit honesty and integrity in all aspects of your work. You are responsible for representing your qualifications, experience, and performance of services in an accurate, truthful manner.

This also applies to any advertising and/or solicitations for professional project management services. Compliance with all applicable laws, regulations, and accepted ethical standards governing the practice of project management is mandatory. Your honesty and integrity reflect on the entire project management profession and your fellow PMP certified practitioners.

Advancement of the Profession

This area concerns the advancement of the profession through support and distribution of the PMI PMP Code of Professional Conduct as well as upholding intellectual property rights. Adherence to and promotion of the ethical standards set forth by PMI follows on the heels of the earlier requirement to report possible ethical violations. The credibility of the project management profession and the value of PMP certification directly tie to the integrity and professional standards upheld by existing practitioners.

In the course of providing project management services, you might come to possess information developed or owned by others. This information, commonly known as intellectual property, is usually copyright protected and can include patents, business methods, and industrial processes. The PMI PMP Code of Professional Conduct instructs you to recognize and respect this property. You must act with discretion and confidentiality when intellectual property is involved. There can be legal repercussions if intellectual property is not adequately safeguarded.

Understanding Responsibilities to Customers and the Public

This is the second and final section of the PMI PMP Code of Professional Conduct. The first section of the Code addresses your responsibilities to the profession. Many of the themes from the previous section are repeated now with an emphasis on customer service and your responsibilities to customers and the public at large.

Professionalism, personal integrity, and a more in-depth discussion of what constitutes a conflict of interest are the focus. This section is comprised as follows:

➤ Qualifications, experience, and performance of professional services

➤ Conflict of interest situations and other prohibited professional conduct

Qualifications, Experience, and Performance of Professional Services

In the previous section, you were instructed to be accurate and truthful in your representations to PMI as well in your professional undertakings. These same responsibilities are reiterated now with specific attention on the transmittal of this information to customers and the public.

You have a duty to properly represent your qualifications, experience, and performance of professional services when soliciting work and advertising. Estimates of costs, services, and expected results should be justly presented. You are accountable for providing accurate, trustworthy information to customers and the public.

You are responsible for accurate and truthful representations in the information you present to PMI and to the public. The concept appears throughout the PMI PMP Code of Professional Conduct. Expect questions on the exam regarding this responsibility.

In performing professional project management services for customers, it is imperative you meet your customer's expectations and complete all work in accordance with the agreed-upon scope and objectives. Your customer should approve any deviations or changes to the work plan.

Confidentiality should be maintained at all times. This applies in the case of intellectual property, noted in the previous section, but also in the context of all professional activities performed.

Conflict of Interest Situations and Other Prohibited Professional Conduct

The importance of identifying conflicts of interest and communicating this information to all impacted parties was stressed previously. The emphasis was placed on conflicts of interest and your consequent responsibility to your profession. This area concentrates on your responsibility to customers and the public when a conflict of interest is known. The focus here is on prohibited conduct.

You have an obligation to acknowledge a conflict of interest but you must also ensure a conflict of interest does not compromise the legitimate business interests of your customer. You cannot allow a conflict of interest to influence nor interfere with your judgment or the fulfillment of your professional project management responsibilities.

This is particularly important when you are accountable for decision-making as the project manager. You have a responsibility to your client to be forthright. If you engage in behavior that is questionable, yet alone improper, you are compromising your credibility as a project manager professional. Your decisions regarding the specific incident can be tainted, as well as your behavior and judgment regarding all facets of the project. Every decision becomes suspect.

Inappropriate payments, gifts, or other forms of compensation for personal gain must be declined. Examples of inappropriate compensation can vary from the seemingly innocuous, such as theatre tickets or lunch paid for by a vendor, to the more extreme, namely cash payments or vacation packages.

Similarly, you should refrain from offering inappropriate payments, gifts, or other forms of compensation to another party for personal gain. You might be familiar with the term *kickback*, which has been used to describe this activity in various industries. The PMI PMP Code of Professional Conduct is explicit in condemning this activity.

An exception is made by PMI in cases where offering or accepting payments, gifts, or other forms of compensation for personal gain conforms with applicable laws or customs of the country where project management services are being performed. In instances where you believe this exception might be valid, consult a legal professional. This practice is not acceptable for companies incorporated within the United States regardless of where they are doing business.

Your obligation to be trustworthy and exemplify a high standard of integrity is implicit within the PMI PMP Code of Professional Conduct. Inflating the number of project hours worked by team members to appear ahead of schedule or even on schedule is inappropriate. Overstating your hourly rates to make the project appear to be operating within budget when you are funneling those funds to other project costs, tinkering with progress/status reports, and manipulating project milestones to appear on-time and on-budget are simply wrong. It is an insult to the profession of project management and it's not ethical.

More often than not you will know if your actions are creating a conflict of interest or if you are engaging in questionable behavior. If you cannot be completely honest with all parties regarding your actions, they are suspect. If you catch yourself thinking, "What the client doesn't know want hurt them," or not fully disclosing information to your own project team, your actions are improper. You might have the greater good of the project at heart when you claim Phase I of the project completed on schedule because you plan to use more resources in Phase II to make up the gap but this is false reporting. You must be honest with your client regarding the true status of the project and then work with the impacted parties to develop strategies for mitigating the problem.

You must also be honest with your project team. Your responsibility in this regard is two-fold: You have an obligation to communicate openly with your fellow team workers; furthermore, as the project manager, you are the team lead for the project and must lead by example.

Communicating honestly, openly, and effectively with your client and your project team can be difficult. It is hard to tell a paying client that a project is facing severe setbacks and obstacles, particularly when the client might (rightly or wrongly) hold you accountable for the problems. A client might continue to make change requests late into development or place unrealistic demands on you and your team in terms of the project budget, scope, and timeline.

Similarly it can be tough to deal with a project team during a stressful implementation. You might have team members you do not personally like and whom you did not select for your team. There might be interpersonal conflicts. All of these situations can lead to a breakdown in communication and are normal scenarios you might be faced with during a project. These problems are compounded when a conflict of interest, real or perceived, is present.

You do not want to compound your workload as the project manager by ignoring or discounting potential conflicts of interest regardless of when they arise during the project. Address as many issues as possible at the beginning of the project during the planning process. You set the tone for the entire project by how you broach issues up front. If your client and project team see you minimizing or negating issues, the die is cast for other team members to do the same. Furthermore, your integrity is compromised.

You must also be vigilant throughout the project, actively identifying and mitigating issues regarding conflict of interest. Sometimes a potential conflict of interest does not arise until midway though the project. Always recognize conflicts of interest at their earliest point of origin. This assures your client and project team that you are above board. If situations arise which were unknown and through circumstances are not immediately addressed and rectified, again make the conflict of interest transparent to all parties as soon as possible. This is essential to maintaining your credibility as a project manager professional to your client, your project team, and the public.

In summary, avoid conflicts of interest. If this is not a viable option, identify and acknowledge conflicts of interest, both real and potential, as soon as possible. Avoid all situations where your honesty and integrity as a project manager can be questioned or condemned. If you question the ethical consequences of an action or feel a decision should be hidden from your project team, you should not engage in the behavior.

Conflict of interest appears in both sections of the PMI PMP Code of Professional Conduct. This is an important topic that will be covered thoroughly in your examination.

Expect scenario-based questions on the exam related to conflict of interest. These questions ask you to determine what you would do in a given situation. Be careful to select the best response in accordance with the PMI PMP Code of Professional Conduct. There may be multiple answers that appear right. In these instances, narrow your choices by determining the clearly incorrect answers and then select the best response from the remaining choices.

Conclusions

Table 8.2 summaries the main topics from this chapter.

Table 8.2 Professional Responsibility

Topic	Professional Responsibilities Summary
Truthful representation	Provide accurate, truthful information to PMI, customers, and the public.
Ethical violations	Report possible violations of the PMI PMP Code of Professional Conduct to PMI and cooperate with investigations.
Conflict of interest	Occurs when personal interests are placed above professional responsibility. Avoid conflicts of interest. If not possible, identify and communicate all potential conflicts of interest to all parties.
Appearance of impropriety	When a conflict of interest is not communicated to all parties, your work and actions might appear improper.
Ethical standards	PMI expects PMPs to exhibit integrity and professionalism.
Intellectual property	A product developed and owned by others with commercial value. Recognize and respect copyrighted material.
Confidentiality	Maintain and respect sensitive information, including intellectual property, obtained in the course of your work.
Professional judgment	Be honest in your work.
Personal gain	Tied to conflict of interest. When someone benefits inappropriately in exchange for influencing a project. This is prohibited.
Inappropriate compensation	Tied to conflict of interest. This can include payments and gifts for personal gain. This is prohibited.

Exam Prep Questions

1. A vendor sends you a holiday greeting card signed by the company's staff using digital signatures. A gift certificate addressed to recipient for $100 at a local steakhouse is included. What do you do?

   ❏ A. Go out to dinner with a friend.

   ❏ B. Return the gift certificate and explain your company's policy on gift acceptance.

   ❏ C. Donate the gift certificate to a 503(c) charity.

   ❏ D. Give the gift certificate to your boss.

2. A colleague overstates her qualifications in her application for PMP certification. PMI selected her application for audit and you have been asked to sign off on her Experience Verification Form. What do you do?

   ❏ A. Explain that the project occurred a few years back and you simply cannot recall the details.

   ❏ B. Ask the colleague what she wants you to do.

   ❏ C. Ask your colleague to submit a new Experience Verification Form accurately stating her experience.

   ❏ D. Do not respond to PMI's request.

3. You have access to proprietary information a vendor included as part of a bid proposal. The information was marked confidential and included to show the vendor would be issued a patent by the end of the month making their bid the best candidate for your company and significantly improving the market share of the vendor. What do you do with this information?

   ❏ A. Invest in the company immediately.

   ❏ B. Tell your friends to invest in this company.

   ❏ C. Wait until the information becomes public knowledge, and then decide if you want to invest in the company.

   ❏ D. Provide the proprietary information to a competing vendor.

4. A meeting with a vendor runs late and a suggestion is made that the meeting should be continued over dinner. When the bill arrives, the vendor offers to pay for your meal. How do you respond?

   ❏ A. You accept and thank him for the meal.

   ❏ B. You accept and tell him you will pay for the next meal.

   ❏ C. You counter and offer to pay for his meal on your expense account.

   ❏ D. You decline and pay for your own meal.

5. Falsification of information at any point during the PMI Certification Program can result in
   - ❏ A. Revocation of your PMI membership
   - ❏ B. Revocation of your PMP certification
   - ❏ C. Notification of your employer
   - ❏ D. Both A and B

6. Your spouse works for a vendor bidding on a project at your company. You are not affiliated with the specific project team evaluating bids but you are part of the executive project management team. What do you do?
   - ❏ A. Inform your company of the relationship
   - ❏ B. Inform the vendor of the relationship
   - ❏ C. Both A and B
   - ❏ D. Disqualify the vendor

7. You work for a U.S.–based company hired to perform project management services in a foreign country. Other companies who have done business in this country inform you that gifts must be made to the government to obtain the necessary project approvals. What do you do?
   - ❏ A. Offer the recommended gifts to obtain project approvals.
   - ❏ B. Do not offer gifts to obtain project approvals.
   - ❏ C. Ignore the need for project approvals.
   - ❏ D. Both B and C.

8. You are responsible for developing a cost estimate to bid on a government contract. The scope was set by the government. Your supervisor says the cost estimate is too expensive and should be reduced by one-third to assure your company wins the contract. Your analysis shows that any reduction to the proposed cost estimate will make the project unable to meet the specified scope. What do you do?
   - ❏ A. Reduce the cost estimate and submit the proposal.
   - ❏ B. Submit your initial cost estimate without reducing the cost.
   - ❏ C. Explain to your supervisor in writing that your analysis shows a reduction in the cost estimate will make the project unable to meet the specified scope.
   - ❏ D. Both A and C.

9. You apply for a position at a company and list PMI membership on your resume. The company wants to hire a PMP. You are scheduled to take the PMP exam in a few days. At your interview, a comment is made implying that you are PMP certified. What do you do?

   ❏ A. Provide no clarification. Your resume states you are a member of PMI. An assumption that you are PMP certified is not your responsibility to correct and you will be certified soon if you pass the exam.

   ❏ B. Clarify you are a member of PMI and are scheduled to take your PMP certification exam soon but are not yet PMP certified.

   ❏ C. Confirm you are a member of PMI but do not address PMP status.

   ❏ D. Confirm you are a member of PMI and PMP certified. You will be certified soon if you pass the exam.

10. You are a project manager working on a project that has had numerous change requests from the customer resulting in scope creep. The project is overtime and over budget. The remaining scope entails preferred user requirements that do not impact the operation of the application. You can complete the project this month if you reduce the scope removing these preferred user requirements. What do you do?

    ❏ A. Continue with the project and complete the remaining scope.

    ❏ B. Explain to the customer the benefits of reducing scope and make the customer sign off on this final change request.

    ❏ C. Reduce the scope, do not document this change, and tell the customer the project has been completed.

    ❏ D. Explain to the customer the preferred user requirements are not possible and get the customer to sign off on this final change request reducing the project scope.

Answers to Exam Prep Questions

1. Answer B is the best response. You have a responsibility to refrain from accepting inappropriate payments, gifts, or other forms of compensation for personal gain according to the PMI PMP Code of Professional Conduct. You might have additional responsibilities in accordance with your company's policies and procedures. Answer A is not correct because accepting the gift would be a violation of the PMI PMP Code of Professional Conduct. Answer C is not correct because the vendor might be lead to believe the gift was accepted and the appearance of impropriety might still exist. Although Answer D might seem acceptable, it is not the best response of the choices given.

2. Answer C is the best response. You have a responsibility to cooperate with PMI concerning ethics violations and the collection of related information. You have a further responsibility to support and disseminate the PMI PMP Code of Professional Conduct. You must provide accurate, truthful representations concerning qualifications, experience, and performance of services. Answers A, B, and D conflict with these responsibilities.

3. Answer C is the best response. You have a responsibility to maintain and respect the confidentiality of sensitive information obtained in the course of professional activities. This responsibility makes answers A and B incorrect. You have a responsibility to recognize and respect intellectual property developed and owned by others, which makes answer D an incorrect choice.

4. Answer D is the best response. You have a responsibility to refrain from accepting inappropriate forms of compensation for personal gain. Answer A is incorrect for this reason. You have a responsibility to refrain from offering inappropriate forms of compensation for personal gain, making answer C incorrect. Answer B is a poor choice because the appearance of impropriety is present.

5. Answer D is the best response. Falsification of any information directly or indirectly related to all aspects of the PMI Certification Program can result in both revocation of your PMI Membership and your PMP Certification. Although answers A and B are both correct, they are not the best responses. Answer C is not correct. PMI will not notify your employer if you falsify information at any point during the PMI Certification Program.

6. Answer C is the best response. You have a responsibility to disclose to both the vendor and your company significant circumstances that could be construed as a conflict of interest or an appearance of impropriety. Answers A and B are both correct but are not the best responses. Answer D is not correct. You have an obligation to disclose the information. Your company and the vendor can decide the best course of action given the information.

7. Answer B is the best response. Answer A is not correct because you have a responsibility to refrain from offering inappropriate gifts for personal gain. The exemption regarding conformity with applicable laws or customs of the country where project management services are being performed does not apply because you are working for a U.S.–based company and subject to U.S. law. Answers C and D are incorrect because you have a responsibility to comply with laws and regulations in the country where providing project management services requires project approvals.

8. Answer C is the best response. You have a responsibility to provide accurate and truthful representations in the preparation of estimates concerning costs, services, and expected results. This responsibility makes answers A and D not appropriate. You have accountability to your management and answer B is not appropriate because you are usurping your manager's authority and undermining your own professional conduct by doing so.

9. Answer B is the best response. You have a responsibility to provide accurate, truthful representations concerning your qualifications, experience, and performance of services. Answer A and C are lies of omission. You are misleading the hiring company about your qualifications. Answer D is a lie of fact that could result in revocation of your PMI membership and your PMP certification.

10. Answer A is the best response. You have a responsibility to maintain and satisfy the scope and objectives of professional services, unless otherwise directed by your customer. Answers B, C, and D require manipulation of your customer and/or falsification of information, which is not in compliance with professional conduct.

Need to Know More?

Brake, Terence, Danielle Walker, and Thomas Walker. *Doing Business Internationally: The Guide to Cross-Cultural Success*, Second Edition. New York: MacGraw-Hill Professional Book Group, 2002.

Ferraro, Gary P. *The Cultural Dimension of International Business*, Fifth Edition. Upper Saddle River, NJ: Prentice-Hall, 2005.

Rosen, Robert (ed), Patricia Digh, Marshall Singer, and Carl Phillips. *Global Literacies: Lessons on Business Leadership and National Cultures*, Fifth Edition. New York: Simon and Schuster, 2000.

Project Management Institute. "PMP Code of Professional Conduct." Project Management Institute. http://www.pmi.org/info/PDC_PMPCodeOfConductFile.asp.

PMP Practice Exam 1

Test-taking Tips

When you sit for the actual PMP certification examination, there will be 200 multiple-choice questions and you will have up to four hours to complete the examination. This breaks down to 50 questions per hour and a little more than a minute per question. Therefore, the practice exams included in this book have 50 questions that you should time yourself to complete within an hour using the same average of a little more than a minute per question. Not all questions require equal time. Don't agonize over every question. Read the question and each possible answer in its entirety prior to selecting an answer. Select the best answer to each question based on the response that seems to adhere to the PMBOK and PMI.

More than one answer might seem plausible and correct. Select the best answer from those provided rather than aiming for the "correct" answer. In some cases multiple choices among the available answers might seem equally valid, so it is important to rule out obviously incorrect choices to narrow your options.

If more than one answer seems logical, look for an answer that includes both responses. Some of your choices include "Both X and Y," "Neither X nor Y," "All of the above," or "None of the above." The inclusion of a choice that includes multiple answers does not mean it is the correct answer. Some of the choices can be tricky in this regard.

Likewise, many of the available choices include terminology, concepts, and processes endorsed by the PMBOK and PMI. Just because you recognize the term does not mean this is the correct answer. The exam uses terms in similar contexts to assure you thoroughly understand and can apply the material. Be sure to read each question carefully to avoid any confusion among terminology or process names.

In your response to every test question, you should strive to select the best answer based on how you believe PMI and the PMBOK would respond given the question and not necessarily from your own project management experience. The best answer as determined by PMI is provided as one of the four possible responses.

Be suspicious of answers offering definitive responses such as never and always. Some answers might tout non-PMI methods and reflect common project management misconceptions. Some answers might offer correct information but the information is not pertinent to the question at hand and is simply included to confuse you. Similarly, some questions might contain factually correct information that has no bearing to the possible answers. If you do not have a firm grasp of the material and immediately know the best answer, you can waste valuable test time trying to figure out a way to use and apply irrelevant information. This is particularly tricky when mathematical calculations are requested in response to an examination question.

It is important to apply the same test conditions to taking this practice exam as you will experience on the day of the actual test. Be aware of your time to avoid having to rush at the end to complete the examination. You will want to leave adequate time to review any responses you were unsure of and/or to return to unanswered questions. If you are spending more than one minute on a question, it is better to skip over the question and mark it for review later than to agonize over the question and lose the opportunity to answer other questions to which you know the answer.

During the actual computerized exam, you can mark questions for later review and/or make multiple passes through the exam. Mark every question you are unsure of even if you have selected an answer. This approach saves you time when you review your responses because you do not need to review any unmarked questions. If on a second review, you determine an answer, unmark the question. Continue this process of going through all the marked questions until they all have answers or you are nearing the end of the allotted time period.

Save the last 20 minutes or so of the test to finalize any unmarked answers and assure you have provided an answer to each question. For the practice test, if you adhere to the suggested 1 minute per question rule of thumb, you will have 10 minutes to review your answers and respond to any marked questions. On the actual exam day, try to make a best guess by ruling out definitely wrong answers as discussed earlier, but do not give up. Select an answer for each question even if you have to guess. There is no penalty for guessing.

Passing the Exam

The PMP certification examination consists of 200 four-option, multiple-choice questions developed by PMPs. Examinees must score 81.7% to pass the test, which requires answering 164 questions correctly. For the practice exam, you are responding to 50 questions and must answer 41 correctly to pass with a score of 81.7%.

Exam Topics

The PMP Certification Examination tests for six knowledge areas as well as professional responsibility. The knowledge areas are

➤ Project initiation

➤ Project planning

➤ Project execution

➤ Project control

➤ Project closing

Exam Questions

1. Your project team is working with a vendor to correct some programming errors found during user acceptance testing. The decision is made to work through lunch and order take-out. When the food is delivered, the vendor says the bill has been taken care of. What do you do?

   ❏ A. You accept and thank the vendor for your lunch.
   ❏ B. You accept and tell him you will pay for lunch for everyone tomorrow.
   ❏ C. You keep working and pretend you did not hear what the vendor said.
   ❏ D. You decline and pay for your own meal.

2. Which of the following statements does not apply to the project charter?

   ❏ A. The project charter formally authorizes the project.
   ❏ B. The project charter provides the project manager with authority to devote organizational resources to project activities.
   ❏ C. The project charter identifies an external project sponsor.
   ❏ D. The project charter includes a work breakdown structure (WBS) and associated WBS dictionary.

3. When should a project manager be assigned to a project?

   ❏ A. Prior to the start of project planning
   ❏ B. After the project charter is approved
   ❏ C. During project planning
   ❏ D. During project execution

4. What does a project scope statement document?
   - ❏ A. What work is to be completed during the project
   - ❏ B. What deliverables need to be produced by the project
   - ❏ C. Both A and B
   - ❏ D. Neither A nor B

5. What does a statement of work (SOW) identify?
   - ❏ A. The business need for the project
   - ❏ B. The project or product requirements
   - ❏ C. The strategic plan
   - ❏ D. All of the above

6. Various models or tools are used during project selection to measure potential benefits associated with a project. Which of the following is not a benefit measurement model?
   - ❏ A. Scoring model
   - ❏ B. Economic model
   - ❏ C. Mathematical model
   - ❏ D. Benefit contribution

7. The change control system is a subsystem of what?
   - ❏ A. Configuration management
   - ❏ B. Project management
   - ❏ C. Risk management
   - ❏ D. Scope management

8. As a project manager, you direct the performance of all planned project activities and manage the technical and organizational resources available to and interacting with your project. Your work is performed in conjunction with whom?
   - ❏ A. The external project sponsor
   - ❏ B. The project management team
   - ❏ C. All of the above
   - ❏ D. None of the above

9. The earned value technique (EVT) measures project performance from project initiation through which of the following phases?
   - ❏ A. Project planning
   - ❏ B. Project executing
   - ❏ C. Project controlling
   - ❏ D. Project closing

10. The project scope management plan, as a component of the project management plan, includes which of the following?
   - ❑ A. Preparation of a detailed project scope statement
   - ❑ B. Creation of the work breakdown structure (WBS)
   - ❑ C. Specifications for formal verification and acceptance of completed project deliverables
   - ❑ D. All of the above

11. Approved change requests can cause a change to which of the following project elements?
   - ❑ A. Scope
   - ❑ B. Quality
   - ❑ C. Schedule
   - ❑ D. All of the above

12. The _____ is a deliverable-oriented hierarchical decomposition of the work to be performed by the project team.
   - ❑ A. Organizational breakdown structure (OBS)
   - ❑ B. Milestone schedule
   - ❑ C. Work breakdown structure (WBS)
   - ❑ D. Master schedule

13. The work breakdown structure (WBS) does all of the following, except:
   - ❑ A. Organizes and defines the entire scope of the project
   - ❑ B. Divides the project into smaller, more manageable tasks
   - ❑ C. Serves as a high-level planning tool for work planned but not yet approved
   - ❑ D. Both A and B

14. _____ is the subdivision of project deliverables into smaller, more manageable components. The final product categorizes project deliverables at the work package level.
   - ❑ A. Baselining
   - ❑ B. Critical path mapping
   - ❑ C. Decomposition
   - ❑ D. Resource leveling

15. The project cost and schedule for deliverables can be reasonably estimated at what level of the work breakdown structure (WBS)?
   - ❑ A. The lowest level
   - ❑ B. The midlevel
   - ❑ C. The work package level
   - ❑ D. Both A and C

16. As the project manager recently assigned to a project in execution, you're asked to rescope the existing project. The project sponsor believes the current scope is unattainable given the budget and scheduled end date. The project is over budget and not meeting schedule milestones. Project cost estimates and timelines were created under the previous project manager. Your analysis of the original project assumptions and constraints show that scope reduction will not enable you to meet the originally estimated end date or budget. What do you do?

    ❑ A. Inform the project sponsor that a scope reduction will not allow the project to meet the original timeline or budget and await further instruction.

    ❑ B. Re-estimate the entire project in terms of scope, timeline, and budget, and then present the project sponsor with each available option given the project assumptions and constraints.

    ❑ C. Reduce the scope and proceed with the direction given by the project sponsor.

    ❑ D. None of the above.

17. One component of the scope baseline for a project is

    ❑ A. The preliminary project scope

    ❑ B. The approved preliminary project scope

    ❑ C. The detailed project scope

    ❑ D. The approved detailed project scope

18. A project is a(n) _____ endeavor undertaken to create a unique product, service, or result.

    ❑ A. Permanent

    ❑ B. Temporary

    ❑ C. Ongoing

    ❑ D. None of the above

19. You're part of a project team constructing a manufacturing plant. You begin using process engineering to define the assumptions and constraints of the manufacturing process to be performed at the plant. This information is then used to design the major manufacturing units within the plant, which in turn serves as the starting point for designing the detailed plant layout and all other associated facilities. Next, design drawings are completed for fabrication and construction requirements. Changes and modifications occur during actual construction, requiring change control management and "as-built" documents. Finally, user acceptance testing and turnover of the completed manufacturing plant results in more adjustments and corrections. This is an example of

    ❑ A. Analogous estimating

    ❑ B. Assumptions analysis

    ❑ C. Fast tracking

    ❑ D. Progressive elaboration

20. The risk of project failure is highest during which phase of a project?
  ❑ A. Initiating
  ❑ B. Planning
  ❑ C. Executing
  ❑ D. Controlling

21. The ability for project stakeholders to influence the project scope and cost of a project is greatest during which phase of a project?
  ❑ A. Initiating
  ❑ B. Planning
  ❑ C. Executing
  ❑ D. Controlling

22. The cost of changes to project scope generally _____ over the life cycle of a project.
  ❑ A. Increase
  ❑ B. Decrease
  ❑ C. Stabilize
  ❑ D. None of the above

23. Project cost and project staffing resources follow a typical pattern during the life cycle of a project. Which of the following is common?
  ❑ A. Cost and staffing levels are high at the beginning of the project, stabilize during the middle phases of the project, and drop rapidly toward project closing.
  ❑ B. Cost and staffing levels are high at the beginning of the project, high during the middle phases of the project, and drop rapidly toward project closing.
  ❑ C. Cost and staffing levels are low at the beginning of the project, peak during the middle phases of the project, and drop rapidly toward project closing.
  ❑ D. Cost and staffing levels are low at the beginning of the project, rise during the middle phases of the project, and peak toward project closing.

24. An organization comprised by a full-time project manager with moderate project authority and a full-time project management administrative staff is an example of what type of structure?
  ❑ A. Functional
  ❑ B. Weak matrix
  ❑ C. Strong matrix
  ❑ D. Projectized

25. One type of progressive elaboration occurs when the work to be performed within the near term is planned in detail while work scheduled for further out is defined at only a high level in the work breakdown structure (WBS). As the task draws nearer, the amount of detail for the task is further defined. Which of the following terms defines this type of progressive elaboration?

   ❑ A. Activity sequencing
   ❑ B. Precedence diagramming method (PDM)
   ❑ C. Activity-on-node (AON)
   ❑ D. Rolling wave planning

26. What is the most common precedence relationship used in the precedence diagramming method (PDM)?

   ❑ A. Finish-to-start
   ❑ B. Finish-to-finish
   ❑ C. Start-to-finish
   ❑ D. Start-to-start

27. Which of the following is not a type of dependency available in activity sequencing?

   ❑ A. Discretionary dependencies
   ❑ B. External dependencies
   ❑ C. Internal dependencies
   ❑ D. Mandatory dependencies

28. When a scheduled activity cannot be estimated with an adequate degree of certainty, the work within the activity can be decomposed. The resource requirements for each lower, more detailed work package can be estimated and aggregated to form a basis for estimating the overarching scheduled activity. What is this type of estimating called?

   ❑ A. Bottom-up estimating
   ❑ B. Decomposed estimating
   ❑ C. Should-cost estimating
   ❑ D. Three-point estimating

29. What does crashing a project imply?

   ❑ A. Project cost and project schedule tradeoffs occur to achieve the maximum schedule compression for the least cost to the project without compromising the intended scope of the project.
   ❑ B. Project cost and project schedule overruns resulting in a project coming in over budget and over time but within the original defined project scope.
   ❑ C. Throwing more resources at the project to meet the planned project end date and planned project scope.
   ❑ D. Another term for fast tracking a project.

30. Cost control of a project entails determining and evaluating which of the following factors?
   - ❑ A. The cause of a cost variance
   - ❑ B. The magnitude of a cost variance
   - ❑ C. Both A and B
   - ❑ D. Neither A nor B

31. Planned value (PV) is
   - ❑ A. The budgeted cost for work scheduled to be completed on an activity up to a specific time
   - ❑ B. The budgeted cost for the work actually completed on the schedule activity during a specific time period
   - ❑ C. The total cost for work on the schedule activity during a specific time period
   - ❑ D. None of the above

32. The most commonly used performance measure for evaluating if work is being completed as planned at any given time point in a project is which of the following?
   - ❑ A. Cost variance (CV)
   - ❑ B. Schedule variance (SV)
   - ❑ C. Both A and B
   - ❑ D. Neither A nor B

33. A cost performance index (CPI) value less than 1.0 indicates a project has which of the following?
   - ❑ A. A cost overrun of the cost estimates
   - ❑ B. A cost underrun of the cost estimates
   - ❑ C. Neither a cost overrun nor a cost underrun
   - ❑ D. None of the above

34. You're managing a project using the earned value technique (EVT) for cost management. The project planned value (PV) is $200,000. The project earned value (EV) is $100,000. The actual value (AV) is $150,000. What is the cost variance (CV) for the project?
   - ❑ A. 100,000
   - ❑ B. −100,000
   - ❑ C. 50,000
   - ❑ D. −50,000

35. You're managing the same project cited in question 34 using the earned value technique (EVT) for cost management. The project planned value (PV) is $200,000. The project earned value (EV) is $100,000. The actual value (AV) is $150,000. What is the schedule variance (SV) for the project?
    - ❏ A. 100,000
    - ❏ B. –100,000
    - ❏ C. 50,000
    - ❏ D. –50,000

36. You're managing the project cited in question 34 using the earned value technique (EVT) for cost management. The project planned value (PV) is $200,000. The project earned value (EV) is $100,000. The actual value (AV) is $150,000. Calculate the cost performance index (CPI) for the project. What is the cost-efficiency of the project?
    - ❏ A. Over budget
    - ❏ B. Under budget
    - ❏ C. On budget
    - ❏ D. Unable to determine from the information given

37. You're managing the project cited in question 34 using the earned value technique (EVT) for cost management. The project planned value (PV) is $200,000. The project earned value (EV) is $100,000. The actual value (AV) is $150,000. What is the schedule performance index (SPI) for the project?
    - ❏ A. 0.5
    - ❏ B. 1.5
    - ❏ C. 1.75
    - ❏ D. 2

38. Comparing planned project practices or actual project best practices from other comparable projects to your project in an effort to improve the quality of your project and establish performance measurement baselines is called what?
    - ❏ A. Benchmarking
    - ❏ B. Continuous improvement
    - ❏ C. Metric creation
    - ❏ D. Quality assurance (QA)

39. A structured, independent review to determine if project activities adhere to your project management plan and other project documentation, including all project policies, procedures, and standards, is called a(n) _____.
    - ❏ A. Assurance review
    - ❏ B. Organizational process assessment
    - ❏ C. Process analysis
    - ❏ D. Quality audit

40. Monitoring project activities and results to evaluate if the findings comply with applicable quality standards as well as identifying mitigation strategies is a _____ activity.
    - ❑ A. Quality assessment
    - ❑ B. Quality assurance
    - ❑ C. Quality control
    - ❑ D. Quality improvement

41. Which of the following is not one of the seven basic tools of quality?
    - ❑ A. Cause and effect diagram
    - ❑ B. Statistical sampling
    - ❑ C. Histogram
    - ❑ D. Scatter diagram

42. Ishikawa diagrams are also known as
    - ❑ A. Cause and effect diagrams
    - ❑ B. Scatter diagrams
    - ❑ C. Fishbone diagram
    - ❑ D. Both A and C

43. A Pareto chart is a type of
    - ❑ A. Cause and effect diagram
    - ❑ B. Control chart
    - ❑ C. Histogram
    - ❑ D. Scatter diagram

44. Project communication planning includes which of the following tasks?
    - ❑ A. Determining and limiting who will communicate with whom and who will receive what information
    - ❑ B. Combining the type and format of information needed with an analysis of the value of the information for communication
    - ❑ C. Understanding how communication affects the project as a whole
    - ❑ D. All of the above

45. Communication technology factors that can affect a project include
    - ❑ A. The urgency of the information need
    - ❑ B. The expected staffing on the project and their individual competencies
    - ❑ C. The length of the project
    - ❑ D. All of the above

46. Which of the following is an accurate statement?
    - ❑ A. Qualitative risk analysis occurs prior to quantitative risk analysis.
    - ❑ B. Quantitative risk analysis occurs prior to qualitative risk analysis.
    - ❑ C. Qualitative risk analysis is performed on risks that have been prioritized during quantitative risk analysis.
    - ❑ D. Both B and C.

47. In evaluating project risk, a decision tree analysis is most helpful in which of the following scenarios?
    - ❑ A. Describing a potential risk and the implications for each available choice and outcome associated with the risk
    - ❑ B. Describing a potential risk and the most likely choice and outcome associated with the risk
    - ❑ C. Describing a potential risk and the least likely choice and outcome associated with the risk
    - ❑ D. None of the above

48. The identification of risks associated with a project happens when?
    - ❑ A. Occurs only at the beginning of a project when the risk management plan is developed
    - ❑ B. Is an ongoing process, regularly scheduled throughout the life cycle of a project
    - ❑ C. Occurs as needed throughout the life cycle of a project
    - ❑ D. Both B and C

49. The responsibility for tailoring a contract for goods and services to the needs of the project lies with whom?
    - ❑ A. The project manager
    - ❑ B. The project management team
    - ❑ C. The attorneys
    - ❑ D. The contract manager

50. The decision on whether a product or service can be produced by the project management team or can be purchased is called what?
    - ❑ A. Buyer assessment
    - ❑ B. Expert judgment
    - ❑ C. Make-or-buy analysis
    - ❑ D. Procurement evaluation

Answers to Practice Exam 1

1. D	**18.** B	**35.** B
2. D	**19.** D	**36.** A
3. A	**20.** A	**37.** A
4. C	**21.** A	**38.** A
5. D	**22.** A	**39.** D
6. C	**23.** C	**40.** C
7. A	**24.** C	**41.** B
8. B	**25.** D	**42.** D
9. D	**26.** A	**43.** C
10. D	**27.** C	**44.** D
11. D	**28.** A	**45.** D
12. C	**29.** A	**46.** A
13. C	**30.** C	**47.** A
14. C	**31.** A	**48.** D
15. D	**32.** C	**49.** B
16. B	**33.** A	**50.** C
17. D	**34.** D	

1. Answer D is the best response. You have a responsibility to refrain from accepting inappropriate forms of compensation for personal gain. Answers A and C are incorrect for this reason. Answer B is a poor choice because the appearance of impropriety is present.

2. Answer D is the correct response. A work breakdown structure (WBS) is not a component of the project charter. Answers A, B, and C are all components of the project charter.

3. Answer A is the best response. A project manager should be assigned prior to the start of project planning. Answer B is incorrect because the project manager should be assigned prior to the creation of a project charter. Answer C is incorrect because a project manager should be assigned prior to, not during, project planning. Similarly, answer D is incorrect because a project manager should be in place before project execution.

4. Answer C is the best response. A project scope statement documents what work is to be accomplished and which deliverables need to be produced. Answers A and B are both individually correct, but answer C is the better response. Answer D is incorrect.

5. Answer D is the best response. A statement of work (SOW) identifies the business need for the project, the project or product requirements, and the strategic plan for the organization. Answers A, B, and C are individually correct, but answer D is the better response.

6. Answer C is the correct response. Project selection methods are used to determine which project the organization will select. These methods fall into two categories: benefit measurement methods and mathematical models. Benefit measurement methods include scoring models, economic models, and benefit contribution, making answers A, B, and D incorrect. A mathematical model is a category of models and not a specific model in itself.

7. Answer A is the correct response. The change control system is a subsystem of the configuration management system.

8. Answer B is the best response. The project manager, along with the project management team, directs the performance of the planned project activities and manages the technical and organizational interfaces necessitated by the project and occurring continuously throughout the project lifecycle.

9. Answer D is the best response. Earned value technique (EVT) measures performance of the project as it moves through the entire project life cycle, from project initiation through project closing.

10. Answer D is the best response. The project scope management plan includes preparation of a detailed project scope statement, creation of the work breakdown structure (WBS), and a process specifying how formal verification and acceptance of the completed project deliverables will be obtained.

11. Answer D is the best response. Approved change requests can cause a change to project scope, project quality, and project schedule.

12. Answer C is the correct response. The work breakdown structure (WBS) is a deliverable-oriented hierarchical decomposition of the work to be executed by the project team to accomplish the project objectives and create the required deliverables.

13. Answer C is the correct response. The work breakdown structure (WBS) provides a detailed definition of work specified in the current, approved project scope statement. Both answers A and B describe the WBS and are therefore incorrect responses to the question.

14. Answer C is the correct response. Decomposition is a planning technique that subdivides project deliverables into smaller, more manageable components until the project work and project deliverables are defined at the work package level.

15. Answer D is the correct response. The project cost and project schedule for work can be reliably estimated at the work package, or lowest, level of the work breakdown structure (WBS). The work package level is the lowest level of the WBS.

16. Answer B is the best response. You have a responsibility to provide accurate and truthful representations in the preparation of estimates concerning costs, services, and expected results. It is your responsibility as a project management professional to give the project sponsor all the information pertinent to make informed decisions regarding the viability and continuation of a project.

17. Answer D is the correct response. The approved detailed project scope is one component of the project scope baseline. Other components are the associated work breakdown structure (WBS) and the WBS dictionary. Answer A is incorrect because it is an unapproved preliminary, not detailed, project scope. Answer B is incorrect because even though it purports to be "approved," it is a preliminary, not detailed, project scope. Answer C is incorrect because it is not an "approved" detailed project scope.

18. Answer B is the correct response. A project is a temporary endeavor undertaken to create a unique product, service, or result. A project by definition cannot be permanent nor ongoing. A project has a specific timeline and duration.

19. Answer D is the correct response. Progressive elaboration is a technique for continuous improvement in your planning efforts. More details are added to your planning documents as the information becomes available, and each successive iteration of your planning process results in a better plan.

20. Answer A is the correct response. The risk of project failure is highest at the start of a project. The certainty for project completion increases as the project continues through its life cycle.

21. Answer A is the correct response. Stakeholders have the ability to influence the project scope and project cost to the greatest extent during the initiating phase of the project. This influence decreases during the life cycle of the project.

22. Answer A is the correct response. Project changes from scope creep or error correction have a more significant impact on project cost as a project continues through its life cycle.

23. Answer C is the correct response. Project cost and project staffing levels are low at the start of a project, peak during the middle phases of the project life cycle, and then drop rapidly toward the conclusion of the project.

24. Answer C is the best response. A strong matrix structure within an organization supports a full-time project manager with considerable project authority, including budgetary and resource allocation ability, as well as a full-time project management administrative staff. Answer A is incorrect because a functional structure within an organization provides a part-time project manager with little to no authority and part-time administrative support. Answer B is incorrect because a weak matrix structure within an organization supports a part-time project manager with limited authority and only part-time administrative staffing. Answer D is incorrect because a projectized structure within an organization provides a full-time project manager with almost absolute authority and a full-time project management administrative staff.

25. Answer D is the correct response. Rolling wave planning is a form of progressive elaboration in which the work to be performed within the near term is planned in detail while work scheduled for further out is

defined at only a high level in the work breakdown structure (WBS). Rolling wave planning is a tool for activity definition. Answer A is incorrect because activity sequencing entails the documenting of logical relationships among scheduled activities and is actually the task following activity definition. Answers B and C are incorrect because the precedence diagramming method (PDM), also called activity-on-node (AON), is a tool for activity sequencing.

26. Answer A is the correct response. Finish-to-start is the most common type of precedence relationship used in the precedence diagramming method (PDM). The initiation of the successor activity is dependent on the completion of the predecessor activity in finish-to-start dependencies.

27. Answer C is the correct response. Internal dependencies are not a type of dependency used in sequencing activities.

28. Answer A is the correct response. Bottom-up estimating is a technique for estimating a component of work through decomposition. The bottom-up estimate is based on the requirements for each lower work package and then combined to estimate the entire component of work. Answer B is incorrect because there is no technique called decomposed estimating. Answer C is incorrect because should-cost estimating is an activity duration estimating technique. Answer D is incorrect because three-point estimating is a procurement estimating technique.

29. Answer A is the correct response. *Crashing* is a schedule compression technique whereby the project cost and project schedule are optimized to obtain the highest degree of schedule compression for the least cost to the project. Crashing does not always result in a viable project solution and can increase the overall cost of your project. Answer B is incorrect because *crashing* is not a term used for a project that is over time and over budget. Answer C is incorrect because crashing does not necessarily allow you to meet the planned project end date. Answer D is incorrect because fast tracking is another schedule compression tool used to perform multiple phases of project development in parallel.

30. Answer C is the best response. Cost control involves determining and evaluating both the cause of a variance and the magnitude of the variance. Answers A and B are both individually correct, but answer C is the best answer. Answer D is incorrect.

31. Answer A is the correct response. Planned value (PV), in the earned value technique (EVT), is the budgeted cost for work scheduled to be completed on an activity up to a specific time. Answer B is incorrect

because the budgeted cost for the work actually completed on the scheduled activity during a specific time period refers to earned value (EV). Answer C is also incorrect because the total cost for work on the scheduled activity during a specific time period defines actual cost (AC). Answer D is incorrect.

32. Answer C is the best response. The most commonly used performance measure for evaluating whether work is being completed as planned at any given time in a project is both cost variance (CV) and schedule variance (SV). Answers A and B are both individually correct, but answer C is the best answer. Answer D is incorrect.

33. Answer A is the correct response. A cost performance index (CPI) value less than 1.0 indicates a project has a cost overrun of the cost estimates. Answer B is incorrect because a cost underrun of the cost estimates is indicated by a CPI greater than 1.0. Answers C and D are incorrect.

34. Answer D is the correct response. Cost variance (CV) is calculated by subtracting the actual cost (AC) from the earned value (EV). CV = EV – AV. In the example given, the AC is $150,000 and the EV is $100,000. $100,000 – $150,000 = -$50,000. Answer A is incorrect. Answer B is the schedule variance (SV), not the CV, so it is incorrect. Answer D is incorrect.

35. Answer B is the correct response. Schedule variance (SV) is calculated by subtracting the planned value (PV) from the earned value (EV). SV = EV – PV. In the example given, the PV is $200,000 and the EV is $100,000. $100,000 – $200,000 = –$100,000. Answer A is incorrect, as is answer C. Answer D is the cost variance (CV), not the SV, so it is incorrect.

36. Answer A is the correct response. The cost performance index (CPI) is calculated by dividing the actual cost (AC) into the earned value (EV). CPI = EV ÷ AC. In the example given, the AC is $150,000 and the EV is $100,000. $100,000 ÷ $150,000 = .06667. A CPI value less than 1.0 indicates a cost overrun of the project budget. Answer B is incorrect because, if the project were under budget, the CPI value would be greater than 1.0. Answer C is incorrect because the CPI would be 0. Answer D is incorrect.

37. Answer A is the correct response. The schedule performance index (SPI) is calculated by dividing the planned cost (PC) into the earned value (EV). SPI = EV ÷ PC. In the example given, the PC is $200,000

and the EV is $100,000. $100,000 ÷ $200,000 = .05. A SPI value allows you to predict the completion date for a project in conjunction with the schedule status. Given the math done to arrive at answer A, answers B, C, and D are incorrect.

38. Answer A is the best response. *Benchmarking* is the practice of comparing your project to other planned project practices or actual project best practices in an effort to improve your project and establish performance measurement benchmarks. Answer B is incorrect because continuous improvement is a plan-do-check-act cycle for improving quality in the product developed by a project. Answer C is incorrect because metrics are specific defined tools for describing and measuring key values for quality control. Answer D is incorrect because quality assurance (QA) is the application of planned, systematic activities to achieve specific quality objectives. QA is the overarching process in which continuous process improvement is practiced. Benchmarking is one task within the process, and metrics are a way to assess quality initiatives.

39. Answer D is the correct response. A quality audit is a structured, independent review providing an assessment of whether a project's activities meet organizational and project policies, processes, and procedures.

40. Answer C is the best response. Monitoring project activities and results to evaluate whether the findings comply with applicable quality standards as well as identifying mitigation strategies is a quality control activity. Answers A, B, and D are incorrect.

41. Answer B is the correct response. Statistical sampling is a quality control technique, but it is not one of the seven basic tools of quality. The seven basic tools of quality are cause and effect diagram, control charts, flowcharting, histogram, Pareto chart, run chart, and scatter diagram. Answers A, C, and D are incorrect because these items are part of the seven basic tools of quality.

42. Answer D is the best response. Answer A is correct because Ishikawa diagrams are also known as cause-and-effect diagrams. Answer C is correct because Ishikawa diagrams are also known as fishbone diagrams. Because both A and B are correct answers, Answer D (both A and C) is the best response. Answer B is incorrect. Scatter diagrams show the pattern of the relationship between two variables, whereas Ishikawa diagrams show how various factors (causes) can link to potential problems (effects).

43. Answer C is the correct response. A Pareto chart is a specific type of histogram, ordered by frequency of occurrence and showing how many defects were generated to show nonconformity. Answers A, B, and D are incorrect.

44. Answer D is the best response. Project communication planning includes all these tasks: determining and limiting who will communicate with whom and who will receive what information, combining the type and format of information needed with an analysis of the value of the information for communication, and understanding how communication affects the project as a whole.

45. Answer D is the best response. Communications technology factors include the urgency of the information need, the expected staffing for the project, the staff members' individual skill sets, and the length of the project.

46. Answer A is the correct response. Qualitative risk analysis occurs prior to quantitative risk analysis and is a method for prioritizing identified risks for quantitative risk analysis. Answers B, C, and D are incorrect.

47. Answer A is the correct response. A decision tree diagram can be used to consider potential risks and all the implications associated with the risk. You can include every conceivable choice and outcome. Every option is considered. Answer B is incorrect because choice and outcome are limited to the most probable scenario. Answer C is incorrect because choice and outcome are limited to the least probable scenario. Answer D is incorrect.

48. Answer D is the best response. Risk assessment is not limited to the beginning of a project's life cycle when the risk management plan is developed. The risk management plan should include a tool for risk assessment as a continuous process throughout the project. Risk reassessment should be a regularly scheduled component of the project but should also have the flexibility to occur as needed at greater or lesser intervals based on the level of risk.

49. Answer B is the best response. The responsibility for tailoring a contract for goods and services to the needs of the project lies with the project management team. The project management team can include the project manager, attorneys, and/or contract manager, but the responsibility does not rest solely with one individual.

50. Answer C is the best response. The decision on whether a product or service can be produced by the project management team or can be purchased is called a *make-or-buy analysis*.

PMP Practice Exam 2

1. The project charter:
   - ❑ A. Is a good thing to have to enter restricted areas
   - ❑ B. Tells the newspapers when the project will end
   - ❑ C. Authorizes equipment acquisition
   - ❑ D. Provides a high-level definition of the effort and its stakeholders
   - ❑ E. Announces who the project engineer is

2. Scorecard modeling, cost benefit analysis, payback periods, and internal rate of return are examples of:
   - ❑ A. Project selection methods
   - ❑ B. Enterprise benefits measurement methods when selecting a project
   - ❑ C. Ways to ensure stakeholder commitment
   - ❑ D. Integral parts of the statement of work

3. Project scope:
   - ❑ A. Defines all the equipment that will be used in the project
   - ❑ B. Is a document that identifies the stakeholder responsibilities
   - ❑ C. Is part of the project charter
   - ❑ D. Defines at a high level the project execution framework and its deliverables

4. Project success can be achieved only if:
   - ❑ A. The project manager is an expert in managing resources.
   - ❑ B. The project manager is part of the executive management team.
   - ❑ C. There is a clear link between the project deliverables and the business strategy.
   - ❑ D. The project sponsor leads the initiatives.
   - ❑ E. None of the above.

5. The project management plan:
   - ❏ A. Are the steps needed to complete a project task
   - ❏ B. Is prepared at the beginning and fixed throughout the execution of the project
   - ❏ C. Not needed until resources have been assigned
   - ❏ D. Is an outline that identifies all the steps and processes that will be used after a project is initiated

6. The work breakdown structure:
   - ❏ A. Is a list of all the tasks needed to complete a meeting
   - ❏ B. Is needed as part of the project charter
   - ❏ C. Is set and does not change throughout the project
   - ❏ D. Is used to break down the project into manageable pieces

7. The project baseline:
   - ❏ A. Encompass all the initial estimates for tasks and resource utilization
   - ❏ B. Is only important in the project initiation phase
   - ❏ C. Is the result of the original plans plus the approved changes
   - ❏ D. Is not needed to successfully manage a project

For questions 8–10, use the following network diagram:

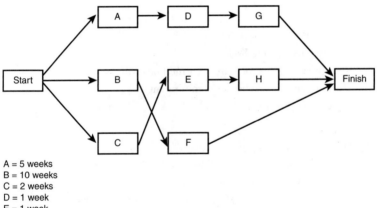

A = 5 weeks
B = 10 weeks
C = 2 weeks
D = 1 week
E = 1 week
F = 3 weeks
G = 11 weeks
H = 1 week

8. What would be the early start for activity H?
   - ❏ A. 11
   - ❏ B. 10
   - ❏ C. 4

9. What is the critical path?
   - ❑ A. Start – A – D – G – Finish
   - ❑ B. Start – B – F – Finish
   - ❑ C. Start – C – E – H – Finish

10. Which project schedule represents the tasks outlined in the network diagram?

   ❑ A.
   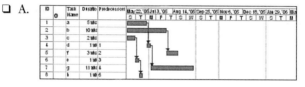

   ❑ B.
   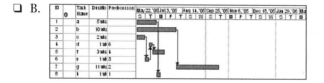

   ❑ C.

11. Which of the following is not a good input to project cost estimation?
   - ❑ A. Work breakdown structures
   - ❑ B. Time estimates
   - ❑ C. Earn value analysis
   - ❑ D. Schedules

12. Which one of the following four cost budgeting tools uses current and historical project information to calculate project cost estimates?
   - ❑ A. Cost cancellation techniques
   - ❑ B. Reserves analysis
   - ❑ C. Parametric estimating
   - ❑ D. Funding limit reconciliation

13. Within the PMI realm, who is ultimately responsible for the project quality?
   - ❑ A. Project team
   - ❑ B. Project manager
   - ❑ C. Quality assurance manager
   - ❑ D. Validation engineer

14. The process group in which detailed resource assignments and responsibilities are formalized is called the:
    - ❏ A. Project management plan
    - ❏ B. Quality assurance plan
    - ❏ C. Project charter
    - ❏ D. Human resources management plan

15. How many communication channels will be required in a project in which 30 individual are participating?
    - ❏ A. 150
    - ❏ B. 270
    - ❏ C. 444
    - ❏ D. 435

16. Who has the ultimate responsibility for making sure that a message in the project team is understood?
    - ❏ A. The project sponsor
    - ❏ B. The sender
    - ❏ C. The project coordinator
    - ❏ D. All

17. The intent of the risk management process group is to:
    - ❏ A. Underwrite all the risks affecting the company
    - ❏ B. Announce project risks
    - ❏ C. Address and implement how risk will be identified and mitigated
    - ❏ D. Increase the probability of positive outcomes in the project

18. Which one of these is not a typical way to deal with negative threats?
    - ❏ A. Avoid
    - ❏ B. Transfer
    - ❏ C. Mitigate
    - ❏ D. Share

19. Which of the following is a recognized contract type within the PMI context?
    - ❏ A. Fixed-price or lump-sum contract
    - ❏ B. Cost-reimbursable contract
    - ❏ C. Time and material
    - ❏ D. All of the above

20. Which one of these is not used when preparing a statement of work?
    - ❏ A. Project scope statement
    - ❏ B. Work breakdown structure
    - ❏ C. Risk management plan
    - ❏ D. Work breakdown dictionary

21. When the project manager receives a project change request, he should:
   - ❏ A. Send it to the change control board for approval
   - ❏ B. Discuss it with the project team and leave it for phase 2
   - ❏ C. Evaluate its risk and potential impact before taking any action
   - ❏ D. None of the above

22. One method to determine how well a project is executing at a specific point in time is by using:
   - ❏ A. Cost variance analysis
   - ❏ B. Historical data
   - ❏ C. Expert judgment
   - ❏ D. The cost performance index (CPI)

23. Quality assurance application in a project is the:
   - ❏ A. Definition of organizational quality practices
   - ❏ B. Ensuring of six sigma compliance
   - ❏ C. Application of Pareto charts to project sample points
   - ❏ D. Application of organizational quality metrics to the project

24. You and your project team determine that external resources are needed. Which method would be best to secure these resources?
   - ❏ A. Acquisition
   - ❏ B. Pre-assignment
   - ❏ C. Negotiation
   - ❏ D. Contract management
   - ❏ E. none of the above

25. As a project manager, you need to know how to manage conflict. Which one of the following is not a way to successfully manage conflict?
   - ❏ A. Problem-solving
   - ❏ B. Compromising
   - ❏ C. Formal
   - ❏ D. Withdrawal

26. How much time should a project manager spend in communication activities?
   - ❏ A. 10%–25%
   - ❏ B. 36%–50%
   - ❏ C. 51%–69%
   - ❏ D. 70%–90%

27. Which of the following is not a basic element for successful communication?
    - ❏ A. Sender
    - ❏ B. Message
    - ❏ C. Analog line
    - ❏ D. Receiver

28. What is the name of the process that uses the procurement documents and the selection criteria as primary inputs?
    - ❏ A. Procurement plan
    - ❏ B. Request seller responses
    - ❏ C. Contract management
    - ❏ D. Sales advisory plan

29. An approved corrective action is:
    - ❏ A. A response to a management request
    - ❏ B. A quality management plan
    - ❏ C. A course correction to bring the project in line with the project plan
    - ❏ D. None of the above
    - ❏ E. Issued by executive management

30. Ishikawa diagrams, see the figure below, are used for:
    - ❏ A. The cost management plan during the project execution
    - ❏ B. Brainstorming
    - ❏ C. Finding the cause and effect in the project quality assurance process
    - ❏ D. All of the above
    - ❏ E. None of the above

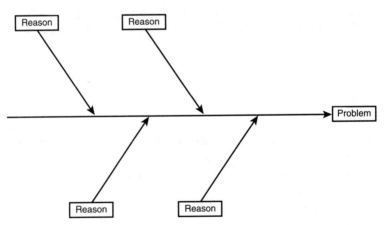

31. The Pareto chart, Ishikawa diagrams, histograms, and six sigma are techniques used for implementing _____ in the project:
    - ❏ A. Quality processes
    - ❏ B. Quality metrics
    - ❏ C. Quality control
    - ❏ D. All of the above

For questions 32–38, use the following problem:

You are the new project manager tasked with taking over for a project manager who left 6 weeks ago. Some of the numbers that you find in your initial research are as follows:

Estimated project cost: $675,000

Project timeline: 24 weeks

This is week 16 and accumulated costs are $300,000. Additionally, only 25% of the work has been completed.

32. What is the budget at completion?
    - ❏ A. $300,000
    - ❏ B. $168,750
    - ❏ C. $675,000
    - ❏ D. There is not enough information.

33. What is the planned value?
    - ❏ A. $300,000
    - ❏ B. $168,750
    - ❏ C. $389,423
    - ❏ D. $452,250
    - ❏ E. There is not enough information.

34. What is the earned value?
    - ❏ A. $300,000
    - ❏ B. $168,750
    - ❏ C. $389,453
    - ❏ D. $483,103

35. What is the cost variance?
    - ❏ A. –$250,000
    - ❏ B. –$483,103
    - ❏ C. –$289,750
    - ❏ D. –$131,250

36. What is the schedule variance?
    - ❑ A. –$157,351
    - ❑ B. –$289,750
    - ❑ C. –$283,500
    - ❑ D. There is not enough information.

37. What will be the estimated at-completion cost?
    - ❑ A. $1,200,000
    - ❑ B. $675,000
    - ❑ C. $3,000,000
    - ❑ D. $1,050,000

38. Because the CPI is .5625, what do we know about this project?
    - ❑ A. It can be finished on time if we crash the schedule.
    - ❑ B. We will need an extra 6 weeks to complete it.
    - ❑ C. The project is at budget risk.
    - ❑ D. None of the above.

39. The project management triple constraint is composed of all these except:
    - ❑ A. Scope
    - ❑ B. Quality
    - ❑ C. Time
    - ❑ D. Cost

40. Maslow's hierarchy of needs talks about how people need to satisfy various personal needs. What is the correct sequence for those needs?
    - ❑ A. Safety, love, esteem and self-actualization, physiological
    - ❑ B. Love, physiological, safety, esteem and self-actualization
    - ❑ C. Esteem, physiological, safety, love, and self-actualization
    - ❑ D. Self-actualization, physiological, safety, love and esteem
    - ❑ E. Physiological, safety, love, esteem and self-actualization

41. Which leadership style would be most common in a car wash?
    - ❑ A. MacGregor's Theory Y
    - ❑ B. MacGregor's Theory X
    - ❑ C. Maslow's hierarchy of needs
    - ❑ D. Ouchi's Theory Z

42. What would be the result of imposing judgment on a project team? The project manager is _____ his recommendations.
    - ❑ A. Smoothing
    - ❑ B. Formalizing
    - ❑ C. Compromising
    - ❑ D. Forcing
    - ❑ E. None of the above

43. S-curves, histograms, and earn value analysis are examples of:
    - ❑ A. Project justification
    - ❑ B. Capital acquisition requests
    - ❑ C. Performance reporting tools
    - ❑ D. None of the above

44. _____ and _____ are two procedures used to perform all the closure activities in a project or a project phase.
    - ❑ A. Management, stakeholder
    - ❑ B. Project team, stakeholder
    - ❑ C. Administrative, contract closure
    - ❑ D. Management, contract closure

45. You work for an organization that has no rules with regard to vendor kickbacks or special gifts. A vendor approaches you with a trip to Paris, provided you help him get the contract with your organization. What would be the most prudent thing to do?
    - ❑ A. Accept the offer and help the vendor get the contract.
    - ❑ B. Ask the vendor for an additional trip for your boss.
    - ❑ C. Decline the offer and advise the vendor on the standard bidding process.
    - ❑ D. Seek legal counsel before accepting the trip.

46. You are offered a job as project manager for a fixed cost project. At the same time, you are approached by another client to work on her project on a time and material basis at a higher hourly rate. What should you do?
    - ❑ A. Tell the new client that you need some time to consider all your options before giving her an answer.
    - ❑ B. Leave your current customer and start on the other project as soon as possible.
    - ❑ C. Discuss the matter with your client and ask for more money.
    - ❑ D. Try to squeeze in both projects without notifying anyone.

47. As a senior leader in the project management field, you receive a voice mail from one of your competitor's junior project managers asking for help in the project management discipline. What is the most appropriate course of action?
    - ❑ A. Tell the other guy to stop complaining and get a couple of project management books.
    - ❑ B. Decide that it is not worth the risk and ignore the call.
    - ❑ C. Start working with him after hours.
    - ❑ D. Talk to your supervisor and appraise her of the situation before initiating contact.

48. You are assigned to lead a corporate project with a lot of diversity and several countries participating. What is your best course of action when it comes to giving assignments and setting up the schedule?

   ❑ A. Try to standardize all activities based on the corporate calendar.

   ❑ B. Tell management that you need to implement a PMO at corporate in order to have everyone local.

   ❑ C. Learn about communication styles and local holidays and plan for process execution across time zones.

   ❑ D. Use external consultants willing to work locally.

49. You are in charge of a project that is going to miss the milestones that were set at the enterprise level by 2 weeks. What do you do?

   ❑ A. Advise management of the revised project plan and timeline.

   ❑ B. Wait and see if they notice when you do not give an update on the item.

   ❑ C. Crash the schedule to make the deadline.

   ❑ D. Do nothing.

50. A good project manager tends to _____ above all else when it comes to active communications.

   ❑ A. Write reports

   ❑ B. Cold-call people

   ❑ C. Listen

   ❑ D. Help

Answers to Practice Exam 2

1. D	18. D	35. D
2. B	19. D	36. C
3. D	20. C	37. A
4. C	21. C	38. C
5. D	22. D	39. B
6. D	23. D	40. E
7. C	24. A	41. B
8. C	25. C	42. D
9. A	26. D	43. C
10. A	27. C	44. C
11. C	28. B	45. C
12. C	29. C	46. A
13. B	30. C	47. D
14. D	31. C	48. C
15. D	32. C	49. A
16. B	33. D	50. C
17. D	34. B	

1. Answer D is correct. The project charter formally authorizes the project, assigns the project manager, and gives a high-level definition of the projects and its deliverables; none of the other answers apply to the project chapter definition.

2. Answer B is correct because projects are seeded from the recognition of a regulatory or business need. However, when it comes to measuring the actual organizational benefit, your client or company needs to make arrangements to secure the capital and reserve assignments. For this type of allocation, the aforementioned models are just a few of the tools at your disposal to find a measure of the enterprise benefit and the cost justification. You could have selected answer A, but it does not express complete reasoning and thorough consideration when selecting, justifying, and launching a project.

3. Answer D is correct. The project scope is one of those live documents. Why? A project is a temporary endeavor, with a specific product, but external factors like your business strategy can have a material impact of determining where the project might or might not go in the future. You may have thought of selecting answer C, but the project charter is the document that formally launches the project and defines at a high level the project deliverables, the project sponsor, and the project manager.

4. Answer C is correct. Rare is the occasion that you get to have a project for the sake of spending money. And, because a project is a temporary endeavor, the authority of the project manager is highly dependent on the support of senior management. Answer D is incorrect because the job of the project sponsor is to represent management interest in the project—not to lead the execution of the project.

5. Answer D is correct. The project management plan is the entire framework and processes that will be used to control the entire project effort. Answer A refers more to the mistaken interpretation that the project plan is the Gant chart that people may prepare using products like Visio, Excel, or Project.

6. Answer D is correct. To have an effective work breakdown structure, you must take time to understand what the project objectives and the risk involved are. When this is accomplished, the next task is to compartmentalize the project into manageable pieces—but not to the extreme. Good examples are to stop at a point where a task is down to 5 days in duration or resource utilization can be measured. If you chose option A you might have been thinking of a meeting agenda but

not the WBS. If you opted for option B, the project charter does not include or make reference to the WBS, remember that the intent of the project charter is to launch the project, announce the project manager, and present a general overview of the project deliverables.

7. Answer C is correct. The harsh reality of project management is that no matter how much time you invest in analysis during the execution of the project, you are going to find missing critical elements, external forcers can influence your project, or organizational changes can force a course correction. The project baseline will help you account for all the course corrections you implement during the execution of your project. You might have been tempted to select answer A, but the project baseline is not something that stays fixed; it changes as changes to the project are implemented.

8. Answer C is correct. Activity H should start on the first day of week 4 because it can't start executing until C (2) and E (1) are complete.

9. Answer A is correct. Answer A = 17 weeks; Answer B = 13 weeks; Answer C = 4 weeks. In general, the critical path is composed of the activities that form the longest path on a project.

10. Answer A is correct. The network diagram gives only three paths of execution: Start – A – D – G – Finish; Start – B – F – Finish; and Start – C – E – H – Finish. Answer A is the only one showing the predecessors in the correct order.

11. Answer C is correct. Earned value analysis is used during the execution of the project to determine resource consumption versus planned. On the other hand, the WBS, time estimates, and schedules are excellent sources for estimation of rate of consumption, timelines, and overall project resource needs.

12. Answer C is correct. Cost aggregation builds its cost estimates by adding the tasks outlined in the work breakdown structures, and parametric estimate uses historical data and project-specific characteristics. Cost cancellation techniques, reserve analysis, and funding limit reconciliation are not considered budgeting tools.

13. Answer B is correct. Within the realm of project management, the project manager has the ultimate responsibility. You might have thought of the quality assurance manager, but quality is something that goes beyond the project and is housed in the organization. The project team and the validation engineer are elements that support both the company quality policies and the processes required during the execution of the project.

14. Answer D is correct. The human resources planning process is where the core project team and the project manager plan for the request of resources from the functional manager and coordinate how to best approach the project demands versus the normal work duties of the resource.

15. Answer D is correct. The number of communication channels can be determined using the formula n(n–1)/2, where n is the number of people participating in a project. In our question, the formula will look something like: $30 \times (30 – 1)/2$; $30 \times (29)/2$; $870/2 = 435$, which is answer D.

16. Answer B is correct. For a message to be clearly understood, two things need to happen: The sender has to make sure that the receiver acknowledges the receipt and reading of the message, and the receiver needs to ensure that the sender received the acknowledgement. None of the other options pertains to the message communication process.

17. Answer D is correct. Risk can be catalogued in qualitative and quantitative terms. The risk management process group serves as the roadmap used to reduce its impact on the project. None of the other answers clearly articulates the scope and importance of the PMI risk management processes.

18. Answer D is correct. Share is a typical way to deal with positive risk. The other answers are examples of how a project manager might deal with a risk that can have a negative impact on the outcome of the project.

19. Answer D is correct. All these are examples of contract types that vary in accordance to the risk the buyer and the seller are willing to assume.

20. Answer C is correct. With the exception of the risk management plan, which identifies how risk will be managed throughout the project, the rest are examples of project plan elements that are used to define the work to be done and the deliverables expected out of the project.

21. Answer C is correct. The project manager is ultimately responsible for the success of the project. As such, she should execute due diligence with regard to a change request before approving a change. Answers A and B might be actions you will take in the process, but the first priority is to evaluate what impact a change will have on the outcome of the project.

22. Answer D is correct. The cost performance index is the most encompassing answer as it divides the earned value by the actual cost of the project. For the CPI calculations, a project with a CPI value greater than 1 signifies that your project is running under budget.

23. Answer D is correct. *Quality assurance* refers to the process of applying and measuring performance against the enterprise quality policies. Six Sigma and Pareto charts are used to represent the execution trending of a process, while organization quality practices refers to how quality is managed and considered in the enterprise.

24. Answer E is correct. In the PMI realm, *virtual teams* and *acquisition* refer to the action of securing nonlocal resources. Preassignment, negotiation, and contract management are activities the project manager might engage in during the process of securing the resources, but they are subprocesses when securing external resources.

25. Answer C is correct. With the exception of formal, the rest are known ways to resolve conflict. The orders of magnitude based on their long-lasting effects are problem-solving, compromising, and forcing. Withdrawal and smoothing are part of this group, but they do not address the problem.

26. Answer D is correct. The project manager is the focal point for information for senior management, stakeholders, and the project team. As such, the project manager spends much of his time ensuring that communication occurs and is effective at all levels affected by product of the project.

27. Answer C is correct. If you stand back and think of what it takes for successful communication, you think of an idea or a concept that needs to be communicated. You must build the entire message (words, syntax, and morphology); then talk to, write, or call the recipient to deliver the message; and wait for confirmation that your message was understood. On the other hand, the individual being communicated with has to do the same process, but in reverse. He needs to receive the message, check if it is in a language or in a frame of reference familiar to him, and then proceed to decipher its meaning. *Analog line* is a technical term associated with old telephone lines used for modulating and demodulating the messages sent via modem.

28. Answer B is correct. After you have defined your procurement plan, the equipment or service to be purchased, and how you are going to evaluate any responses, you are ready to request a seller response to your statement of work (SOW).

29. Answer C is correct. From time to time, external events such as business strategy change or regulatory compliance have a direct impact on the day-to-day execution of the project. Approved corrective actions are recognized changes throughout the entire organization of the project plan. It's ultimately approved and authorized by the project sponsor and the project manager.

30. Answer C is correct. The Ishikawa (also called the fishbone or cause-and-effect) diagram was first developed by Kaoru Ishikawa in 1969. It is used to identify the root cause of why a process might have gone out of control. Answer A refers to how costs might be managed through the life of the project. Answer B, brainstorming, is an activity with the express purpose of collecting ideas.

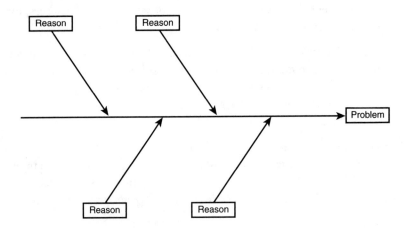

31. Answer C is correct. Part of the quality plan requires tools that will enable the successful implementation of control programs that provide quality assurance. Quality processes and metrics are used in support of the quality control activities.

32. Answer C is correct. Budget at completion (BAC) equates to the original cost estimate of the project.

33. Answer D is correct. Planned value (PV) or budget cost of work schedule (BCWS) equates to the percentage of work that should have been completed according to the plan. In this case, you divide the 16 weeks by the 24 in the original plan; this equals 67%. You then multiply $675,000 (the budget at completion) by 67% and get $452,250.

34. Answer B is correct. Earned value (EV) or budgeted cost of work performed (BCWP) equals the actual percentage of work performed times the budget at completion (BAC). EV = .25 × $675,000 = $168,750.

35. Answer D is correct. Cost variance equals earned value minus actual cost. $168,750 - $300,000 = -$131,250.

36. Answer C is correct. Schedule variance equals earned value minus planned value. $168,750 - $452,250 = -$283,500.

37. Answer A is correct. Estimated at completion equals budget at completion divided into cost performance index (EV/AC). $675,000 ÷ (168750 ÷ 300000) = $675000 ÷ .5625 = $1,200,000

38. Answer C is correct. A CPI less than 1.0 suggests that the project is executing at budget risk.

39. Answer B is correct. Even thought it is a good thing to think of quality as part of your project daily execution, quality it is not part of the triple constraint of execution.

40. Answer E is correct. As project manager, you need to be aware of what makes employees and team members happy. One way to do this is to apply Dr. Abraham Maslow's hierarchy of needs. This theory postulates that the performance of the individual is predicated by the need of satisfying his personal needs. These range from basic needs (physiological) like a roof over his head and food on his table to self-actualization needs like finding self-fulfillment. You must recognize these as cyclical in the sense that self-actualization is only the destination—most individuals tend to treasure the journey as well.

41. Answer B is correct. MacGregor's Theory X postulates that people must be constantly watched and that they are incapable, avoid responsibility, and avoid work.

42. Answer D is correct. The forcing conflict resolution technique forces the project manager's opinion(s) on the project team. This can solve the short-term need to make a decision but tends to create discord.

43. Answer C is correct. Within the context of project communication management, these reports can assist in presenting the project's performance and resource utilization.

44. Answer C is correct. As the name suggests, contract closure addresses all the processes pertaining to contract closures and administrative deals with the processes internal to the organization.

45. Answer C is correct. With the growth in the number of corporate standards in recent years, you need to avoid any act that might be construed as a conflict of interest or as unethical.

46. Answer A is correct. The PMP code of ethics clearly states that it is your responsibility to provide, maintain, and satisfy the scope and objectives of professional services unless otherwise directed by the customer.

47. Answer D is correct. As a PMP, you are expected to help in the advancement of the project management discipline.

48. Answer C is correct. You are the project manager and need to move away from making decisions solely based on the corporate environment. Probably the main reason for this international virtual team is to leverage the expertise of internal resources available to your client or employer within the corporate environment.

49. Answer A is correct. You are ultimately responsible to your project sponsor and the rest of the executives affected by this delay. You need to have a meeting with management to inform them of the new delivery date and offer crashing the schedule as an option.

50. Answer C is correct. Only good listeners are capable of keeping long-term active communication with all the members of the project team up and down the chain.

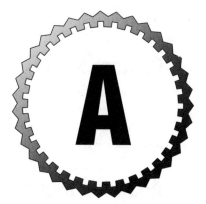

CD Contents and Installation Instructions

The CD features an innovative practice test engine powered by MeasureUp, giving you yet another effective tool to assess your readiness for the exam.

Multiple Test Modes

MeasureUp practice tests are available in Study, Certification, Custom, Adaptive, Missed Question, and Non-Duplicate question modes.

Study Mode

Tests administered in Study mode allow you to request the correct answer(s) and explanation(s) to each question during the test. These tests are not timed. You can modify the testing environment during the test by clicking the Options button.

Certification Mode

Tests administered in Certification mode closely simulate the actual testing environment you will encounter when taking a certification exam. These tests do not allow you to request the answer(s) or explanation(s) to a question until after the exam.

Custom Mode

Custom mode allows you to specify your preferred testing environment. Use this mode to specify the objectives you want to include in your test, the timer length, and other test properties. You can also modify the testing environment during the test by clicking the Options button.

Adaptive Mode

Tests administered in Adaptive mode closely simulate the actual testing environment you will encounter when taking an Adaptive exam. After answering a question, you are not allowed to go back—you are only allowed to move forward during the exam.

Missed Question Mode

Missed Question mode allows you to take a test containing only the questions you have previously missed.

Non-Duplicate Mode

Non-Duplicate mode allows you to take a test containing only questions not previously displayed.

Question Types

The practice question types simulate the real exam experience.

Random Questions and Order of Answers

This feature helps you learn the material without memorizing questions and answers. Each time you take a practice test the questions and answers appear in a different randomized order.

Detailed Explanations of Correct and Incorrect Answers

You'll receive automatic feedback on all correct and incorrect answers. The detailed answer explanations are a superb learning tool in their own right.

Attention to Exam Objectives

MeasureUp practice tests are designed to appropriately balance the questions over each technical area covered by a specific exam.

Installing the CD

The minimum system requirements for the CD-ROM are as follows:

➤ Windows 95, 98, Me, NT 4, 2000, or XP

➤ 7MB of disk space for the testing engine

➤ An average of 1MB of disk space for each test

To install the CD-ROM, follow these instructions:

 NOTE If you need technical support, please contact MeasureUp at 678-356-5050 or email support@measureup.com. Additionally, you'll find frequently asked questions (FAQs) at www.measureup.com.

1. Close all applications before beginning this installation.

2. Insert the CD into your CD-ROM drive. If the setup starts automatically, go to step 6. If the setup does not start automatically, continue with step 3.

3. From the Start menu, select Run.

4. Click Browse to locate the MeasureUp CD. In the Browse dialog box, from the Look in drop-down list, select the CD-ROM drive.

5. In the Browse dialog box, double-click Setup.exe. In the Run dialog box, click OK to begin the installation.

6. On the Welcome screen, click MeasureUp Practice Questions to begin the installation.

7. Follow the Certification Prep Wizard by clicking Next.

8. To agree to the Software License Agreement, click Yes.

9. On the Choose Destination Location screen, click Next to install the software to C:\Program Files\Certification Preparation.

 If you cannot locate MeasureUp Practice Tests through the Start menu, see the section later in this appendix titled "Creating a Shortcut to the MeasureUp Practice Tests."

10. On the Setup Type screen, select Typical Setup. Click Next to continue.

11. On the Select Program Folder screen, you can name the program folder your tests will be in. To select the default, simply click Next and the installation will continue.

12. After the installation is complete, verify that Yes, I Want to Restart My Computer Now is selected. If you select No, I Will Restart My Computer Later, you will not be able to use the program until you restart your computer.

13. Click Finish.

14. After restarting your computer, select Start, Programs, MeasureUp, MeasureUp Practice Tests.

15. On the MeasureUp Welcome screen, click Create User Profile.

16. In the User Profile dialog box, complete the mandatory fields and click Create Profile.

17. Select the practice test you want to access and click Start Test.

Creating a Shortcut to the MeasureUp Practice Tests

To create a shortcut to the MeasureUp Practice Tests, follow these steps:

1. Right-click your desktop.

2. From the shortcut menu, select New, Shortcut.

3. Browse to C:\Program Files\MeasureUp Practice Tests and select the `MeasureUpCertification.exe` or `Localware.exe` file.

4. Click OK.

5. Click Next.

6. Rename the shortcut `MeasureUp`.

7. Click Finish.

After you have completed step 7, use the MeasureUp shortcut on your desktop to access the MeasureUp products you ordered.

Technical Support

If you encounter problems with the MeasureUp test engine on the CD-ROM, please contact MeasureUp at 678-356-5050 or email support@measureup.com. Technical support hours are from 8 a.m. to 5 p.m. EST Monday through Friday. Additionally, you'll find frequently asked questions (FAQs) at www.measureup.com.

If you'd like to purchase additional MeasureUp products, telephone 678-356-5050 or 800-649-1MUP (1687) or visit www.measureup.com.

Additional Resources

Websites

 Project Management Institute (http://www.pmi.org)—The PMI website offers a variety of information related to PMP certification as well as membership in the organization.

Web-based Study

 An Applied Framework for Project Management (http://www.pmi.org/info/PDC_AppliedFramework. asp?nav=0405)— *An Applied Framework for Project Management*, a module-based, online course, is offered by PMI in support of A Guide to the Project Management Body of Knowledge (PMBOK). This course includes project management templates, checklists, and worksheets for projects of all sizes and complexities. You are given real-world scenarios allowing for interaction and explanatory sessions. Eleven modules are provided in a sequential order. You have no set time limit for completing the materials, although there is an overall deadline of 1 year of access to the course. The cost of the course is $425 for PMI members and $475 for non-members. Members receive two CEU and PDU credits.

 Business Balls (http://www.businessballs.com)—A resource website offering free materials and articles related to organizational development and leadership skills.

Carnegie Mellon Software Engineering Institute (http://www.sei.cmu.edu/cmmi/cmmi.html)—The Carnegie Mellon Software Engineering Institute (SEI) is a federally funded research and development center sponsored by the United States Department of Defense and operated by Carnegie Mellon University. SEI was established in 1984 to support process improvement in software engineering. It offers a maturity model referencing mature practices in a specific discipline to improve a group's ability to perform that discipline. The original model— Capability Maturity Model (CMM)—has since evolved into the Capability Maturity Model Integrated (CMMI) and offers an integrated set of models to provide a structured framework for process improvement throughout an organization. In many professional settings, CMMI and PMBOK are tailored to support the business goals of the organization. CMMI supports project management and the goals of PMI and the PMBOK with an emphasis on continuous improvement.

Value Based Management (http://www.valuebasedmanagement. net/)—A resource website consolidating the various management methods, management models, and management theories applicable to project management.

Books

Bell, David E., Howard Raiffa, and Amos Tversky (editors). *Decisionmaking: Descriptive, Normative, and Prescriptive Interactions.* New York: Cambridge University Press, 1988.

Brake, Terence, Danielle Walker, and Thomas Walker. *Doing Business Internationally: The Guide to Cross-Cultural Success, Second Edition.* New York: McGraw-Hill Professional Book Group, 2002.

Cooper, Cary L., Chris Argyris, and Derek F. Channon (editors). *The Concise Blackwell Encyclopedia of Management.* Malden, MA: Blackwell Publishers, 1998.

DePaoli, Tom. *Common Sense Purchasing: Hard Knock Lessons Learned from a Purchasing Pro.* Charleston: BookSurge Publishing, 2004.

Ferraro, Gary P. *The Cultural Dimension of International Business, Fifth Edition.* Upper Saddle River, NJ: Prentice-Hall, 2005.

Frame, J. Davidson. *The New Project Management: Tools for an Age of Rapid Change, Complexity, and Other Business Realities.* New York: Jossey-Bass, 2002.

Graves, Samuel B., and Jeffery L. Ringuest. *Models & Methods for Project Selection: Concepts from Management Science, Finance and Information Technology.* New York: Springer Publishing, 2002.

Ireland, Lewis. *Quality Management for Projects and Programs.* Newton Square, PA: Project Management Institute, 1991.

Keeney, Ralph L., Howard Raiffa, and Richard Meyer (contributor). *Decisions with Multiple Objectives: Preferences and Value Tradeoffs.* New York: Cambridge University Press, 1993.

Kerzner, Harold. *Project Management: A Systems Approach to Planning, Scheduling, and Controlling, Eighth Edition.* Indianapolis: John Wiley and Sons, 2003.

Kliem, Ralph L., Irwin S. Ludin, and Ken L. Robertson. *Project Management Methodology.* New York: Marcel Dekker, 1997.

Meredith, Jack R., and Samuel J. Mantel. *Project Management: A Managerial Approach, Fifth Edition.* New York: John Wiley and Sons, 2002.

Pritchard, Carl. *Risk Management: Concepts and Guidance.* Arlington: E S I International, 2001.

Project Management Institute. *A Guide to the Project Management Body of Knowledge, Third Edition.* Newton Square, PA: Project Management Institute, 2004.

Rosen, Robert (editor), Patricia Digh, Marshall Singer, and Carl Phillips. *Global Literacies: Lessons on Business Leadership and National Cultures, Fifth Edition.* New York: Simon and Schuster, 2000.

Software Engineering Institute. *The Capability Maturity Model: Guidelines for Improving the Software Process.* Pittsburgh: Software Engineering Institute, 1995.

Verzuh, Eric. *The Fast Forward MBA in Project Management, Second Edition.* New York: John Wiley and Sons, 2005.

Verzuh, Eric (editor). *The Portable MBA in Project Management, Second Edition.* New York: John Wiley and Sons, 2003.

Weiss, Joseph W., and Robert K. Wysocki. *Five-Phase Project Management: A Practical Planning and Implementation Guide.* Newton Square, PA: Project Management Institute, 1992.

 Wysocki, Robert K., and Rudd McGary. *Effective Project Management, Third Edition.* Indianapolis: John Wiley and Sons, 2003.

Glossary

acceptance
Formal receipt of something to include judging the item true, sound, suitable, and complete.

acceptance criteria
Requirements and conditions set forth as criteria which must be met prior to acceptance of a project deliverable.

activity
Work that is performed during a project.

activity sequence
The order in which activities must be accomplished.

activity-on-arrow (AOA) diagramming
Diagramming method using nodes and arrows in which duration information is depicted on the arrows. Also called the arrow diagramming method (ADM).

activity-on-node (AON) diagramming
Diagramming method using nodes and arrows in which duration and scheduling information is depicted on nodes. Also called the precedence diagramming method (PDM) or fishbone diagramming.

actual cost (AC)
Total cost of work performed on a project for a given reporting period. Also referred to as actual cost of work performed (ACWP).

actual cost of work performed (ACWP)
See actual cost.

administrative closure
Performing activities (creating, organizing, and reporting information) to close a project or phase.

analogous estimating
Uses actual duration, cost, or budget figures from similar activities. Also referred to as top-down estimating.

appeal

A request or demand for consideration or payment by one party (either the seller or buyer) from another party, in accordance with the terms and conditions of a legally binding contract.

appearance of impropriety

Outward indication of not acting properly.

arbitration

Formal process for settling contractual disputes. An impartial person or arbitrator is appointed by mutual consent to make a final judgment based on the facts of the dispute.

arrow diagramming method (ADM)

Diagramming method using nodes and arrows in which duration information is depicted on the arrows. Also called the activity-on-arrow (AOA) diagram.

assumptions

For project planning purposes, assumptions are assumed true and real without need of proof. Assumptions are validated and documented during the planning process.

bidder conference

A meeting of potential bidders to present information on the product or service offered for bid and to allow bidders to ask questions.

bottom-up estimating

The process of creating estimates for midlevel to upper-level activities by aggregating the individual estimates for each work package in the activity.

budgeted cost of work performed (BCWP)

Value of completed work expressed in terms of the expended budget. Also referred to as earned value (EV).

budgeted cost of work scheduled (BCWS)

Approved budget for the scheduled work to be accomplished. Also referred to as planned value (PV).

claim

A request or demand for consideration or payment by one party (either the seller or buyer) from another party, in accordance with the terms and conditions of a legally binding contract.

co-location

Physically locating all team members in the same proximity for the project duration.

confidentiality

Discretion in maintaining and transmitting secret information.

conflict of interest

When personal interests are placed above professional responsibility.

constraint
Any condition that restricts a performance aspect of a project. For example, a schedule constraint limits the amount of time available to work on the project.

continuous improvement
Cycle of evaluating and improving processes. A quality assurance and quality control component.

contract management
Performing activities to manage a contract.

contract closure
Performing activities to formally close a contract.

contract negotiations
Discussions between both contract parties to determine the parameters of the contract and finalize contract terms and conditions. Contract negotiations usually result in a signed contract.

control charts
Graphical representations depicting process data over time and against specific control limits. As a component of quality control, control charts allow the project team to evaluate if a process needs adjustment.

corrective action
Changes made to bring expected future performance of a project inline with the project management plan.

cost performance index (CPI)
A measure of cost efficiency. The earned value (EV) of a project divided by the actual cost (AC) of a project.

$$CPI = EV/AC$$

A value equal to or greater than one indicates a favorable condition, whereas a value less than one is deemed unfavorable.

cost variance (CV)
A measure of cost performance. The earned value (EV) of a project minus the actual cost (AC) of a project.

$$CV = EV - AC$$

A positive value indicates a favorable condition and a negative value is unfavorable.

criteria
Standards used to base decision making and evaluations of products, services, results, or processes.

critical path
The shortest path to complete a project from the starting task to the ending task. Any delay encountered with any task on the critical path affects the overall project schedule.

defect repair
A document that describes a defect, or deficiency, in a project component and the suggested course of action to repair or replace the component.

dependency
A relationship between activities requiring that one activity cannot start or finish until a predecessor activity has started or finished.

dispute
A disagreement between seller and buyer related to the terms and conditions of a legally binding contract.

earned value (EV)
Value of completed work expressed in terms of the expended budget. Also referred to as the budgeted cost of work performed (BCWP).

earned value management (EVM)
Measuring project performance and progress using project scope, project schedule, and project resource data. Performance measurement compares the earned value of the project to the actual value of the project. Progress measurement calculates earned value compared to the planned value.

ethical standards
Acting professionally in the conduct and execution of work performance to include integrity, honesty, and respect.

expected monetary value (EMV)
The statistical calculation of the average future value of money given multiple possible scenarios.

feasibility study
Document presenting analysis and research related to the viability of a proposed project based on the operational environment, available technology, existing marketplace conditions, and internal resources. A feasibility study might support the initiating of a project, or it might prove the project unjustifiable.

functional manager
Someone with management responsibility over a group of specialized staff within a hierarchical, or functional, organization.

functional organization
A hierarchical organization grouping staff by specialization where each employee has a designated manager.

go/no-go decision
A decision whether to continue a project or project phase based on accessing various project factors. This decision point can present itself at multiple points in the project life cycle.

holistic project management
An all-encompassing approach to project management within an enterprise or organization. Organizations practicing this approach practice and apply the project management methods to all their initiatives.

inappropriate compensation
Payments, gifts, and/or other consideration given to an individual for personal gain in exchange for favorable professional treatment. Tied to conflict of interest.

intellectual property
A product with commercial value developed and owned by others, usually copyrighted material.

lessons learned
Knowledge gained during the performance of the project. Tied to post-implementation review.

management by objectives (MBO)
Management technique that sets forth specific objectives and then measures performance based on progress toward those objectives.

matrix organization
Any organizational structure supporting a project manager sharing management responsibility with a functional manager for assigning work and directing the activities of staff assigned to the project. In a matrix organization, the functional manager retains responsibility for the entire specialized group while the project manager has authority only in tasks and work related to the project.

milestone
A notable point in time or an event in a project.

objective
Goal toward which work is directed, a purpose to be achieved, a result to be obtained, a product to be produced, or a service to be performed.

organizational breakdown structure (OBS)
Tool depicting work packages in their hierarchical relationship to the performing organizational units.

organizational process assets
Any process assets of an organization that are not directly related to a project and that can influence the success of a project.

parametric estimating
Calculates duration estimates by multiplying the quantity of work by the productivity rate.

payment system
Process and procedures used to pay vendors

personal gain
When someone benefits inappropriately in exchange for influencing a project. Tied to conflict of interest.

planned value (PV)
Approved budget for the scheduled work to be accomplished. Also referred to as the budgeted cost of work scheduled (BCWS).

portfolio
A group of projects or programs that work together to achieve an organization's strategic objectives.

post-implementation review
An assessment performed after project completion comparing actual versus planned results. This review usually includes an evaluation of lessons learned on the project and their applicability to future projects.

precedence diagramming method (PDM)

Diagramming method using nodes and arrows in which duration and scheduling information is depicted on nodes. Also called the activity-on-node (AON) or fishbone diagramming.

preventive action

Proactive response to reduce or minimize the impact of a project risk occurring.

procurement management plan

Documents detailing the procurement process from solicitation planning to procurement (contract) closeout. A subsidiary management plan to the project management plan.

procurement planning

Process for determining what to procure, from whom to procure, and when to procure.

professional judgment

Applying ethical standards and reasoned decision making in the execution of your work.

program

A collection of projects that are related to one another and managed in a coordinated fashion.

project

A temporary activity undertaken to produce a unique product, service, or result.

project archives

Repository for all project-related information. Archived documents may include project plan, lessons learned, contracts, performance metrics, and project team performance evaluation.

project boundaries

The points in time at which a project begins and ends.

project charter

Document providing formal authorization for a project. The project charter is issued by the project sponsor and empowers the project manager to use organizational resources for project activities.

project initiation

Process group in which a new project can be formally authorized and scope defined.

project initiator

Person or group providing the resources and authority for a project. Also referred to as the project sponsor.

project life cycle

Sequential project phases, from inception through completion, used to manage the project.

project management

According to PMI's PMBOK, "the application of knowledge, skills, tools, and techniques to project activities to meet project requirements."

Project Management Body of Knowledge (PMBOK)

According to PMI, an inclusive term describing "the sum of knowledge within the profession of project management." PMBOK commonly references the PMI's publication *A Guide to the Project Management Body of Knowledge.*

project management information system (PMIS)

Tools and techniques used to gather, integrate, and disseminate project management process outputs. Both manual and automated systems can be included throughout the project life cycle.

Project Management Institute (PMI) Code of Professional Conduct

Ethical standards for the practice of project management promulgated by PMI.

project management knowledge area

A specific area of project management defined by its required knowledge and differentiated from other areas by the defined inputs, tools, techniques, and outputs.

project management methodology

Tools, techniques, templates, processes, and procedures providing a framework for managing projects.

project management office (PMO)

An entity within an organization whose primary responsibility is to provide centralized and coordinated management services for projects.

project management plan

Collection of all subordinate plans and a document describing how work will be accomplished to satisfy project goals.

project management process

Any one of the 44 unique processes defined by the PMBOK.

project management process groups

The grouping of project management processes into five distinct groups, as defined by the PMBOK. These five progress groups are initiating processes, planning processes, executing processes, monitoring and controlling processes, and closing processes.

project management professional (PMP)

A person certified by the PMI as a project management professional. PMP certification implies adherence with the PMI Code of Professional Conduct, experience performing project management duties, continuing education credits, and an understanding of the PMBOK.

project management team

Individuals directly responsible for project management activities. The project management team includes the project sponsor, project manager, and all project staff.

project manager (PM)
Individual assigned by the sponsoring organization responsible for achieving project objectives.

project planning
Development and maintenance of a project plan.

project schedule
Planned dates for performed planning project activities and meeting schedule milestones.

project schedule network diagram
Any visual display of the relationships between project schedule activities.

project scope
Work to be performed to deliver a product, service, or result according to specified requirements.

project selection
Process for determining whether a project should be initiated based on organizational criteria.

project sponsor
Person or group providing the resources and authority for a project. Also referred to as the project initiator.

projectized organization
Any organizational structure giving the project manager complete authority to assign work, apply resources, and direct the performance of individuals working on the project.

qualitative risk analysis
Prioritizing risks, based on probability of occurrence and impact, for future analysis or action.

quality assurance
Process for routinely evaluating project performance to assure adherence with quality objectives.

quality audit
Structured review to determine if a project complies with quality objectives.

quality management plan
Documents detailing the relevant sponsoring organization's quality objectives and implementation of those objectives. A subsidiary management plan to the project management plan.

quantitative risk analysis
Numerically analyzing the effect of identified risks on project objectives.

resource breakdown structure (RBS)
A hierarchical diagram of resources necessary for a project used to create schedules for projects that are limited in resources.

responsible, accountable, consulted, informed (RACI)
Form of a responsibility assignment matrix (RAM). Each project team member is assigned a role as the responsible, accountable, consulted, or informed person for project tasks.

responsibility assignment matrix (RAM)
Tool linking the organizational breakdown structure (OBS) to the work breakdown structure (WBS), ensuring each component of the project's scope of work is assigned to a project team member.

risk
Any event that results in a positive or negative affect on a project if the event occurs.

risk acceptance
Risk response planning technique in which the project management team takes no action to deal with an identified risk. Risk acceptance results in no change to the risk management plan.

risk avoidance
Risk response planning technique in which the project management team takes action to eliminate the identified risk or minimize the impact to the project. Risk avoidance results in changes to the risk management plan. Strategy for negative risks or threats.

risk enhance
Risk response planning technique in which the project management team increases the probability and/or positive impacts. Strategy for positive risks or opportunities.

risk event
Discrete occurrence of a project risk.

risk exploit
Risk response planning technique in which the project management team ensures the opportunity is realized. Strategy for positive risks or opportunities.

risk identification
Determining which risks might affect a project and documenting their characteristics.

risk management plan
Documents detailing how to approach, plan, and execute risk management activities for a project. A subsidiary management plan to the project management plan.

risk mitigation
Risk response planning technique in which the project management team takes action to reduce the probability of the occurrence or affect of a risk to below an acceptable threshold. Risk mitigation might result in changes to the risk management plan. Strategy for negative risks or threats.

risk register
Document listing project risks, the results of risk analysis, and the risk responses.

risk response planning
Developing options and actions to enhance opportunities and reduce threats to a project's objectives.

risk share

Risk response planning technique in which the project management team shares the benefits of a risk with a third party. Strategy for positive risks or opportunities.

risk transfer

Risk response planning technique in which the project management team takes action to shift the affect of a threat to a third party. Risk transfer might result in changes to the risk management plan. Strategy for negative risks or threats.

rolling wave planning

A planning technique in which the level of planning detail depends on how close the current date is to the planned start date of the work. Work that is planned for the future is planned at a high level, where work that is planned to begin soon will have more detailed plans. As the start date of work gets closer, the plans for that work will need to be revisited to provide more detail.

root cause analysis

Technique to determine the underlying cause of a risk, defect, or variance.

scheduled performance index

A measure of schedule efficiency. The earned value (EV) of a project divided by the planned value (PV) of a project.

$$SPI = EV/PV$$

A value equal to or greater than one indicates a favorable condition whereas a value less than one is deemed unfavorable.

schedule variance (SV)

A measure of schedule performance. The earned value (EV) of a project minus the planned value (PV) of a project.

$$SV = EV - PV$$

slack

The difference between the early start date and late start date for an activity.

staffing management plan

Documents detailing how and when to met human resource requirements. A subsidiary management plan to the project management plan.

stakeholder

Any person or organization involved in the project or who might be impacted (either positively or negatively) by the project's execution or completion.

subsidiary plans

A subcomponent of the project management plan that addresses a particular knowledge area or topic.

three-point estimates

Uses three separate estimate values for each activity: most likely, optimistic, and pessimistic.

top-down estimating
Uses actual duration figures from similar activities. Also referred to as analogous estimating.

triple constraint
The three classic attributes of projects that a project manager must properly manager: scope, time, and cost.

truthful representation
Providing accurate, truthful information to PMI, customers, and the public.

vendor management
Performing activities to manage a vendor.

WBS dictionary
Document supporting the work breakdown structure (WBS) by providing detailed information for each work package.

weighted system
Assigning mathematical values to criteria for the purpose of scoring seller proposals.

work breakdown structure (WBS)
Tool depicting work packages in their hierarchical relationship to the performing organizational units.

Index

D

How can we make this index more useful? Email us at indexes@quepublishing.com

How can we make this index more useful? Email us at indexes@quepublishing.com

How can we make this index more useful? Email us at indexes@quepublishing.com

R